FERNANDO CORTES and the MARQUESADO in MORELOS, 1522–1547

FERNANDO CORTES AND THE MARQUESADO IN MORELOS, 1522–1547

A Case Study in the
Socioeconomic Development of
Sixteenth-Century Mexico

G. Micheal Riley

UNIVERSITY OF NEW MEXICO PRESS

Albuquerque

Portions of Chapters 2, 4, and 5 of this book first appeared in
The Americas: A Quarterly Review of Inter-American Cultural History,
25:1 (July 1968); 27:3 (January 1971); and 28:3 (January 1972).

For France V. Scholes

Table of Contents

List of Maps and Illustrations

List of Tables

Preface

In the quarter-century immediately after the conquest of the Aztec Confederacy (1519–21), Fernando Cortés* the principal figure in that epic achievement of Spanish arms and ambition, acquired and developed extensive property holdings in central and southern Mexico. These holdings comprised populous tribute and labor-providing encomienda towns, lands, mines, Indian and Negro slaves, livestock, and business enterprises. After Charles V conferred upon Cortés the title of Marqués del Valle de Oaxaca in 1529, they were collectively known as the Marquesado de Cortés. In 1535 Cortés established the Marquesado as a *mayorazgo* or entailed estate. Following the conqueror's death in 1547, the estate passed in inheritance to his legitimate son Don Martín Cortés, born of his second marriage. Subsequently and throughout the colonial era, the Marquesado, although subjected to various modifications and vicissitudes, remained in the hands of Cortés' descendants.

After 1529 Cortés' properties and interests in New Spain were concentrated in the valleys of Mexico and Oaxaca, in the Tehuantepec district, and in the modern states of Morelos and Veracruz. The title of nobility secured by Cortés, Marqués del Valle of Oaxaca, suggests that during the years 1522–29 he placed special importance on his holdings in the Oaxaca area. The encomienda dues of numerous Indian towns and gold that was mined by gangs of Indian slaves there had yielded a very handsome income. The value of these Oaxaca interests was sharply reduced early in the 1530s, however, as several encomiendas were lost in governmental action of 1529–31 and as the area's placer gold deposits

---

* Cortés' name is properly Fernando and not Hernán or Hernando. That fact was long ago established by Henry R. Wagner in his *The Rise of Fernando Cortés* (Los Angeles, 1944). In the preface to that book (page vi), Wagner wrote "Cortés wrote his name as Fernando, and all the early documents read in the same way, indicating plainly that such was his name and not Hernando or Hernán. I, therefore, follow in his footsteps. Cortez, as the English write it, is a barbarism."

were exhausted. During the 1530s and the 1540s the conqueror's holdings in the Morelos area constituted the most lucrative part of the Marquesado. Cortés clearly recognized as much, for in 1531, after his return from Spain, he began concentrating much of his attention on that area.

Up to now scholars have devoted little attention to the development of the Marquesado in their treatment of Cortés and have provided insufficient account of New Spain's early socioeconomic and political development. Important and relatively unknown aspects of the Cortés story, as well as the early history of Colonial Mexico, include the means by which the conqueror was able to gain and retain control of a considerable portion of his original holdings and interests despite restrictive measures inspired by the crown and by Cortés' competitors and instituted by colonial agencies of government; the establishment of the Marquesado; the nature and utilization of the unusual jurisdictional powers and privileges accorded the conqueror by the Spanish crown; and the economic development and exploitation of the estate. The later history of the Marquesado (after Cortés' death) likewise forms a relatively unknown and significant feature of the administrative, social, and economic history of New Spain.

This study presents a detailed account of the development of the Marquesado in Morelos from 1522, when the conqueror first acquired interests in the area, to his death in 1547. We will consider the definition, consolidation, and use of encomienda grants; the acquisition and development of land holdings; the formation and utilization of a management organization and labor force; and the sources, extent, and relative value of revenues produced.

Although other parts of the Marquesado differed slightly in general composition—they included mining in some instances and provided special problems of management and control resulting from local conditions—the development of the Morelos properties may be regarded as fairly typical of that of the entire estate during Cortés' lifetime. The story of the Marquesado in Morelos also serves as a case study illustrating important aspects of Mexican history during the first decades of the sixteenth century.

This study was initially undertaken as a doctoral dissertation under the direction of Professor France V. Scholes, Research Professor Emeritus at the University of New Mexico. Its preparation included utilization of unpublished documentation housed in Spanish and Mexican archives. Research was pursued during the summers of 1961 and 1965 in the Archivo General de la Nación (Mexico City), particularly the extensive Marquesado records dating from the 1520s through the early years of the nineteenth century and contained in the Hospital de Jesús section. The great manuscript collection of the Archivo General de Indias in Seville and especially the very valuable Sección IV, Papeles de Justicia, wherein numerous *procesos*, or lawsuits, relating to Marquesado land, encomienda, and other property-interest conflicts are recorded, was investigated during 1962–63. Funding for these and related bibliographical endeavors was generously supplied by the University of New Mexico (Fellowship, 1961), the Social Science Research Council (Research Training Fellowship, 1962–63), and Colorado State University (Faculty Improvement Committee Grant, 1965). Also utilized were pertinent materials from the Harkness Collection of Spanish Manuscripts in the Library of Congress, Washington, D.C.; the Joaquín García Icazbalceta Collection in the University of Texas Library (Austin, Texas); the Hispanic Documents Collection (Cortés Papers) in the Gilcrease Institute (Tulsa, Oklahoma); the Bibliothèque Nationale (Paris); and Professor France V. Scholes' private collection of Cortesian documents in microfilm copy (from Spanish, Mexican, and other archives). Funds for acquiring copies of some items in these collections, in-place use of others (Gilcrease Institute, Professor Scholes' Collection, and the University of Texas Library), and the completion of this study was generously provided by Marquette University's Committee on Research (Grants, 1968 and 1969) and the University of New Mexico (Fellowship, 1960).

Among the individuals who lent vital encouragement and gave essential time and assistance to the preparation of this study are the staff of the Archivo General de la Nación and its director, Sr. Ignacio Rubio Mañe; Sr. Miguel Saldaña, Mexico City; the staff of the Archivo General de Indias and its former director, Sr. José María de la Peña; the late Sr. Santiago Díaz Montero, Seville; Professors Stanley S. Newman, Edwin Lieuwen, and the late Frank D. Reeve of the University of New Mexico; Mrs. Mary Wicker, Albuquerque, New Mexico; and Fr. Francis P. Prucha, S.J., Marquette University.

A special note of gratitude must go to four who truly made the effort possible: Professor France V. Scholes, generous mentor, critic and friend; Mr. and Mrs. Randolph R. Riley, enthusiastic parents; and Denise Ann Riley, loving wife, critic, and editor.

The title and appropriate archival designation of the major manuscript sources utilized are given in the first footnote citations of each. Thereafter only archival designations are cited. The spelling of Indian (Nahuatl) place names follows, in general, modern Mexican practice; exceptions are rendered as found in sixteenth-century Spanish references. Readers are directed to the List of Abbreviations included as a means of simplifying the citation of important printed and manuscript materials.

1

Introduction

The Land

The encomiendas, landholdings, and varied enterprises which eventually constituted the richest part of Fernando Cortés' great estate in New Spain, the Marquesado, were located in an area generally comprising the present Mexican state of Morelos. Two major geological formations, the Cordillera Neovolcánica and the Depresión del Balsas (or Austral) encircle the Morelos area with mountains and hills and provide the high ridges and rugged barrancas (canyons) which divide it into sections distinctly diverse in climate and terrain.[1] Shaping the northern boundary of the area are the volcanic, almost interlocking Ajusco and Sierra Nevada de Popocatépetl ranges. Ridge lines extend southward from the Ajusco range and link with the Miacatlán, Cacahuamilpa, and Taxco mountains to form the area's western and southern limits. In the east, ridges and hills reach southward from the slopes of the Sierra Nevada de Popocatépetl to the Nexapa River and its tributary, the Río Tepalcingo. The Nexapa flows through the rough country of the Sierra Huautla (part of the Sierra Ocotlán) and into the Amacuzac River, which carries the area's southern extremities to the Taxco Mountains. The Amacuzac is a major tributary to the great Balsas River for which the Morelos area acts as a watershed.[2]

Within these mountain walls, which vary in altitude from about 6,000 to more than 17,500 feet, are numerous valleys which are narrow and of high altitude in the north and broad and low in the south. The largest and most important are the Valle de Cuernavaca in the west and the Valles de Yautepec (or San Gaspar), Jojutla and Cuautla (or Las Amilpas) in the east. Some of the northern valleys and the high altitude mountains around them are the *tierras frías* or temperate cold lands of Morelos. Other valleys in the north, the upper reaches of the Valles de Cuernavaca and Cuautla, and the Yautepec Valley are *tierras templadas* or temperate lands of moderate climate. The lower altitude southern mountains, the southern extensions of the Cuernavaca and Cuautla valleys and the Valle de Jojutla are the subtropical, hot, and humid *tierras calientes* of the area.[3]

In the northern mountains and valleys snow is not uncommon in the winter or dry season, and during the six month wet or summer season rains are frequent. Annual rainfall is, however, moderate, and there are few springs or continuously running streams except in the northwestern corner, the Zempoala-Huitzilac region, where several small mountain lakes provide tributaries to the Tembembe and Tetlama rivers.[4] A descending semiarid strip separates the high-altitude north of the area from its lower and warmer central and southern regions. This strip also marks the dividing line between formations which are a part of the Cordillera Neovolcánica and the valleys, mountains, and plateaus which are a part of the Depresión del Balsas. Fernando Cortés described the mountains and hills of this strip, through which he marched in 1521, as pine-covered, unpopulated, and waterless. For want of water, he wrote, and because movement through a pass in this area was so difficult, some of the Indians who accompanied him died of thirst.[5]

The temperate to subtropical valleys and surrounding ridges and hills in central and southern Morelos are areas of snowless, warm, even hot, winters. Except for some stretches in the rough terrain of the far south and southeast, summer rains are frequent and moderate to heavy. Virtually all of the valleys are fed by numerous continuously running streams and rivers. In the west the Tembembe and the Tetlama (or Jojutla) rivers drain the Cuernavaca Valley and form the only important lakes in the area, large Tequesquetengo and the smaller and swampy Coatetelco. In the east the Río Yautepec waters the Yautepec and Jojutla valleys and the long Valle de Cuautla is drained by the Cuautla, Nexapa, Tepalcingo, and Tenango rivers. All of these streams form or join major tributaries to the Amacuzac River.

Groves of cedar, pine, spruce, madrono (strawberry tree), ocote (Mexican pitch pine), live oak, and in places maguey and *amaquavitl* (the *"árbol de papel"* or paper tree) abound in the northern mountains and valleys.[6] To the south are forests of pine, live oak, Mexican juniper and various subtropical and tropical bushes and trees. Here and there in the semiarid strip of the north-central part of the area and in the southeastern plateaus and hills plant life is all but nonexistent. The major valleys of the region as well as many of the lesser ones are rich in volcanic soils and plant life interrupted by numerous hills, rock outcroppings, and deep barrancas. Among these, the northern and centrally located fit the description a sixteenth-century Spaniard, Juan Ximénez, applied to a part of one of them, the upper Cuernavaca Valley. He described it as "templado, viciosa, y sana," or temperate, lush, and healthful.[7] The valleys in the south are equally rich and frequently more verdant as they are much hotter and more humid. A Franciscan priest stationed at the mission of Tlaquiltenango in the Jojutla Valley late in the 1560s informed the Council of the

Indies that his area was "tierra caliente" and ". . . que todo el año sudan en ella," that all the year they (its inhabitants) sweat there.[8] The southern half of the Cuautla Valley was described in 1571 as ". . . de calor y templado y es buena tierra," hot and temperate and good land.[9]

The numerous well-watered, fertile valleys; the great diversity of climate, flora, and fauna; and the surrounding protective mountains rich in timber, lime, and stone make the Morelos area a desirable place to live. Perhaps it was so regarded by its human inhabitants of 1521; they did claim it as a homeland, theirs for generations.

The People

In 1521 the people of the Morelos area had advanced beyond the first men who had lived there by means of 8,000 or more years of experimentation, innovation, and learning.[10] As time passed, nonfarming hunters were replaced by agriculturalists who were also proficient as potters and architects. To invaders from the north who displaced them, they bequeathed earth, rain, and maize gods and a tradition of urbanlike life in a stratified society based upon intensive land cultivation. A quarrelsome lot, the northern invaders made the Morelos area a battleground for centuries. Two groups among them, the Tlahuicas and the Xochimilcas, established a claim to the area between 1000 and 1300 and by the latter date were permanently settled and dominant there.

These two related tribes, both speakers of the Nahuatl language, split the area, the Tlahuicas securing the southern three-quarters, the Xochimilcas, the northern, mountainous quarter. The arid strip which so vexed Cortés' army in 1521 marked, more or less, the boundary between them. Until after 1440 their activities revolved around almost continuous warfare with neighbors to the north, east, and west, with one another, and with outsiders who penetrated the Morelos country. At times during the turmoil one or both lost independent status and were forced to pay tribute of one sort or another to conquerors, but these were generally short periods of limited vassalage.

There were several such periods between 1395 and 1429 as mercenaries moved through the Morelos area collecting tribute for the tribal group then dominant in the region, the Tecpanecas of Azcapotzalco. These mercenaries, the Tenochas or Mexicans, were Nahuatl-speaking relatives of the Tlahuicas and Xochimilcas. Huitzilhuitl II, their chieftain from 1395 through 1414, led one of the excursions into the Morelos area in the course of which he selected as one of his wives the daughter of the señor (ruling lord) of the major *señorío* or lordship in the area, the pueblo and province of Cuernavaca. Huitzilhuitl's interest in the Tlahuica princess may have been stimulated by his desire for the excellent cotton textiles produced by her father's vassals.[11]

Tecpaneca tribute demands on the Morelos towns came to an end as the Mexicans, newcomers to the great basin-valley complex north of the Ajusco-Popocatépetl mountains, began their rise to power in the development of a conquest state, the Aztec Confederacy. The Mexicans and their recently acquired allies in the Confederacy (or Empire) of the Triple Alliance, the cities of Texcoco and Tlacopan, successfully challenged and replaced their dominating valley neighbors, the Tecpanecas, in 1429. Subsequently, forces led by Moctezuma I, chieftain of the Mexicans from 1440 until 1469 and possibly the son of the Tlahuica princess, brought the Morelos area under effective Confederacy control with the conquest of the Xochimilca towns between Xiutepec and Totolapan and the Tlahuica towns of Cuernavaca, Oaxtepec, Yautepec, Tepalcingo, and Acapistla. Apparently at least Cuernavaca stoutly resisted subjugation, and some of its people were forcibly displaced by Mexican and allied colonists.[12]

Moctezuma's conquest of much of their country terminated the relatively independent development enjoyed by the peoples of Morelos. Thereafter, increasing dependence upon the Confederacy and, finally, its Mexican members was theirs. Initially they paid tribute probably to the Confederacy's partners, among whom mutual agreement determined the division; later payment was probably made to the Mexicans who provided such shares as they saw fit to Texcoco and Tlacopan.[13]

Following the example of earlier Mexican rulers, perhaps including his father, Moctezuma I may have taken as one of his wives a Tlahuica princess, daughter of Cuauhototzin, señor of resistive Cuernavaca.[14] He also secured lands in lush, well-watered Oaxtepec where he developed beautiful gardens much admired by Cortés and at least one of his followers, Bernal Díaz.[15] Of the gardens where he rested in 1521, Cortés wrote:

> . . . and at 10:00 a.m. we arrived in Oaxtepec, of which I made mention above, and in the garden-home of the señor there we all took lodging. That garden is the largest, most beautiful, and most refreshing I have ever seen. It is two leagues in circumference and through its center flows a gentle rivulet of water. At intervals measuring two long-bow shots there are refreshing lodgings and gardens, innumerable trees of various kinds and a great many plants and fragrant flowers . . .[16]

More direct Confederacy control over the Morelos towns was instituted by Moctezuma I's successors, Axayácatl (1469–81) and Tizoc (1481–86). They subjected the area to troop levies to fulfill Confederacy war needs and assigned resident tribute collectors to four of its cabecera (head) towns: Cuernavaca, Yautepec, Oaxtepec, and Acapistla.[17] The ruling chieftains of these towns were invited to participate in the coronation of Ahuitzotl, son of Moctezuma I and successor to Tizoc as ruler of the Mexicans.[18] During his reign, 1486–1502, the Tlahuicas and Xochimilcas of Morelos were rapidly integrated into the Confederacy, which was just as rapidly becoming a conquest-empire dominated by the Mexicans. Ahuitzotl initiated construction, completed after his death, of a major temple in the Morelos town of Tepoztlan.[19] In 1490 he made important sacrifices in Cuernavaca and may have participated in the selection of a new señor for that town and its *sujetos* (subject settlements). Tehuehuetzin, the señor selected, founded a new dynasty when he took office the following year.[20]

The Confederacy—or perhaps more accurately the Mexican—subjugation of the peoples of Morelos begun by Moctezuma I was completed by his namesake, Moctezuma II, who succeeded Ahuitzotl in 1502. Before his death as a captive of Spanish conquerors and on the eve of their conquest of the area, Morelos had become an integral part of the Aztec state. Its peoples regularly provided tribute and labor services thereto; the señoríos to which they belonged comprised provinces therein; even the religious rituals they performed were, in part, directed at placation and worship of Aztecan deities.

Aztecan Morelos

The Tlahuica and Xochimilca peoples of Morelos, perhaps numbering as many as 725,000 in 1520, were included in three of the tributary provinces of Moctezuma II's Aztec state.[21] Comprising two provinces of more than forty cabecera towns and their sujetos (see Appendix 1) were most of the Tlahuicas and some of the Xochimilcas. Two of the more important cabeceras, Cuernavaca and Oaxtepec, served as administrative centers for the provinces. Perhaps Tepoztlan and certainly several of the other northern Xochimilca pueblos and their sujetos formed a part of the Chalco-Tlalmanalco province which was administered from an Aztecan center in the great valley north of the Ajusco-Popocatépetl ranges.[22]

As Aztecan tributaries the peoples of Morelos were required to make regular tribute payments to Aztecan officials (*calpixques*) one of whom was stationed in Cuernavaca and another in Oaxtepec. These payments consisted of stated amounts of maize, beans, and other foodstuffs; cotton textiles; war costumes and shields; and amaquavitl paper (see Appendix 1). They were also expected to make occasional contributions of men and supplies to conquest and other war activities, to provide laborers for various projects, and to maintain the Aztecan *calpixques* and others, including garrisons of troops, permanently or periodically assigned to their area. Outside of these requirements the artisans and farmers—the ruled— and the lords and priests—the rulers—of Aztecan Morelos enjoyed a considerable measure of autonomy.

This autonomy did not, however, as perhaps it had not in earlier times, preclude the participation of Moctezuma II or his agents in the selection of local ruling lords; in some instances, apparently, Moctezuma appointed them directly. Izcoatzin, dynastic successor to Tehuehuetzin in the señorío of Cuernavaca, may have been replaced at the time of his death in 1512 by an appointee of Moctezuma. The age of the hereditary heirs (and perhaps other factors) may have prompted that and successive appointments up through that of Yoatzin, señor of Cuernavaca at the time of the Spanish conquest. Shortly after the conquest, Yoatzin was replaced by his son, Don Hernando.[23]

Dominating the affairs of the cabecera towns and their sujetos in Aztecan Morelos were señores such as Yoatzin and the other, lesser members of the local nobility, the principales and priests. Supporting these nobles were free commoners (*macehuales*), *mayeques,* who appear to have been tenant farmers or serfs on the lands of the señores and principales, and chattel slaves. Except for the smallest sujetos, where everyone, from noble to slave, lived, the settlements, whether cabecera or sujeto, were apparently subdivided into sections, or barrios as they were known after the Spanish conquest. These barrios were evidently administrative units over which principales exercised hereditary jurisdiction. The farming commoners in a barrio enjoyed use-right to its lands. Barrios were assessed the tribute required to meet Aztec demands and to support the local nobility. The commoners, artisans and farmers, and the mayeques were responsible for producing the tribute (the commoners seem to have provided much of that due the Aztec state; the mayeques, much of that due the local nobles); the principales, for collecting it.[24]

The households of the barrios varied considerably in size and composition, with the average probably comprising between five and six persons.[25] In some instances several households of related family groups constituted a sort of compound unit in which the head of one of the households was dominant. The largest households, generally those of señores and principales, often included two or more nuclear families and other related folk, some mayeques or other servants, and chattel slaves. The smaller households of the commoners and mayeques consisted of a nuclear family and a relative or two.

Barrio and cabecera-sujeto landholdings were of three basic types: individual, communal, and community.[26] Individually held or owned lands, often worked by mayeques, were those of the local and Aztecan nobility. Communal lands were those to which commoners had virtually inalienable use-right but over which governing principales and señores exercised jurisdiction. These lands were worked and occupied by individuals and commonly used, as in the case of woodlands. Community lands supported local and Aztec religious establishments and, in some instances, were utilized by local nobles, particularly señores, and Aztec officials who had title thereto by virtue of the offices they held.

The numerous, productive peoples of Morelos were valuable vassals for Moctezuma II. Theirs was a well-ordered, magnificently varied garden in his Aztecan state. Over several decades preceding his second, fateful one as ruler of the Confederacy, they had become economically and politically, even dynastically, Aztecan. To some of them, then, Moctezuma turned in 1519 for consultation as his conquerors approached. Two years later—although by then evil portents were having their way and Moctezuma was no more—they met those conquerors as loyal Aztecan vassals, with arrow, stone, and blood.

The Spanish Conquest[27]

The Aztec Confederacy was not a century old in April 1519 when Fernando Cortés disembarked on its eastern shores near the coastal town of Chalchiuhcuecan (facing the island of San Juan de Ulúa). Runners sped to its ruler, Moctezuma II, with news of his arrival. Long plagued by portents of disaster, Moctezuma summoned priest-magicians for advice as to the origins and purposes of the invader. Among those who responded were several from Cuernavaca, Yautepec, and Oaxtepec, important towns in Morelos. Anxiously they sought the meaning of the appearance of the Spaniard and his followers.[28] Within months they had their answer as the audacious Spaniard undertook mastery of their confederacy and portions of the world that surrounded it.

For almost two years the priest-magicians of Morelos, their people, and their area escaped direct exposure to the shattering ambitions of the conquering Spaniard. Then, in the spring of 1521, as he relentlessly pursued his campaign to reduce the defenders of the Aztec state in numbers and strength and to isolate them in their capital city of Tenochtitlan, Cortés sent an invasion force into Morelos. In late February or early March the town of Chalco—a recently acquired ally that straddled the primary transport route to his principal outside supply base, the coastal town of Villa Rica, and that formerly had been an important source of Tenochtitlan's food supply—appealed for help in resisting an anticipated retaliatory attack by Confederacy forces.[29] From Texcoco, his newly acquired base of operations for the coming seige of Tenochtitlan, Cortés sent his able *capitan,* Gonzalo de Sandoval, and a force described by

Bernal Díaz del Castillo, as ". . . two-hundred infantrymen, twenty cavalrymen, ten or twelve crossbowmen and about the same number of musketeers, our friends the Tlaxcalans, and another company of Texcocans. . . ."[30]

In Tlalmanalco, a pueblo near Chalco, where he camped for a night, Sandoval was advised by his Indian spies that the threatening Confederacy troops were to the south in the mountainous country around the town of Chimalhuacan Chalco. His army augmented with soldiers from Chalco and nearby Huejotzingo and Cuauhquechollan, Sandoval marched south engaging in a running battle with the enemy, who were retreating steadily into the rough country southwest of the great volcano, Popocatépetl. After a night in Chimalhuacan Chalco, Sandoval, with the advice of Chalcan spies, marched his forces through difficult ridges and gorges and into the Morelos area.

The town of Oaxtepec was the primary objective of this first invasion in the Spanish conquest. Following Chalcan spy reports, the Spanish and allied troops entered the rough ridges between the Ajusco and Popocatépetl Ranges and advanced through mountain valleys into the northwestern corner of the long Cuautla valley. There they found Oaxtepec, an old Tlahuica establishment, site of Moctezuma I's famous gardens and, as the spies had reported, an Aztec garrison.

Chastisement and elimination of the garrison was not an easy task. Making effective use of easily defended hills and ravines, the Aztecs fought with skill and determination. Even after they were forced to surrender Oaxtepec and retreat in defeat, some returned and attempted unsuccessfully to dislodge Sandoval's exhausted troops from the gardens and homes where they were resting. Subsequently the Spanish and their allies spent two days encamped in Oaxtepec, which they found delightful. Years later, remembering reports of their stay and his own later visit there, Bernal Díaz wrote:

> And after Captain Sandoval saw himself free of the skirmishes [with the Aztecs who returned after their initial defeat and retreat] he gave thanks to God and went to rest and sleep in a garden, which there was in that town, the most beautiful garden, with large buildings and many things to see, I have ever seen in New Spain (I), and having so many things to see it was an admirable thing, certainly a garden for a great prince [doubtless that of Moctezuma I] . . . it was more than a quarter-league in length.[31]

Although he felt that the primary threat to Chalco's security had been eliminated and that his troops were in no condition to engage in another major bout, Sandoval was persuaded to attack the Aztec garrison housed in Acapistla, located across from Oaxtepec in the northeast corner of the

Cuautla Valley. Apparently his Chalcan allies and some of his Spanish captains argued that the contingent of Aztecs there should be rendered impotent, perhaps because they could provide a continuing threat to the over-all Spanish-Allied conquest effort. Sandoval requested peaceful submission by the garrison and people of Acapistla, but their leaders responded negatively and in a fashion which he seems to have deemed insulting and necessitating forceful action.

Acapistla, another of the old Tlahuica towns in Morelos, was well protected by surrounding ravines and proved more difficult to subdue than had Oaxtepec. Apparently its peoples and the threatened Aztecs fought as one in bloody determined resistance. Their stand was not broken until after Sandoval's Spanish troops, inspired by his and Captain Andrés de Tapia's exemplary bravery, succeeded in scaling the ravine walls and entering the fortified town. The hand-to-hand combat which followed was joined by Sandoval's allied troops, who turned it into a slaughter so vicious as to horrify even the more-than-calloused Spaniards. Later, in a letter to his king, Cortés wrote of the incident:

> . . . and that pueblo was very strong and placed on a height and where they [its defenders] could not be attacked by cavalry; and as the Spanish arrived those of the town fearlessly began to fight with them and threw rocks from [the heights] above . . . there was much fighting and resistance and there were many injuries . . . all of those who found themselves there affirm that a small stream which almost encircles the town was, for more than an hour, stained with blood. . . .[32]

The Spanish were not sufficiently horrified by the slaughter to refrain from participation in pillage of Acapistla. Leaving the defeated town for the return trip to Texcoco, they (like their allies returning home) were loaded with plunder including slaves, not a few of whom were pretty females. But they were probably mortified by their reception in Texcoco, for their plunder went unattended, their tired bodies unrested, and their feat unrecognized as Cortés curtly ordered them to return to Chalco: Sandoval's troops had scarcely unbuckled their swords when that town again appealed to Cortés for help in the face of a new threat. Aztecs, evidently out to avenge the defeats they suffered in Morelos and especially in the Acapistla affair, were again attacking. Cortés, feeling that Sandoval and his soldiers had failed in their mission, abruptly ordered them to fulfill it. They were spared, however, as the Chalcans managed to fend off the attack before the Spanish reached their city.

About a month elapsed between Sandoval's effort and the second, decisive Spanish invasion of Morelos. During that month vital men and supplies delivered by three ships which docked at Villa Rica reached

Cortés' headquarters in Texcoco. As welcome as these were delegations from towns which, impressed with recent Spanish successes, abandoned Aztecan tutelage and tendered their allegiance to Cortés. That month did not, however, bring submission to Spanish authority by the Aztecan chieftains in Tenochtitlan. In early April, exasperated by their defiant refusals to surrender what remained of their conquest state, Cortés set out to weaken their resistance by further reducing their sphere of influence and activity. Renewed probing of the Chalco area by their troops provided him with an immediate objective: effective subjugation of Morelos, which was the base of operations for the probes and still a supplier of essential foodstuffs and other goods to Tenochtitlan.

Leaving Sandoval in command in Texcoco, Cortés, with a number of allied troops and a Spanish force of 30 cavalry and 300 infantry, marched to Tlalmanalco on April 5, 1521.[33] Proceeding to Chalco the next morning, he stopped briefly for conferences with Chalcan leaders and to add allied troops to his army and then continued on to Chilmalhuacan Chalco, departure point for Sandoval's invasion of Morelos.

The following day, April 6, as his army filed southward through mountains and into the northern valley of Totolapan, Cortés began the long process of acquiring land and peoples in Morelos that would be his and his heirs' for generations. Almost twenty years later he would leave his great supporting estate in Morelos to take final leave of his conquests in a trip to his native land, the scene of his death. But his reception that day in April did not promise a fruitful relationship. Some of the people, Xochimilcas for the most part, cast stones and shot arrows at him and his army from *peñoles* (promontories) to which they had fled as he approached. Initially Cortés chose to ignore their harassment, but early in the afternoon as he entered the Tlayacapan valley and discovered a fairly large number of its residents, probably including some from the town of the same name, atop a fortified peñol, he decided to attack them.

Cortés' attack on this peñol has been described as "a fit of insensate folly" undertaken because "he [Cortés] seemed to think the honor of his army demanded it."[34] Folly it may have been, as the peñol might have been bypassed as unessential to his primary objective; but perhaps it was not folly, for, as the conqueror knew well, the large numbers of peoples over whom he and his Aztecan antagonists enjoyed or sought authority equated suzerainty with success in force of arms. His already commanding stature among many of them had been earned by meeting challenges forcefully.

The ferocity with which the defenders of the peñol met his attack cost Cortés the lives of at least eight of his Spanish soldiers and an unaccounted number of allied troops. He was, in fact, unable to overcome the defense before he was forced to withdraw his troops In order to meet a large army which entered the valley and bore down upon him. That army, perhaps comprising Xochimilca, Tlahuica, and Aztec warriors, was successfully routed through adroit maneuvers by his cavalry and the greatest effort by his foot soldiers. Spent by thirst, wounds, and fatigue, his troops then collapsed for the night beside some springs unfortunately located just below an occupied and fortified peñol. Throughout the night the people on the hillock, evidently townsmen of Tlayacapan, tormented them with arrows, stones, and shouted insults.

Reconnoitering the surrounding terrain early on April 8, Cortés placed some of his musketeers and crossbowmen on a peñol adjacent to that occupied by the Tlayacapanecas.[35] From that position his superior weapons and the Indians' lack of water finally forced the Indians to capitulate. A store of maize was secured in the surrender, along with a number of captives, who would soon be enslaved. The following day, that, judged folly, had its desired result. Some of the principales whom he had recently attacked without success surrendered themselves and their people. A group of slaves were then sent to Texcoco, and Cortés prepared his army for departure southward, the first stage in his invasion and the effective conquest of Morelos completed.

Reaching Oaxtepec in the upper Cuautla Valley on April 10, Cortés was peacefully received with offerings of food by Tlahuica chieftains. Evidently no Aztecan troops were then garrisoned in Oaxtepec, and its residents, having been humbled by Sandoval, were convinced that submission to Cortés was expedient if not entirely profitable. Taking advantage of the welcoming reception, Cortés and his army rested in gardens and homes which they found refreshing and praiseworthy.[36] The following morning they marched southwest into the Yautepec Valley and, approaching the town of that name, encountered a hostile army of Tlahuicas and, perhaps, Aztecs. Cortés reported,

> And as we arrived, it appeared that they wanted us to make some sign of peace or that they were afraid or they deceived us. But very shortly, without more remonstrance, they began to flee, abandoning their pueblo [Yautepec], and I, not recovered from restraining myself in it [the remonstrance], with thirty cavalry gave them chase for a good two leagues until they entered into another pueblo called Gilutepeque [Xiutepec] where we lanced and killed many [of them].[37]

Apparently those not killed in the foray as the fleeing army entered Xiutepec continued through the town and beyond it. The town's population offered little resistance to the invaders as they entered. Its adult male members, including principales, were evidently in flight with the army or had been killed in the preceding foray. After two days in the pueblo awaiting the return and surrender of its missing warriors and principales, Cortés took punitive action against them, enslaving the remaining males and a number of women and children.[38] Finally on April 13 as he took leave for a march to nearby Cuernavaca he fired the town. His action elicited no obvious response from the departed of Xiutepec, but before he was gone representatives from Yautepec appeared to pledge him the allegiance of their peoples.

The advance northward from Xiutepec through the magnificence of the Cuernavaca valley's northern reaches to his next objective was a short one. Cuernavaca, long the Tlahuica capital for a part of Morelos and an Aztecan administrative center, still housed a garrison of Confederacy troops.[39] That garrison, with the aid of local troops, used the town's excellent natural defenses to make conquest difficult. A contemporary chronicler, relying on Cortés' description, said the place was "strong and large and surrounded by deep barrancas"; another, three and a half centuries later, recounted:

> . . . as they approached the Spaniards stopped, separated from their enemies [the defenders of Cuernavaca] by the deep barranca and receiving from the opposite side [of the barranca] a rain of arrows and stones, thrown and slung, accompanied by a thundering clamor.[40]

A courageous act by one of his allies finally provided Cortés access to the fortified town: an enterprising Tlaxcalan crossed the protecting barranca at the town's rear by climbing through an overhanging tree.[41] As the Spanish and allied troops followed him into the town, its defenders, unnerved by the unexpected presence of their antagonists at their rear and in their midst, began to flee. Some, unable to go far, fought their enemies with knives or killed themselves to resist capture. Others escaped into the surrounding countryside but were pursued by their more mobile attackers. The result was a slaughter.[42]

Defeated Cuernavaca was then subjected to a burning and plundering in which Cortés and his forces secured rich rewards for their efforts. Bernal Díaz said of the booty in which he shared, "In this pueblo we had great plunder, very large cotton textiles as well as good women [presumably taken as concubines and slaves] . . .[43] Having secured blankets and women, the Spaniards and their allies took rest in surroundings as pleasant as those of Oaxtepec. As they rested, the señor and principales of the defeated town who had fled during the invasion returned and surrendered to Cortés.[44] Years later a Hispanicized descendant and namesake of the Texcocan leader (allied with the Spanish) who had effected the capitulation of Cuernavaca's Tlahuica chieftains wrote of it:

The lord named Yoatzin went retreating into the mountains and [Cortés] sent Ixtlilxochitl [leader of the Texcocans] to reprehend his [Yoatzin's] rebelliousness and to tell him that he should come to give and ask pardon for that which had transpired; presently, therefore, as dawn broke, they [Yoatzin and others] came to offer the Christians service and support, promising to aid them and to be forever, insofar as they could effect it, in his [Cortés'] favor.[45]

The final stage in Cortés' invasion of Morelos, the acquisition of Cuernavaca, was also the last step in the conquest phase of the Spanish subjugation of the area. The morning the Tlahuica chieftains came to offer him what would become a quarter of a century of supporting service, Cortés marched his army northward out of their valley through the arid, elevated zone beyond, where thirst and overexertion severely taxed his troops and even overcame some of his allies, and into the Ajusco Mountains. Emerging in the great basin-valley home of his principal antagonists, Cortés successfully attacked one of their important lakeside centers, Xochimilco, on April 15. He then triumphantly circled the lake site from which the Aztecs still defied him, much as he had the February before, and returned to Texcoco.

Having once again returned to Texcoco in the face of Aztecan defiance, Cortés undertook to tighten the noose he had patiently laid around the city. The siege of Tenochtitlan was begun in earnest. Using ships newly built in Tlaxcala and hauled laboriously overland to Texcoco, Cortés combined naval warfare with repeated infantry and cavalry attacks on the city. Through May and June and well into July the Aztecs were equal to their challenger. Their stout defense was sufficient to create doubt in some quarters as to the outcome of the struggle. Towns which had previously abandoned Aztecan domination now denied their pledges of allegiance to the Spanish. Other towns in outlying districts, some of which had never been under Aztecan domination or allied with the Spanish, took advantage of the occupation of both to acquire territories for themselves.

It was an instance of this kind of acquisition which drew Cortés' attention once again to Morelos. In the first week in July, as he fought the Aztecs from Xoloc, a settlement on the Ixtapalapan causeway into Tenochtitlan, he received a plea for assistance from the Tlahuicas of Cuernavaca. Warriors from Malinalco and the Cohuica towns northwest and southwest of Morelos were making incursions into their territory. Determined to prevent any further depletion of his allied support, Cortés responded with the dispatch of about one hundred Spanish soldiers and an undefined number of allied troops under the command of Andrés de Tapia. With the assistance of forces from Cuernavaca, Tapia was able to overcome the threatening groups in their own territory and return to the siege operations in less than the ten days allotted him for the foray.[46]

The siege of Tenochtitlan ended on August 13, 1521. Thoroughly trampled by Fernando Cortés and his apocalyptic horsemen, the Aztecs were conquered. Disease, thirst, starvation, and the scourge of war had weakened them for months. In their weakness they were renounced by subject peoples, orphaned by their gods, and forced to surrender, bit by bit, their conquest state. Finally they gave themselves and the rubble of their great city to Fernando Cortés.

Although Cortés had conquered them, the Aztecs and many others of their world, including the peoples of Morelos, were not yet really his in August 1521. Defeated and conquered they were, but subjugated and converted—politically, economically, socially, and spiritually—they were not. The task of making them and theirs a domain for himself, his king, and his God—the creation of a Spanish colonial state—remained.

Spiritual Subjugation[47]

In their commitment to mastery of the Aztecan world two years and some months before the defeat of Tenochtitlan, the Spanish sought not only the political and socioeconomic domination of its peoples but also their conversion to the truth faith, Spanish Catholic Christianity. Although other aspects of their conquest enterprise might preclude or precede their religious objective, it was ever essential to the sum of their efforts.

Responsibility for Christianization of the heathen was not confined to the priestly among them—initially Fray Bartolomé de Olmedo, a Mercedarian, and Juan Díaz, a secular clergyman—but was shared and exercised by Cortés, his captains, his soldiers and even their servants. The principals in the spiritual subjugation of the Aztec world, however, were men like Díaz and Olmedo, trained as spokesmen and interpreters of doctrine, dogma, and ritual.

Olmedo and Díaz, who landed with Cortés in 1519, were joined before the fall of Tenochtitlan by several other clerics including two Franciscan friars, Diego Altamirano and Pedro Melgarejo. The latter, whose primary function was to provide papal indulgences for the conquering Spaniards, is credited with the first step in the spiritual subjugation of Morelos. His endeavors seem to have consisted primarily of accompanying and encouraging the Cortesian force which conquered the towns of Totolapan, Tlayacapan, Oaxtepec, and Cuernavaca in April of 1521.[48]

Effective conversion of the Aztecan state did not begin until after the defeat of Tenochtitlan. The appearance in 1523 of three Franciscans—

Friars Juan de Aora, Juan de Tecto, and Pedro de Gante—marked the actual beginning of the replacement of Aztecan by Christian deities in the rebuilt Tenochtitlan. The conversion effort in outlying areas did not begin until after the arrival, in May 1524, of the twelve "Mexican Apostles." These Franciscans, together with the five who preceded them and their Dominican counterparts who reached the city in 1526, set the pattern for Christian missionization in the Aztecan world. They adapted Spanish Catholic doctrine, ceremony, and custom to the languages, needs, and attitudes of the Aztec peoples.

Eight or nine months after their arrival and barefoot walk from Villa Rica to the rebuilt Tenochtitlan, the twelve apostles were joined, according to Fray Jerónimo de Mendieta, by several fellow Franciscans including Fray Alonso de Herrera, Fray Antonio Ortiz, Fray Antonio Maldonado, and Fray Diego de Almonte.[49] Monasteries and churches were under construction and conversions begun in Texcoco, Tlaxcala, Huejotzingo, and Tenochtitlan at the time of the arrival of this fourth group of Franciscans. It is also possible that four of their predecessors were already working, from quarters in Tenochtitlan, in the Morelos area.[50]

Mendieta, successor and chronicler to the early mendicant missionaries, reported that the apostles, with the help of their recently arrived brethren, presumably in 1525,

> . . . founded the fifth convent [monastery, fifth of the Franciscan establishments] in the pueblo of Cuernavaca . . . from that Cuernavaca convent they [the friars stationed there] visited [in the ecclesiastical sense] Ocuila and Malinalco and all the hot lands situated to the south as far as the Mar del Sur [Pacific Ocean].[51]

In further discussion of early Franciscan missionization in the "pueblos de tierra caliente (towns of the hot country)," Mendieta wrote:

> . . . from the Cuernavaca monastery, which was the fifth where they placed friars, they [the friars] went out to visit through the territory of that which is called the Marquesado and they found the people as well disposed and willing to be Christians as in the pueblos of which I made mention above, especially in those [pueblos] called Yacapichtla [Acapistla] and Guastepec [Oaxtepec] . . .[52]

He noted that cooperation of the principales in the Morelos area facilitated the conversion effort, and that the vices of the Indians, particularly drunkenness, were rapidly eliminated.

The *Códice Municipal de Cuernavaca* (see Appendix 2), evidently composed after 1550 and based upon information gleaned from that town's Indian leaders, describes the implantation of the Christian faith in Cuernavaca and its sujetos.[53] One of the principales who contributed to the preparation of the *Códice,* Don Toribio de San Martín Cortés, listed ten friars who came with Cortés in 1524 to baptize the people of the area. The date he gave for the baptism was obviously an error, as his list included seven of the Franciscans who came to New Spain in that year and one who came with the fourth group in 1525. Probably the other two friars on the list were also members of the group that arrived in 1525.[54]

Mendieta, relying on the history written by his fellow Franciscan and predecessor, Fray Toribio Motolinía, indicated that the convento (and probably church) of Cuernavaca was founded in 1526, and that the friars there served the Cohuica and Taxco areas.[55] He added that the padres were unable to visit every settlement in the areas mentioned, and that the Indians frequently came to the larger towns from smaller pueblos and estancias to hear Mass, be instructed in the faith, and have their children baptized. He noted the difficulties in missionary labors in the area during the rainy season, which he cited as April through September, when the deep barrancas ran full with flood waters and were formidable obstacles to travel.[56]

The data supplied by Mendieta, Motolinía, the authors of the *Códice,* and Indians who testified in various legal proceedings during the 1550s and in the compilation of the *Relaciones* of the 1570s and 1580s indicate that the initial phase of the spiritual subjugation of Morelos was the work of Franciscan friars.[57] These mendicants began operating from their headquarters in Cuernavaca as early as 1525 and, no doubt, built temporary churches in the major towns of the area.[58] Evidently they erected in Acapistla a church and monastery which was rebuilt and operated by the Augustinians after 1535. Later, between 1535 and 1540, they built a permanent church in Tlaltenango.[59] In later years they added to these structures a church-monastery in Xiutepec, built before 1569, and similar edifices in Mazatepec and Xochitepec, both apparently constructed in the last decade of the seventeenth century.[60]

Although they were later participants in the spiritual subjugation of Morelos, Dominican and Augustinian friars built more missions and probably worked among a larger group of neophytes in the long-term conversion effort there than did the Franciscans. The Dominican endeavor began at least as early as 1529, three years after the first of the order reached New Spain.[61] In chronicling the deed of these and other Dominicans, Fray Agustín Dávila Padilla noted that some of the first among them went to Oaxtepec soon after their arrival and there built the order's first church in an Indian town. That establishment, he recorded, subsequently served as one of three major Dominican mission headquarters in New Spain.[62]

From Oaxtepec the preachers labored among the Indians of Yautepec,

Tetela del Volcán, Hueyapan, and Tepoztlan.[00] In Tepoztlan—an important Aztec ceremonial center, site of the temple built during the reigns of Ahuitzotl and Moctezuma II—the friars encountered stubborn resistence to abandonment of preconquest religious beliefs.[64] In later years, perhaps after 1550, the Dominicans built convento-churches in each of these towns and in Tlaltizapan. About 1580 they apparently replaced the Franciscans in Tlaltenango, and much later they assumed responsibility for a secular and evidently Spanish parish in Cuautla.[65]

The Augustinians did not join in the missionization of New Spain until 1533, more than a decade after the fall of Tenochtitlan.[66] In Morelos, as they did in several other areas, these friars moved into towns and estancias with which, for want of manpower, the Franciscans and Dominicans had been able to maintain only occasional contact. Among the first of these towns was Totolapan where, between 1533 and 1536, they built a monastery and a church.[67] At about the same time they apparently erected similar missions in Ocuituco and Zacualpan de Amilpas and took over and rebuilt the Franciscan church in Acapistla.[68] From these centers they carried out a conversion program in the northern Tlayacapan-Atlatlahuacan valleys and southward through the broad Cuautla Valley.[69] In the 1550s they evidently constructed missions in that valley at Jonacatepec, Jumiltepec, and perhaps at Jantetelco.[70] To these they added another before 1570, in the north at Atlatlahuacan.[71]

All of these missionaries and particularly the Franciscans were given aid in their spiritual subjugation of Morelos by Cortés.[72] Although considerable work remained in the conversion process, much had been accomplished before his death in 1547.

2

Encomiendas

Acquisition, 1522–1524

The Aztec Confederacy expired on August 13, 1521, as the city of Tenochtitlan conceded defeat to Fernando Cortés and his Spanish and allied Indian army. Following a victory celebration in Coyoacan, headquarters for the last days in the siege of the city, the conqueror and his followers undertook to create a colonial state out of the ruins of the Aztec domain. They selected ruined Tenochtitlan as the island site for the capital of their new state, the kingdom of New Spain, and reconstruction was immediately begun. Labor and materials for the huge project were requisitioned from settlements in the surrounding countryside, including some in Morelos.[1]

As Tenochtitlan-México, in later times more often called La Ciudad de México (Mexico City), was reconstructed and a governing body formed for it, Cortés began dispatching subjugation expeditions to areas, within and without the boundaries of the old Aztec Confederacy, not yet under Spanish domination. Some of the expeditions so dispatched served as exploratory parties seeking knowledge of the mineral wealth, fertile soils, and peoples of the areas they penetrated. Some also sought information about the sea to the west (Mar del Sur) and possible water routes to it from the eastern ocean.

Two such expeditions returned Cortesian soldiers to Morelos. Juan Rodríguez de Villafuerte led one, the principal objective of which was the Mar del Sur. Villafuerte's force evidently marched through Morelos in 1521, perhaps following its river system southward, to the town of Zacatula, located not far from the mouth of the Las Balsas River.[2] In the same year, troops under the command of Francisco de Orozco penetrated the northeastern corner of Morelos in pursuit of threatening Mixtecas. During the siege of Tenochtitlan several among the tribal groups not committed to support of either the Spanish or the Aztecs (some having denied earlier declarations of allegiance) attempted to acquire areas uncontrolled or left unprotected by the fully engaged antagonists. Among these were the Mixtecas of the Oaxaca region who sought control of the area surrounding and including Segura de la Frontera, the Spanish villa established at Tepeaca in 1520. Following Tenochtitlan's capitulation, Cortés sent reinforcements to Orozco, his commander in Segura, who then moved against the Mixtecas. Orozco's campaign took him into Morelos where the towns of Tetela del Volcán and Hueyapan were drawn into the fighting.[3]

These military-exploratory ventures were essential to the establishment of the political entity of New Spain and constituted a preliminary step in the economic subjugation of the territories it was to encompass. Cortés, a participant in the early development of Spain's Cuban colony, realized that effective economic subjugation meant Spanish settlement and exploitation of the human and natural resources of his new domain.[4] Earlier he had assigned *solares* (ground plots or lots) in Villa Rica and Segura de la Frontera to his followers, himself, and the Spanish crown; he now did so in Tenochtitlan, as he would subsequently, either in person or through lieutenants, in newly founded villas. He also requested, in reports to the Spanish crown, that seeds, plants, animals, and colonists be sent to New Spain as rapidly as possible.

As early as March 1522, Cortés began granting encomiendas to his followers despite his admitted knowledge of the misuse and disastrous result of such grants in Cuba and his belief that many of the peoples of the Aztecan world were sufficiently competent to become free vassals of the Spanish crown.[5] His grants authorized individuals, as encomenderos, to collect tribute and secure labor services from the Indians of assigned towns.[6] In establishing the encomienda system in New Spain, Cortés was influenced by a number of circumstances, including the demands of his soldiers for rewards for their service in the conquest and the fact that a tribute payment and labor service system was a feature of Aztecan administration in the Confederacy of the Triple Alliance and was in operation when he landed on its shores in 1519.[7]

In his third Letter of Relation (May 22, 1522) Cortés informed the king that he had been obliged to make encomienda grants to his soldiers in recognition of their conquest services. He realized he had no legal authority to do so but hoped that his action, prompted by necessity, would receive crown approval. The response to this letter was consistent with royal policy formulated in 1520: instructions to Cortés dated June 26, 1523, explicitly forbade grants of encomienda and ordered revocation of any grants he had made. The conqueror withheld compliance with these instructions and on October 15, 1524, again wrote the crown arguing that the encomienda system provided the only satisfactory means of supporting (and rewarding) worthy conquistadores and colonists and guaranteeing the stability of the colony.

Cortés' arguments, rooted in colonial realities and augmented by the opinions of fellow local officials, many of New Spain's missionary clergy, and some of the royal advisors in Spain, produced a modification of crown policy during the years 1525–29. The encomienda, subject to alteration and control by royal agencies of government, was gradually accepted as a necessary feature of administration in New Spain.[8] Cortés' position was thereby justified, and his grants as well as those of his successors in the governorship of New Spain were given tacit recognition. But the confused legal status of the grants made before 1525, especially those Cortés made without explicit instruction or in contravention of the royal order of 1523, provided occasion and excuse for his political rivals in the colony to challenge the validity of a number of grants, including those which constituted his personal holdings.

Allotment of lands for agricultural enterprise was undertaken as encomiendas were assigned. The lands Cortés and his fellows assigned themselves were, in most instances, in use at the time of the conquest and were from all five of the major classes of Aztecan holdings.[9] Lands which gave promise of mineral wealth, in use or otherwise, were taken by the Spanish for development by individuals who were obliged to share their profits with the crown. The earliest of these were evidently exploited in placer operations such as those undertaken in the Oaxaca and Michoacán areas.[10]

For these and all phases of the socioeconomic development of New Spain, Cortés, as the colony's crown-appointed (in a royal decree of October 15, 1522) political and military administrator, issued ordinances in 1524.[11] These regulations evidence the conqueror's knowledgeable interest in economic activity, particularly agrarian enterprise, beyond the exploitation of mineral resources. In light of his later endeavors, however, perhaps (as Bancroft suggests) his primary concern was acquisition of precious metals for himself and his king.[12]

As the principal agent and virtual dictator in the economic subjugation of the Aztecan world during the years 1522–24, Cortés reserved for himself numerous encomienda towns and took possession of sizable tracts of land for what became his *granjerías* (holdings) and haciendas. These properties and similarly acquired mining interests formed the beginning of his estate in New Spain. The encomiendas, generally speaking, provided the capital and the labor, while the landholdings provided the rich soils, the mineral and water resources, and the construction materials out of which the estate was developed.

No grants of encomienda issued by Cortés to himself have as yet come to light, but it is clear that his encomienda towns were among the most productive and populous in New Spain.[13] The 42,800 *pesos de oro* of annual revenue in tribute payments which his attorneys reported as the minimum figure he was receiving in 1524 suggests the value of these holdings (see Appendix 3).[14] They were located in practically every area then included within the boundaries of the colony, in all parts of the Aztecan Confederacy and in places not a part thereof, in the Valley of México, Michoacán, Pánuco, Oaxaca, Tehuantepec, Soconusco; around the towns of Villa Rica, Tlapa, Tuxtla, Huejotzingo, Tlaxcala, Atotonilco; and in Morelos (see Appendix 3). Many of them were potential or actual port sites and trading centers or were in the vicinity of mines.[15]

The encomiendas Cortés reserved for himself in Morelos, Cuernavaca, Oaxtepec, Acapistla, Tepoztlan, and Yautepec formed the heart of his estate there. As defined by Cortés, these encomiendas encompassed all of the settlements, cabecera and sujeto, in Aztecan Morelos except the towns in its northeastern corner: Tetela del Volcán and Hueyapan and their surrounding sujetos.[16] Acapistla and Yautepec (with their sujetos) were to pay their tribute directly to Cortés or his agents rather than delivering it to collectors in Oaxtepec as they had in making payments to the Aztecs. The cabecera towns of Totolapan, Tlayacapan, and Atlatlahuacan together with their sujetos were included in the encomienda of Acapistla. Before the Spanish arrived, they had paid their tribute directly to Aztec agents in Oaxtepec in what appears to have been a capacity equal to that of Acapistla and Yautepec. Tepoztlan, which may have rendered the Aztecs tribute through Chalco-Tlalmanalco, was to pay encomienda dues directly to Cortés or his agents.[17] These assignments reflect Cortés' use—with significant alteration—of the Aztecan taxation system in making his repartimiento encomienda grants.[18]

Cortés probably reserved the Morelos towns for himself as he began assigning encomiendas to his followers in early 1522. There is no evidence that any among them were involved in the changes he made both in his personal holdings and in those set aside for the crown after he was appointed governor and captain-general of New Spain in 1523.[19] In 1524, he was receiving tribute from these towns and, no doubt, labor services as well, and apparently had been for some time.[20]

Conflict and Losses, 1524–1530

Cortés occupied an enviable, almost all-powerful position in the affairs of New Spain in early 1524. As governor and captain-general he enjoyed virtually unlimited authority over the political, social, and economic development of the colony, the territorial enlargement of which his lieutenants were pursuing with vigor. He had successfully vanquished powerful rivals and had secured a vast personal estate comprised of properties in most of the richest districts of the new colony.

A succession of events during the years 1524–26 produced an abrupt shift in the conqueror's fortunes and left him shorn of much of his power, influence, and property. In the spring of 1524 his political and economic authority was curtailed with the arrival in New Spain of four crown-appointed treasury officials and the receipt of a royal decree disapproving his grants of repartimiento-encomienda. Although Cortés and his lieutenants in the government of New Spain chose to ignore the directive, it prompted controversy in the colony, the repercussions of which limited Cortés' influence and led, ultimately, to his loss of some properties. The following autumn he undertook his heroic but ill-fated two-year expedition to Honduras. During his absence New Spain was beset by bitter factional rivalries which severely reduced both his influence and his wealth. Finally, soon after his return to Tenochtitlan-México in May of 1526, he was obliged to relinquish his governing powers to a recently appointed successor who had been instructed to subject him to residencia proceedings.

Prior to 1524 Cortés, as governor, exercised superior authority in the supervision and management (including expenditure) of crown revenue in New Spain. In the spring of 1524 that authority was assumed by four royal treasury officials: Alonso de Estrada, *tesorero* (treasurer), Gonzalo de Salazar, *factor* (collections and disbursements agent), Pedro Almindes Cherino, *veedor* (inspector), and Rodrigo de Albornoz, *contador* (auditor). The last of these, Albornoz, may also have been entrusted with a secret commission as a kind of personal intelligence officer for the Emperor Charles V. Jealous of their legal authority, personally ambitious, and eager for power, these men collectively and individually represented a serious challenge to the rather freewheeling authority and influence previously enjoyed by the conqueror. Within a few months competition for power divided them into two conflicting pairs, Estrada and Albornoz versus Salazar and Cherino, each allied with dissident factions in the colony.

The state of affairs in New Spain rapidly deteriorated from 1524 to 1526 while the conqueror was absent on his fruitless expedition to Honduras and the colony was deprived of his forceful leadership.[21] Before his departure in the last days of October 1524 he appointed the royal treasurer, Alonso de Estrada, and the contador, Rodrigo de Albornoz, to serve in his absence as cogovernors of New Spain. To assist them in the task he gave Licenciado Alonso Zuazo, a respected crown official from Cuba, the responsibility of administering justice and selected Rodrigo de Paz (Cortés' cousin), who had joined him in Mexico in 1523, to serve as *alcalde mayor* and aid to Zuazo. Paz was also entrusted with supervision and management of Cortés' estate.[22] After his arrival at Espíritu Santo in the Coatzacoalcos area in December, 1524, Cortés received a report from his cousin which described increasing differences between Estrada and

Albornoz and their apparent inability to work together. On the journey to Espíritu Santo Cortés had been accompanied by Salazar and Almindes Cherino, the royal factor and veedor respectively, and, probably with their encouragement, he now ordered them to return to Tenochtitlan-México with new instructions for the government of the colony in his absence. These instructions provided that all four of the royal treasury officials should share authority as cogovernors of New Spain, but in case Estrada and Albornoz were still engaged in dispute, Salazar and Cherino were authorized to assume control of the administration of the colony in cooperation with Zuazo and the alcalde mayor.

Armed with these instructions, Salazar and Cherino, between Christmas 1524 and August 1525, succeeded in removing Albornoz, Estrada, and Zuazo from their governmental positions, gained control of the cabildo of Tenochtitlan-México, and rendered Rodrigo de Paz ineffective in his role as alcalde mayor. In these maneuvers the factor and veedor shrewdly won the support of an anti-Cortés faction comprised of conquistadores and colonists who felt that their services had not been accorded fair recognition by the conqueror in his allocation of encomienda grants. Salazar and Cherino also lent official credence to reports that Cortés had been killed on his journey to Honduras. They thus obtained formal recognition by the cabildo of Mexico City as Cortés' successors in the governorship of New Spain and took action to assume control of his estate in the name of the crown.

As justification for the move to take possession of his properties and interests, the factor and the veedor asserted that the conqueror did not have legal or personal right or claim to his encomienda holdings, but that he held them for and in the name of the crown as governor of New Spain. After the official pronouncement that Cortés was dead, they therefore called upon Rodrigo de Paz to render account to the royal treasury of the revenues received from these encomienda holdings and to release the vast riches supposedly accumulated from them and kept in Cortés' palace in Tenochtitlan-México. Paz resisted these demands, and the palace was brought under attack by troops assembled by the factor and the veedor. Paz surrendered and was promptly brought to trial on the charge of treason, subjected to rigorous torture, and hanged on October 16, 1525.[23]

With Paz out of the way, Salazar and Cherino began taking over Cortés' encomienda holdings and other properties in the name of the crown. Some of the encomiendas were reassigned to conquistadores and colonists of the anti-Cortés faction who had supported the veedor and the factor in their seizure of power, and agents (*procuradores*) were dispatched to the royal court in Spain to defend the action. These agents argued:

. . . that the governor Hernando Cortés had the greatest part of
the Indians of this land and the best of the others [Indians], those
that were profitable, he gave to his relatives, servants, and allies, so
that all the towns [Spanish] lived in extreme need and that now
Gonzalo de Salazar and Pedro Almindez Cherino who remained in
the government have distributed [reassigned in encomienda grants]
the Indians and [thereby] supported the towns and increased the
[property owning] citizens and inhabitants [thereof] . . .[24]

The complaints of the procuradores were not without substantive basis.
Cortés had extensive, perhaps excessive, holdings in New Spain, and in
granting encomiendas, he did favor relatives and personal associates, often
at the expense of deserving conquest veterans.[25] For the sake of harmony
within the colony, if for no other reason, a redistribution of encomiendas
was undoubtedly necessary. Like Cortés, however, Salazar and Cherino
were not legally empowered to make encomienda assignments. Their
reassignments, including some involving Cortés' holdings, were, moreover, characterized by obvious, almost exclusive, partiality for personal
allies.

On October 8, 1525, they formally granted the Morelos encomienda of
Cuernavaca to Antonio Serrano de Cardona. Serrano was a regidor in the
cabildo of Tenochtitlan-México and had actively collaborated with
Salazar and Cherino, especially in the arrest and trial of Rodrigo de Paz.[26]
Somewhat later he served as one of their procuradores in Spain.[27] Cortés'
other encomiendas in Morelos, Oaxtepec, Yautepec, Acapistla, and
Tepoztlan, were taken from him by the veedor and the factor between
late August and the end of October in 1525.[28] To whom these towns were
reassigned is not known, although Yautepec and Tepoztlan appear to
have been granted to Diego de Ordaz, the messenger who brought from
the Tabasco area the welcome report, later proven false, that Cortés was
dead.[29]

News that he was, in fact, very much alive was carried to Tenochtitlan-
México in January 1526 by one of Cortés' servants. His allies, led by
Andrés de Tapia and Gonzalo de Sandoval, had long been plotting and,
armed with news of his probable return, joined Estrada and Albornoz in
deposing and jailing Salazar and Cherino. Five months later Cortés
returned, resumed full authority as governor and captain-general, and
quickly recovered most of his encomienda holdings (some had already
been restored to his agents by Estrada and Albornoz).

The conqueror's regained power and property in the colony was
immediately lost again. In June 1526, Licenciado Luis Ponce de León
came from Spain with instructions to relieve Cortés of the office of
governor and to subject him to residencia proceedings. Ponce's appoint-

ment and instructions reflected the crown policy that had first been firmly implemented in the case of Columbus. Leaders of discovery and conquest enterprises were to be curbed in their ambitions; they were to be replaced as colonial administrators by royal officials entirely dependent upon the king and his councils in Spain. Ponce's appointment, and especially its timing (November 4, 1525), also suggest the impact in court circles of a flood of complaints against Cortés from dissident elements in New Spain.

Cortés dutifully relinquished his governing powers to the licenciado on July 4, 1526. Sixteen days later, Ponce, who had contracted a serious illness en route to Mexico City died, but only after naming as his successor Marcos de Aguilar, a West Indian official who had accompanied him to New Spain. The cabildo of the capital city and representatives from other Spanish settlements joined with leading colonists and clergy in urging Cortés to deny Aguilar's claim to authority and to resume leadership of the colony, but he refused their entreaties and formally accepted Aguilar as governor of New Spain. Aguilar, in turn, permitted him to continue, for several weeks, as arbitrator in Indian affairs, including encomienda assignments. Sometime in the autumn of 1526 Aguilar forced Cortés to surrender this remnant of civil power, and the conqueror withdrew from Tenochtitlan-México to his recovered Morelos encomienda town, Cuernavaca.[30]

When the aged and infirm Marcos de Aguilar died in March 1527, the cabildo of Tenochtitlan-México and many of Cortés' allies again asked the conqueror to resume the governorship. Once more he refused, whereupon the cabildo formally recognized Alonso de Estrada, the royal treasurer, and Gonzalo de Sandoval, longtime friend and loyal lieutenant of Cortés, as cogovernors. Subsequently, on August 23, 1527, Estrada appeared before the cabildo of Tenochtitlan-México with a royal decree that provided him sole authority in the governing of New Spain pending future action by the crown. On the basis of the decree Estrada assumed, probably without explicit legal right, the authority to make encomienda grants.[31] It would appear, however, that until his departure for Spain in 1528 Cortés still claimed some authority in encomienda matters (see the following paragraphs).

Estrada, alone in the governorship of New Spain, evidenced a rather contemptuous attitude toward the conqueror and his associates. After several months of difficulties between Cortés and Estrada, Fray Julián Garcés, the newly arrived Bishop of Tlaxcala, arranged a friendlier relationship, but Cortés, painfully aware of the steady deterioration of his power and influence, decided early in 1528 to take his case, directly and personally, to his monarch. Contributing to this decision were letters from his agents in Spain concerning new hostile reports received in the royal court from his enemies and discussions in the Council of the Indies as to the possible reorganization of the government of New Spain.

Cortés made twenty or more grants of encomienda in various parts of New Spain before his departure in 1528.[32] Some of these grants were made in areas where he had no personal properties; others were a sacrifice of some of his holdings. He used these assignments to pay accumulated debts, to secure funds for his trip to Spain, and to satisfy and silence previously unrewarded followers whose support he could thereby retain.

Several of his Morelos encomiendas were so employed. Oaxtepec was assigned to Juan de Burgos as a debt settlement. Burgos was to receive the revenues from this encomienda until Cortés returned from Spain, at which time he was to be awarded, presumably by Cortés, another encomienda of equal or greater worth. If Cortés did not return, Burgos was to seek crown confirmation of his title to Oaxtepec and was to enjoy its dues indefinitely—that is, at the crown's pleasure. The encomienda of Acapistla, including its Cortesian-defined sujetos of Atlatlahuacan and Totolapan, was granted to Diego Holguín and Francisco de Solís in what appears to have been a political payoff made at their request and based upon need and past service to Cortés and the crown.[33] Evidently Diego de Ordaz still held Tepoztlan and Yautepec (probably with Cortés' approval), so it would appear that Cortés, at the time of his departure from New Spain, retained only one encomienda in the Morelos area: Cuernavaca.

Accompanied by Gonzalo de Sandoval and other loyal soldiers of his conquest campaigns, Cortés departed for Spain in March 1528. Left in charge of his affairs in New Spain, including the management of his estate, were trained overseers and lawyers (*licenciados*). Foremost among these was a relative, Licenciado Juan Altamirano. Altamirano came to New Spain in 1527 from Cuba, where he had recently served as judge of residencia for Diego Velásquez.[34]

Cortés reached Spain in early May 1528 and shortly afterward sought and secured royal directives (the first issued late that month) prohibiting the seizure or disturbance of his colonial properties. These directives proved virtually worthless in the succeeding two years, as most of his holdings were expropriated by the First Audiencia of Mexico, a new governing agency created in 1527–28 for the purpose of stabilizing administration in New Spain and strengthening royal control over it.

The new Audiencia officials arrived in November and December of 1528 and promptly relieved Alonso de Estrada of his interim governorship. Two of the officials died shortly after they reached the colony, leaving Nuño de Guzmán, the president, and the surviving *oidores*, Juan Ortiz de Matienzo and Diego Delgadillo, to execute the Audiencia's powers and functions. These three, in accordance with their instructions, began early in 1529 to take the long-delayed residencia of Cortés, postponed since the death of Luis Ponce de León in 1526. During the *pesquisa secreta* (preliminary hearings) witnesses previously identified with the Salazar-Cherino faction produced considerable testimony detrimental to Cortés.[35] His agents attempted to refute this and other unfriendly commentary and conducted a defense sufficiently spirited to postpone final decision by the Audiencia. In other matters these agents were not as successful with the new governors. Most of Cortés' Mexico City property— including building supplies, horses and other livestock, household furnishings, and even items of clothing—was placed under embargo and sold at auction in the summer of 1529 to pay the fines levied against him.[36] The Audiencia also transferred to the crown most of the encomiendas still held by him as it did many of those held by conquistadores and colonists who were his political allies.

The Audiencia's action was based on secret royal instructions ordering redistribution of New Spain's encomienda properties in order to insure the crown a greater share of tribute revenues and to reserve for it potential port sites, mining centers, and other important settlements.[37] Apparently Guzmán and the oidores felt that these secret instructions allowed them to disregard the royal directive secured by Cortés in May 1528. They had received formal notification of the directive, which prohibited expropriation of any of the conqueror's properties in New Spain during his absence, from his attorneys, to whom it was dispatched immediately after issue.

By taking action in 1529 and 1530 to contravene the directive, the Audiencia nullified all Cortés' rights and interests in the Morelos area. Antonio Serrano de Cardona, having ingratiated himself with the members of the Audiencia (as had his allies, Pedro Almindes Cherino and Gonzalo de Salazar), claimed, in a suit against Cortés brought before the group in late 1528, that Cuernavaca was rightfully his. Cortés' attorneys contested the validity of Serrano's arguments, but the Audiencia upheld Serrano's claim in April 1529.[38] The loss of Cuernavaca left Cortés without any encomiendas in Morelos, although two there, Acapistla and Oaxtepec, were to revert to his control if and when he returned to the colony.[39]

By late 1530 the Audiencia had definitively removed one of these encomiendas—and probably both of them—from Cortés' control. Juan de Burgos' request that he be made the legitimate encomendero of Oaxtepec rather than simply the receiver of its tribute revenues at Cortés' pleasure was granted by the Audiencia in October 1530.[40] Similar action seems to have been taken in the case of Acapistla; that town was reassigned to Francisco de Solís and Diego Holguín.[41] In addition, although Cortés and Diego de Ordaz had worked out a plan in Spain whereby Yautepec and Tepoztlan became the conqueror's once again, the Audiencia, acting on its secret instructions from the crown—or so it maintained—took these towns from Ordaz, thereby abrogating his exchange agreement with Cortés.[42] Tepoztlan and Yautepec were subsequently reassigned by the oidores to Licenciado Barerra and Ordaz's former mayordomo, Francisco de Verdugo.[43]

So by 1530, when Cortés returned to New Spain, his estate amounted to very little. Shortly thereafter he was able to reestablish it, although in modified form, on the basis of a direct grant from the crown of certain encomienda towns and some 23,000 tributary vassals.

The Marquesado and the 23,000 Vassals

Cortés set sail for his homeland in the spring of 1528 with the expressed purpose of regaining the privileged status—social, economic, and political—which he had achieved prior to 1524 but which had steadily deteriorated thereafter. In 1527 he dispatched two agents, Pedro de Salazar and Fray Diego Altamirano, to Spain in an attempt to improve his position in court circles. Salazar and Altamirano were only partially successful in their efforts; they failed to convince the royal court that Cortés was willing to subordinate his interests to those of the crown. A cedula ordering him to return to Spain, issued April 5, 1528, reflected their failure and the crown's continuing suspicious hostility.[44]

That cedula was scarcely dispatched—and certainly could not have reached the Indies—when the crown was both startled and favorably impressed by Cortés' spectacular appearance in Spain. The enviable receptions subsequently given him by prominent court figures such as the Duque de Medina Sidonia, the Conde de Aguilar, and the Duque de Béjar apparently further enhanced his position. Indicative of a more favorable attitude toward him were the royal decree of May 28, 1528, mentioned above, prohibiting any disturbance, legal or otherwise, of his properties while he remained in Spain, and the elaborate welcome extended him in Monzón by the emperor Charles V.

Following his arrival in Monzón in late June or early July 1528, Cortés began a series of consultations with the emperor and his advisors which were continued intermittently until Charles left Barcelona for Italy in July 1529. Evidently colonial policies in general, Cortés' future status, and his difficulties with New Spain's royal officials, including the Audiencia, were among the subjects of these discussions.[45] Some of the legislation enacted in late 1529 and 1530 which recognized the encomienda as a necessary feature in the administration of New Spain was probably formulated during these sessions and was based in part on Cortés' advice.[46]

Despite the crown's demonstration of increasingly friendly confidence, the conqueror did not gain then, nor would he later, all that he desired. It is clear that one of his political objectives was reappointment to the governorship of New Spain. That objective was not realized, as the crown intended that a Second Audiencia would govern New Spain until such time as a viceregal system could be established for the colony. A cedula drawn in April 1529 notified Cortés that the Second Audiencia had been selected.[47] The same cedula did promise him, however, that he would be reappointed captain-general of New Spain and that he would be given the same authority over the more or less undefined area known as the Mar del Sur. This promise was carried out in cedulas issued on July 6, 1529, which were in part redefined in 1531.[48]

In the same month (April) that he was promised the captaincy-general, the first of a series of acts which enabled him to regain a large measure of his earlier economic prominence was signed by the emperor. That act directed royal treasury officials to compensate him for expenses incurred in sending an expedition to the Malaccas in 1526 and 1527.[49] Those which followed (in July and October of that year and March 1530) called for the return to him of funds taken in fines and seizures by the Casa de Contratación and the Audiencia.[50] In addition, immediate consideration by crown authorities of the long-standing dispute over payment of the costs of his Honduras expedition was ordered.[51]

In the spring of 1529 his social prestige was enhanced by marriage, previously arranged by his late father, with Doña Juana de Zúñiga, daughter of the Conde de Aguilar and the niece of the Duque de Béjar. Shortly thereafter, on July 6, 1529, Charles V conferred upon him the title of Marqués del Valle de Oaxaca and formally granted him 23,000 tributary Indian vassals in twenty-two pueblos of New Spain. On July 27, 1529, he and Doña Juana were given authorization for the establishment of their Marquesado as a *mayorazgo*, or entailed estate.[52]

As compared with his acquisitions from 1522 to 1524, the 23,000 tributary vassals in twenty-two pueblos of New Spain represented a sharp reduction in the conqueror's encomienda holdings. No longer his, for example, were the tributes and labor services of Texcoco and Tlacopan—two of the three towns comprising the Aztec Triple Alliance—Tzintzuntzan (the capital city) and other towns of the Tarascan state, the rich mining district of Tlapa (in modern Guerrero), several important towns in the Oaxaca area, and the Soconusco district, to mention only the major holdings not included in the grant. He retained by virtue of the royal decree, however, the tributes and services of Coyoacan in the Valley of México, important centers in the fertile agricultural Valley of Toluca, four major towns in Oaxaca, the Zapotec settlements of Tehuantepec and Jalapa on the Pacific coast of the Isthmus of Tehuantepec, and Tuxtla and Cotaxtla in the Gulf area south of Veracruz. Most important of all from a territorial standpoint, the decrees of July 1529 included all of Cortés' earlier holdings in the Morelos area: the towns of Cuernavaca, Oaxtepec, Acapistla, Yautepec, Tepoztlan, and their sujetos. Cortés was not granted the entire tributary population of all of these areas, however, as the royal decree specified 23,000 vassals in the towns listed. This restrictive provision created innumerable problems in the definition of the grant and in the administration of the estate developed on the basis of the grant.

There were other highly significant features of the grant, some of which were equally troublesome. The grant was perpetual: it was to be passed on to Cortés' heirs and successors, the future Marqueses del Valle. This privilege other encomenderos of New Spain sought, in later decades of the sixteenth century, without success. Moreover, Cortés and his heirs were granted jurisdictional powers, civil and criminal, over the towns of the Marquesado that were never accorded to other encomenderos. In the course of time, the nature of these powers was the subject of considerable dispute. It was the contention of Cortés and his successors that the authority accorded in 1529 included civil and criminal jurisdiction in the first instance, control of water resources, woodlands, and unoccupied lands within the Marquesado, and the appointment of local officials.

The titles and concessions granted the conqueror by Charles V assured him first rank among the conquistadores and colonists of New Spain. His almost insatiable desire for status and special privilege was not satisfied, however, as was evident in his dispatch to Rome, during the sojourn in Spain, of agents who sought papal recognition and favor. In response to petitioning by these agents, Clement VII issued bulls granting him patronage powers, including the right to collect *diezmas* and *primicias* (ecclesiastical tithes and firstfruits) within the confines of his estate in New Spain.[53] Inasmuch as these concessions constituted a potent infringement on the patronage powers of the crown in the New World, it is not surprising that the king and the Council of the Indies took action to prevent Cortés from exercising them.[54]

In the spring of 1530 the Marqués and Marquesa del Valle set out on the long journey to New Spain. En route they tarried for two months in Española but finally reached Veracruz on July 15. They were greeted with rejoicing and celebration provided, for the most part, by colonists and Indians who had suffered injustices, real or imagined, at the hands of Nuño de Guzmán and his colleagues in the First Audiencia. Before his departure from Spain, Cortés received a royal order notifying him of the appointment of the members of the Second Audiencia and directing him not to enter Tenochtitlan-México until the new officials arrived and took office.[55] Accordingly, for several months Cortés and his retinue resided in

Texcoco. Sometime after the Second Audiencia was established in office in January 1531, Cortés moved into his palace on the *plaza mayor* of Mexico City. A few months later, probably in November 1531, he transferred his household to the town of Cuernavaca in Morelos, henceforth the administrative headquarters of the Marquesado.

The Second Audiencia was charged with the responsibility of preparing the way for the establishment of a viceroyalty in New Spain. To this end it was called upon to eliminate as far as possible the colony's decade-old discord and unrest. Its major function was to secure control in the name of the crown of some aspects of local administration. In pursuit of these objectives the Audiencia, by royal directive, sought to reduce the influence of Cortés while maintaining at the same time a friendly relationship with him, adjudicating in a fair manner lawsuits in which he was plantiff or defendant, and implementing by appropriate legal or administrative procedures the sweeping royal concessions that the crown had granted to him.

Beginning in 1531 Cortés' attorneys instituted numerous *pleitos* before the Audiencia for recovery of tribute revenues produced by encomiendas expropriated by Guzmán and his associates. These lawsuits involved (1) claims for revenues from expropriated towns restored to Cortés by the royal decree of July 6, 1529, and (2) claims for revenues from towns which he did not recover by virtue of the decree but which had been taken from him in contravention of the cedulas of May 28, 1528, that is, for revenues from the date of expropriation until formal relinquishment by him of right and title to the same. The Audiencia's decisions in these suits eventually accorded the conqueror some recompense. Cortés was also named defendant in numerous lawsuits, several of which involved title and claim to the encomienda towns conceded to him by the royal cedula of July 6, 1529.[56] Some of these *procesos* were in progress even as the royal decree was formulated, while others followed during succeeding years. Among the encomienda towns which were the subject of these lawsuits were two in Morelos: Cuernavaca and Oaxtepec.

On December 16, 1528, the First Audiencia agreed to hear a lawsuit initiated by Antonio Serrano de Cardona who sought to regain title to the encomienda of Cuernavaca.[57] Serrano's claim was based primarily upon the grant provided him in October 1525 by Gonzalo de Salazar and Pedro Almindes Cherino and upon two royal cedulas. The first of these cedulas, dated July 26, 1526, ordered officials in New Spain to provide appropriate rewards for the services of the three conquistador-procuradores, of whom Serrano, then in Spain representing the Cherino-Salazar faction, was one. The second, dated August 23, 1527, prohibited alienation of Serrano's properties in New Spain. Cortés' attorneys defended their client's claim to the encomienda by arguing that (1) Serrano deserved no such compensation for his conquest services; (2) Serrano's grant was illegal because Cherino and Salazar did not have the authority to make it; (3) the crown had never ordered Cortés to surrender his encomienda claims; and (4) the Audiencia did not have jurisdiction over such matters and therefore could not legally decide the case.

The First Audiencia's decision in Serrano's favor was delivered on April 30, 1529, and was promptly appealed by Cortés' attorneys. That appeal, carried to the Council of the Indies, was in progress in the fall of 1530. On November 7 the council announced its decision, which validated Cortés' claim to the encomienda without prejudice to Serrano or his claim, on the basis of the 23,000 vassal grant made to Cortés by the crown on July 6, 1529. It was on the same grounds that the council upheld the Second Audiencia's recommended decision in favor of Cortés in the suit brought against him by Juan de Burgos over title and claim to the Oaxtepec encomienda.

Burgos, on August 17, 1530, requested that the First Audiencia restrain Cortés from interfering with his collection of tribute and labor services from the Indians of Oaxtepec until such time as his title and claim to the encomienda were sustained, or he was granted another of equal value.[58] He argued that he deserved reward for his conquest services and that Cortés had agreed, in granting him the encomienda of Oaxtepec in January 1528, that he could either seek crown recognition of his claim to the encomienda (if Cortés failed to return from Spain), or that Cortés would grant him another of equal value when he returned to New Spain and reclaimed Oaxtepec. The attorneys for Cortés, in refuting Burgos' case, insisted that Cortés' claim to Oaxtepec, based on the crown's grant of July 6, 1529, negated that of Burgos. In addition, they insisted that it was not the conqueror's place to suffer for Burgos, that he did not owe the plaintiff payment for any past services, and that, despite their previous agreement, Cortés did not have the authority to grant encomiendas to Burgos or anyone else.

On October 10, 1530, the First Audiencia ordered Cortés to refrain from any attempt to take over the encomienda, thereby sustaining Burgos' claim. Cortés' attorneys appealed that decision immediately, and the Second Audiencia heard the appeal testimony. That body, on May 7, 1531, recognized Cortés' claim to Oaxtepec without prejudice to Burgos or his claims and subsequently forwarded the appeal to the Council of the Indies with the recommendation that the decision be sustained by the council, which it apparently was some time thereafter.

Formal recognition of Cortés' claim to encomienda rights in the five cabecera towns of Morelos and to the other towns listed in the royal decree of July 6, 1529 did not resolve all the issues related to the concession. The decree specified that Cortés should enjoy the tributes of 23,000 vassals in the twenty-two towns named. Charged with assignment of the vassals—to be made on the basis of some sort of count or census—was the Audiencia. Early in 1531 a special commission of six members, three named by the Audiencia and three by Cortés, was formed to take such a census. As a first step the commissioners visited Morelos, and there basic differences as to method and procedures developed. For example, should each family head be counted as a tributary unit, or, as the representatives of Cortés insisted, should each household, which might include several families, constitute such a unit? Should the population of all of the semi-independent subdivisions (barrios) and settlements comprising or subordinate to the five encomienda towns be included in a count of tributaries, and if so, which of these actually comprised the towns, and which were subordinate, or sujeto, to them?[59]

It soon became apparent that legal resolution of these issues, also pertinent to other parts of the Marquesado, would take considerable time. The Audiencia, therefore, arranged a temporary contractual agreement with Cortés whereby he was to assume possession, as encomendero, of the towns named in his grant pending final decision in the several questions in dispute. By the terms of this agreement, he obligated himself and his heirs to pay to the crown any revenues collected from the number of vassals in those towns in excess of the specified 23,000.[60]

Controversy and litigation continued throughout the 1530s and 1540s over the questions surrounding Cortés' Marquesado, with few of them adequately answered even by the time of his death in 1547. The Second Audiencia and later Viceroy Mendoza, on crown instructions, attempted to cope with these questions but made few major revisions in the temporary agreement of 1532. Of the few changes made, one involved the Morelos encomienda of Acapistla. In the late summer or fall of 1532 the Audiencia investigated the boundaries between the encomiendas of Chalco and Acapistla, attempting in the process to determine exactly what the sujetos of Acapistla were. The oidores determined that Totolapan was a cabecera town and should not be considered a sujeto to Acapistla as it had been since the conquest. They therefore took Totolapan and its sujetos away from Cortés, and despite his protests, legal and otherwise, it never again constituted a part of the Marquesado.[61]

The unresolved issues relating to definition of Cortés' Marquesado grant were brought before the Council of the Indies for review and decision during the 1550s. After lengthy hearings the council decided (the exact date of this decision is not recorded in available documentation): (1) that the total number of tributary vassals in the towns of the entire Cortés estate in New Spain as listed in the royal cedula of 1529 should not exceed 23,000; (2) that for a count or census of these vassals each house and hearth (*casa y fumo*) should constitute a vassal in accordance with Castilian custom; and (3) that all tribute revenues received by Cortés and his heir, the second Marqués del Valle, from vassals in excess of the 23,000 therein defined should be refunded to the royal treasury of New Spain. Attorneys for the second Marqués, Don Martín Cortés, promptly asked for a review of this order. Finally, Philip II, in a decree issued at Toledo on December 16, 1560, resolved all of the issues that had been pending since 1531 and 1532. In this royal order the king took cognizance of the extraordinary achievement of Cortés in the conquest of the Aztecan state and also of the services of his son, Don Martín, as a soldier in Europe during the 1550s, and ordered that the Cortés estate in New Spain should enjoy the tributes and services of all of the towns, except Tehuantepec, mentioned in the royal concession of 1529, without limitation as to the number of tributary vassals in those towns. Tehuantepec, as a potential port settlement, was reserved as a crown town, but as recompense the Cortés estate was accorded stipulated annual revenues from towns in the Chalco area.[62]

Philip's order of 1560 terminated almost three decades of controversy and litigation over the Cortés estate in New Spain, including the Morelos encomiendas, and constituted a considerable victory for Cortés' heirs and, posthumously, for the conqueror. The legal tributary-vassal value of the Marquesado as originally defined in the grant of 1529 was more than doubled in the decree. Henceforth the estate was to enjoy, legally and without encumbrance, the tributes and labor services of vassals numbered by assessments of the 1550s in excess of 50,000, at least 25,000 of which were located in the Morelos towns.[63]

3

Tribute

The Early Years, 1522–1529[1]

In establishing the encomienda system in New Spain, Fernando Cortés followed the precedent set by the Spanish, who had used a repartimiento-encomienda system on islands in the Caribbean during the previous two decades. The precedent was not, however, worthy of repeat, since the Caribbean institution proved so seriously abusive as finally to prompt crown disavowal in 1520. A royal order of that year forbade any further assignment of encomiendas in the Indies and provided for gradual termination of existing grants. Cortés controverted crown policy, therefore, when he made his first grants in March 1522. He may have done so unknowingly, as it is quite possible that he was unaware of the policy enunciated in 1520. He was not unaware, however, of the circumstances which provoked the royal order. As his correspondence clearly indicates, he was well acquainted with the destructive failure of the Caribbean institution.[2]

As he informed the crown, the conqueror found justification for instituting his encomienda system in practical necessity, local circumstances, and the belief that the abuses which had occurred in the islands could be avoided in his new colony.[3] He doubtless acted with what he felt was at least quasi-legal right in making assignments. Governing officials in the Caribbean—including his forsaken superior, Diego Velázquez—exercised such authority, and he was, in 1522, de facto governor of New Spain, having been so commissioned two years earlier by the cabildo of Veracruz.

Cortés' representations were not entirely unfounded, as conditions and tradition in the Aztec world, in marked contrast to those in preconquest Española and Cuba, facilitated, perhaps encouraged, introduction of the encomienda. In the islands, implementation of the system had necessitated concentration of the native population in villages or towns subject to Spanish control, whereas in the Aztec area many peoples, particularly those in central and southern Mexico, were established in relatively compact settlements before the Spanish arrived. Unlike the Arawak and other peoples of the islands, much of New Spain's native population, in areas over which the Spanish gained control in the 1520s, had long supported a

complex socioeconomic and political structure through tribute payment
and labor service. Cortés and his followers gained access to pictorial
records showing that even before the defeat of Tenochtitlan tribute and
services were provided to the Aztec state by some of its tributary peoples.[4]

The encomienda system Cortés devised for New Spain resembled, then,
that extant in the Caribbean colonies but was based upon an established
and functioning scheme of revenue collection and labor utilization. The
obligations of Cortés' grantees were similar to those of island encomenderos—namely, responsibility for the general welfare, security, and
Christianization of the Indians assigned them. Island grants authorized
use of labor services from a stated number of Indians; an encomendero in
New Spain was assigned a specific Indian town or portion thereof from
which he received both tribute and labor. During the 1520s the tribute
and labor services Indians were to pay their assigned encomenderos were
not defined by Cortés or his successors in the government of New Spain;
presumably they were to provide the amount and kind of tribute that
had been rendered the overlord or overlords he replaced.

Although obviously based in some measure on preexisting norms, the
quotas of services and tribute in kind demanded by most of New Spain's
encomenderos were regarded by the Indians as excessive in comparison
with customary requirements. During the 1530s crown officials sought to
alleviate what appeared to be abuses, often excessive, in this area by
formulating fixed assessments (*tasaciones*) of tribute and services, which
were to be rendered to encomenderos at stated intervals.[5] The length of
these intervals varied from area to area but generally followed a pattern
reflecting preconquest custom and the practices implemented during the
1520s. Tribute payments in maize and other cereals were normally assessed, for example, on an annual basis, consistent with the harvest in an
area of specific dimensions. Manufactured or crafted goods paid in
tribute, such as cotton textiles, mantas (mantles, sometimes blanketlike
lengths of cloth), *naguas* (skirts), and huipiles (dresses), were payable in
defined quantities four times annually, or (as the interval was frequently
cited) one payment every eighty days ("cada ochenta días"). These assessments also stipulated daily quotas of food, firewood (*leña*), and fodder
(*yerba*) to be delivered to the encomendero or his local agents and included provision for consistent household or burden-bearing service or
both by specified numbers of Indians.

Cortés appears to have secured his first tribute and laborers from
towns in Morelos in mid-1522. Certainly he was receiving some of each
from them in 1523.[6] In organizing these towns into encomiendas, he made
the Aztecan tributary province of Quauhnahuac (Cuernavaca) a single
encomienda unit, incorporating as sujetos therein (and technically to the
town of the same name) a number of settlements which previously prob-

ably enjoyed cabecera status. He split the Aztecan province of Huaxtepec (Oaxtepec) into three encomienda units: Oaxtepec, Yautepec, and Acapistla. In each of these encomiendas he also included as sujetos a number of towns which were probably cabeceras before 1521 (see Appendix 4). His fifth encomienda in Morelos comprised Tepuztlan (Tepoztlan) and its sujetos, which, before the Spanish conquest, may have been a part of the Aztec province of Chalco-Tlalmanalco (see Appendix 4).

Collection of tribute and utilization of labor services in the Morelos area during the years 1522–25 was supervised by a Cortesian agent stationed in Cuernavaca or dispatched there from time to time from Mexico City. After 1525, Cortés and the area's other encomenderos often lived in Morelos but continued to use agents permanently resident not only in Cuernavaca but also in Yautepec, Oaxtepec, and Acapistla. The señor and principales of each of the encomienda towns and their sujetos were charged, as they had been in Aztecan times, with the actual gathering of tribute goods. They assigned responsibility for production of defined tribute items and for fulfillment of labor requirements in specific projects to groups and individuals among their macehuales. The señores and principales apparently left the task of collecting much of the tribute, the *comida* or foodstuff items in particular, to individuals who were not members of the local nobility but were in their employ and named as mayordomos, calpixques or *tequitlatos*.[7] These mayordomos and others occupying similar positions also supervised the macehuales in performance of the required labor services.[8]

A report prepared by Cortés' attorneys provides the only exact information available on the kinds and amount of tribute paid by the Indians of the Morelos encomiendas in the years before 1525. That report, presented in 1531 as a memorial whose validity was attested to by Indian and Spanish witnesses, indicates that as of 1524 the Indians were paying tribute in cotton textiles, gold, and grains and were providing services valued annually at "more than 6,000 gold pesos."[9] At about the same time principales from Cuernavaca and several Spanish residents of Tenochtitlan-México, all witnesses essentially hostile to Cortés, reported that when the conqueror first held Cuernavaca in encomienda, presumably before 1525, macehuales there were required to carry foodstuffs, primarily maize and beans, from the town to his mines in Michoacán, a distance of some forty leagues (about 156 miles). The round trip took about forty days in dry weather and fifty during the rainy season and was so rigorous that many of the *tamemes* died or were killed before it was completed.[10]

Others who held encomiendas in Morelos between 1525 and 1531 apparently secured tribute and labor services which were generally similar in kinds and amounts to those Cortés collected in the pre-1525 period and during the years 1526–29 (see Tables 1 and 3). Indians, a majority of whom were from Cuernavaca, and some Spaniards testified in 1551 that Antonio Serrano de Cardona received 200 cargas (bundles of 20 items each) of mantas of good quality, 4 *piernas* (strips or widths) each in size, and a piece of gold jewelry four times each year from Cuernavaca.[11] The payment intervals were of 80 days each or, as a greater number of witnesses said, two were of 80 days and two of 100 days.[12] Daily, the Indians evidently delivered 8 to 10 turkeys, 6 or 7 cargas each of fodder and firewood (a carga of either was probably the amount an Indian could carry on his back), and unspecified amounts of chile, salt, *frutas* (fruit), cacao, and *codornices* (quail) to his house in Mexico City.[13] They supplied his mozos and *criados* (servants) living in Cuernavaca with *"servicios de comida,"* literally food services or food supplies, including *aves* (birds, probably pigeons or quail), cacao, and tortillas and served as *"indios de servicio,"* or service personnel, in his Mexico City household and in the houses maintained by his agents in Cuernavaca. The labor and materials—*cal* (lime), *piedra* (rock), and *madera* (lumber)—used in construction of his residence in Mexico City were supplied by Cuernavaca, as were the large number of tamemes he used daily in various transportation tasks. Each year some of the town's macehuales also prepared, cultivated, and harvested one field of maize and one of wheat for Serrano.

As encomendero of Oaxtepec, Juan de Burgos (like Cortés before him) received an unspecified number of cargas of mantas, described as those of Cuernavaca were, and an item of gold jewelry. Testimony in judicial records of 1551 indicates that these goods were provided him four times each year in quarterly payments the same as those made to Serrano by Cuernavaca.[14] Six or seven cargas of fodder, six or seven cargas of firewood, and varying amounts of chile, salt, frutas, codornices, and cacao were also delivered each day by the Indians of Oaxtepec to his residence in Mexico City. They also supplied Burgos with indios de servicio daily, tamemes on demand, and the labor and materials required in the construction of his house in Tenochtitlan-México. The Indians may also have supplied his mozos and criados in Oaxtepec with servicios de comida and indios de servicio as well as performing labors for him in his mines.[15]

Francisco de Verdugo declared in 1551 that as Diego de Ordaz's mayordomo in Yautepec he collected twenty-five cargas of cotton mantas from the Indians there and fifteen of the same from Tepoztlan four times each year.[16] Indians and other Spaniards testifying at the same time agreed with Verdugo's figures. The Indians insisted, however, that the mantas paid, unlike those of Oaxtepec and Cuernavaca, were small, *"pequeñas y mantillas."*[17] All agreed that the Indians from the two encomiendas delivered daily to Ordaz's home in Mexico City four, five, or more turkeys, six or seven cargas of fodder, six or seven cargas of firewood, and various quantities of codornices, chile, salt, frutas, and cacao. Along with these servicios de comida, *tlapixques* (labor supervisors) and indios de servicio were sent to his capital city residence to carry water and perform other tasks.[18] Each day two *gallinas de tierra* (turkeys), *tortillas de maíz, ají* (chile), *sal,* codornices, frutas, leña, maíz, and yerba, as well as indios de servicio, were placed at the disposal of Ordaz's calpixque in Yautepec (probably Verdugo) and his servants (one or two) who lived in Tlalhuitongo, a sujeto to Yautepec where an orchard had been developed by Ordaz. The people of Yautepec and Tepoztlan also supplied the labor and materials Ordaz employed in building his house in Tenochtitlan-México, carried maize and other supplies to his *"minas de los Yopes,"* worked there, and planted, cultivated, and harvested two fields of wheat and one of maize for him each year.[19]

In the years prior to 1529, Cortés and the other encomenderos of Morelos evidently also received a number of Indian slaves delivered to them as tribute (see Table 1). These slaves were evidently taken from those owned by the Indian nobility of the area's five encomiendas and were brought to the encomenderos from time to time in lieu of certain tribute items normally paid or in addition thereto, according to the demands of the encomenderos. Some witnesses who testified on this subject in 1551 indicated that the slave payments were often made in order to relieve the macehuales of some of the heaviest labor services demanded by the encomenderos.[20] *Penachos de plumas* (bundles of feathers from tropical and other birds) and *joyas y joyuelas* (large and small items of jewelry) were evidently also given the Morelos encomenderos and particularly Cortés from time to time not as tribute but as gifts. According to Indian witnesses, this gift giving to overlords was a custom carried over from Aztecan times (see Table 1).[21]

The encomienda system into which Cortés organized the settlements of Aztecan Morelos between 1522 and 1525 was continued, then, with little apparent modification until the early 1530s. It provided revenues in tribute and labor of very considerable value for Cortés, Juan de Burgos, Antonio de Serrano, Diego de Ordaz, Francisco de Solís, Diego Holguín, Francisco de Verdugo, and others among New Spain's encomenderos to whom the Tlahuica-Xochimilca communities it encompassed were assigned during these early years. The goods and services secured by these new lords were not unlike those the peoples of Morelos had earlier rendered the rulers of the Aztec state, although the Spanish appear to have required larger numbers of laborers for differing, perhaps more difficult, types of work and fewer crafted ceremonial or "war," utensil, and paper goods but larger amounts of foodstuffs than had their predecessors.

The annual value of these revenues was estimated by Cortés' attorneys as 6,000 pesos de oro de minas.[22] That figure was probably a conservative one that did not include the value of labor performed by tamemes and workers employed in nonhousehold tasks, slaves apparently delivered to the conqueror from time to time, or the comida items regularly supplied him. The encomienda revenues Cortés secured from his holdings in Morelos during the years 1522–29 totaled at least 37,200 pesos de oro de minas and perhaps exceeded that amount by as much as 3,000 pesos for an average yearly take of between 6,200 and 6,700 pesos de oro de minas.[23]

The Later Years, 1530–1547

When Cortés sailed for Spain in the spring of 1528 he was receiving tribute and labor services from only one of the Morelos encomiendas, that of Cuernavaca. Since 1525 Tepoztlan and Yautepec had paid their dues to another, and, on the eve of his departure, Cortés personally surrendered the other two, Oaxtepec and Acapistla, in temporary assignments. He had been absent from New Spain little more than a year when receipt of revenues from Cuernavaca also ceased.[24] When he returned to New Spain in July 1530 as Marqués del Valle de Oaxaca, he was not in effective control of any of the Morelos encomiendas, but he possessed recently obtained royal title to them. On the basis of that title he was able, by early 1531, to acquire all five anew.

While living temporarily in Texcoco in the summer and autumn of 1530, the Marqués evidently attempted to assert his claim to the Morelos encomiendas but was prevented from doing so by the First Audiencia. Certainly he was denied both Cuernavaca and Oaxtepec by that body.[25] The following spring, after the Second Audiencia was installed as the governing agency for New Spain but before it took action on his claim to the encomiendas there, Cortés seems to have dispatched agents to Morelos.[26] These criados apparently made arrangements with the señores and principales of Cuernavaca, Yautepec, Tepoztlan, Oaxtepec, and perhaps Acapistla for supply of the labor and materials needed in construction work, particularly the making of new doors and windows and the addition of a new room, on his house on the plaza mayor in Tenochtitlan-México.[27] Evidently that work was undertaken immediately and was continued until early 1533. The lumber, stone, lime, vigas (beams), and other materials, and the labor required were supplied by the Indians, or so some of them testified later, in lieu of regular tribute payments for which provision had not been made at the time his agents initiated their requests.[28]

After the Second Audiencia formally recognized his title to the Morelos encomiendas (May 2) and after his household had been transferred in the summer of 1531 to the refurbished palace on the plaza mayor in the capital city, Cortés began employing some of his tributary vassals from Cuernavaca, Yautepec, Tepoztlan, Oaxtepec, and probably Acapistla in construction of a *casa nueva* (new house) in the town of Cuernavaca.[29] As in the Mexico City project, the Indians supplied materials and labor, in this case in quantities sufficient to the stages of work completed in the summer and autumn of 1531, in lieu of tribute and some of the services they would have provided as regular encomienda dues. The Cuernavaca project was pursued with consistently decreasing priority until 1535 or 1536.[30] Some of the Indians of Yautepec performed a special service in this effort, that of painting the vigas with designs and figures.[31]

Shortly after he moved the Marquesa and his household to Cuernavaca in November 1531, the Marqués began collecting tribute from the Indians of his five Morelos encomiendas on a regular basis. The time schedule and item specification (amount and kind) for tribute payments announced by Cortés at that time were apparently applied—but not without complaint and attempted change—until April 1536. Delivered to Cortés' agents in Mexico City four times each year, apparently at the same intervals as were observed in pre-1529 payments, were: from Cuernavaca, 4,800 mantas described as of four piernas each and measuring two *brazas* (a braza was the equal of about sixty six inches) square, 20 naguas, 20 camisas (blouses), and about 40 colchas (coverlets); from Yautepec and Tepoztlan, 1,500 mantas like those of Cuernavaca, 20 naguas, and 20 camisas; from Oaxtepec, 2,000 mantas like those of Cuernavaca, 40 naguas, 40 colchas, and one *medalla de oro* (gold medal); and from Acapistla, 800 mantas like those of Cuernavaca, 40 naguas, and 40 camisas. These items in quarterly payments amounted to 36,400 mantas, 480 naguas, 320 camisas, 320 colchas and four medallas de oro, each worth 82 mantas.[32] At contemporary price rates for cotton goods the annual tribute was worth between 6,336 and 6,948 pesos de oro de minas.[33] The price of cotton goods in New Spain remained reasonably stable until 1536; therefore the revenues Cortés enjoyed from the tribute in textiles paid him by his Morelos encomiendas for the period 1532 through the spring of 1536 amounted to from 26,928 to 29,529 pesos de oro de minas.[34]

Of great worth to Cortés but difficult to estimate accurately in peso value were the foodstuffs and crafted utensils provided by his Morelos encomiendas. These comida items were delivered to Cortés' house in Cuernavaca beginning in 1532 and continuing through 1533 as described by the principales of Cuernavaca in a declaration made in January 1533:

> . . . they give the said Marqués comida for his dispensation and house as required each day of the week for which they are responsible for service, that is of two weeks, the one, and the other week, the other pueblos of the valley [Oaxtepec, Acapistla, Tepoztlan, and

Yautepec] give, in such fashion that the comida for all the year is divided in half, and one week only Cuernavaca gives it and the other, all the other pueblos of the valley . . .[35]

In 1534 or early 1535 this biweekly arrangement was changed to a monthly system in which Cuernavaca supplied the comida items required each day for fourteen days, Tepoztlan and Yautepec for five days, Oaxtepec for five days, and Acapistla for four days.[36] Many of the items supplied were much like those delivered to the encomenderos of these towns during the years prior to 1529 but were, in most cases, delivered in increased daily quantities. The number of specific items to be delivered daily varied from town to town with the heaviest demands made upon Cuernavaca and Oaxtepec, the least on Acapistla.[37]

Some of the items supplied to Cortés after 1532 were apparently not among the comida requirements of the pre-1529 holders of the encomiendas. Among these items were *manojos de ocote* (bunches of pitch pine splinters for kindling), *cestillas de carbón* (baskets of charcoal), *mecapallis* (headbands used in carrying burdens), *sogas grandes* (large ropes), *braseros* (brasiers), *comales* (pans used in making tortillas), *conejos* (rabbits), *palomas de la tierra* (doves), *tortillas de pan* (wheat flour tortillas), *aguacates* (avocados), and on fast days *huevos* (eggs), *ranas* (frogs), and *pescados y pescadillos* (large and small fish).[38]

Each day, along with the comida items delivered to Cortés, the Indians provided indios de servicio. According to Indian witnesses (1533 and 1536) from 20 to 100 men and from 20 to 50 women from the five towns were utilized daily in household chores in and around the Marqués' palatial establishment in Cuernavaca. On their assigned days Oaxtepec and Cuernavaca each supplied 100 men and from 40 to 50 women; Yautepec, Tepoztlan and Acapistla each supplied 20 men and 20 women.[39] Daily comida items and indios de servicio were also made available to those among Cortés' agents and criados living and working in or near each of the five towns. The amounts of supplies and the numbers of Indians involved in these instances were not large, although both Cuernavaca and Oaxtepec seem to have supported several overseers and quite a number of Spanish *labradores* (skilled farm laborers).

Many other labor services of various kinds were performed for Cortés by the Indians of his Morelos encomiendas, but apparently only one additional major item of tribute was paid him. Cuernavaca's principales testified in 1533 that they had supplied him with forty slaves the preceding year. These slaves were requested to fulfill an increased requirement for *sementera* (field, probably in this instance sugarcane) workers and were to relieve the macehuales who normally tended his fields. Apparently these were the only slaves given the Marqués in tribute in the years following 1531. Among the numerous services large numbers of the Morelos macehuales rendered, either continuously or occasionally, were the planting, cultivating, and harvesting of fields of maize, beans, and cotton, as well as *huertas* (gardens) and *viñas* (vineyards); tending livestock; transporting, as tamemes, sizeable amounts of foodstuffs to Cortés' Taxco mines and working in those mines; transporting large quantities of foodstuffs to Acapulco and to Tenochtitlan-México; and carrying loads of sugarcane from all parts of Morelos to his mill in Cuernavaca. The Indians also sought and collected *hojas y plantas de moreras para criar seda* (mullberry leaves and plants for breeding silkworms) and *salitre para pólvora* (saltpeter or potassium nitrate for gunpowder). These efforts took them as far from their home area as Pánuco and Coyoacan.[40]

Within months after Cortés initiated these requirements they were labeled excessive by the Indian leaders of the Morelos towns. In their complaints, the officials also accused Cortés and his agents of abuse in treating with them and the macehuales of their pueblos. They charged that Cortés' mayordomos and tribute collectors, as well as the administrative and judicial officers he appointed for the area, demanded cotton cloth and other items from the Indians for their personal use. The principales and señores also insisted that during Cortés' absence in 1532 (probably after he left for Tehuantepec) the Marquesa and Hernán Rodríguez, who was responsible for supervising the collection of tribute, added to the encomienda burdens of the Morelos macehuales by ordering improvement in the quality of the cotton textiles they were delivering, demanding that the items be woven more tightly.[41]

Doubtless several factors including the immediate aggravations stimulated the Indians' complaints. Marquesado encomienda demands were greater then those imposed upon the peoples of Morelos by encomenderos, including Cortés, of the 1520s. Tribute increases seem to have been mainly in quantities and varieties of foodstuffs, with relatively small increases, if any, in amounts of other items expected. Systematic collection may have meant, however, more consistent, and thereby increased, payment of some goods than was necessary between 1522 and 1531, but probably not more than was required for satisfaction of pre-1522 Aztecan assessments. Fulfillment of Marquesado labor levies apparently called for continuous involvement of a considerably larger number of Indians in tasks not related to personal and community maintenance or the production of tribute goods than had been required in earlier years. Disabling of the Indians—because of actual population decline as well as loss of physical vitality due to the impact of the conquest years (warfare and the serious epidemic of 1521-22, probably smallpox), the subsequent disasters of 1528-29, caused by heavy rain ruination of maize and other crops, and in 1531 and 1532, widespread, death-dealing epidemics (probably of smallpox and measles)—must have been obvious in the Morelos towns by 1532–33.[42] Finally, unsettled questions as to Cortés' encomienda and other rights in Morelos and elsewhere within the Marquesado, resulting in agitation, debate, and investigation, did not go unrecognized as opportunity for complaints by the Indian leaders and their towns.

Word of the complaints evidently reached the Second Audiencia in late 1532 or early 1533. That body, already formally charged with precise definition of the Marqués' vassal grant of 1529, immediately solicited a formal declaration of the tribute and services provided him by Cuernavaca. Such a declaration was made by the town's principales on January 24, 1533.[43] A little over a week later, on February 4, the oidores heard a report which repeated, with elaborations, the complaints already expressed by the Cuernavaca Indians. Lope de Saavedra, who had been in Cuernavaca and other areas in Morelos two months earlier, delivered the report.[44] Subsequently the Audiencia seems to have undertaken a more extensive investigation into the conditions which prompted the Cuernavaca complaints and to have advised the crown of the circumstance and its action. Exactly what information, including additional complaints, the Audiencia secured before it took action to alleviate the Indians' distress is not clear. Certainly it did receive one more complaint, that of a Dominican friar, Francisco Mayorga, which was prepared on August 12, 1533.[45]

In the spring of 1534, following receipt of a royal cedula authorizing prescription of a fair tribute and labor service requirement for the Morelos encomiendas, the oidores called the principales of the towns and the Marqués before them.[46] Apparently after careful consideration of the pintura (picture or codex) records of their tribute assessments presented by the Indians and of testimony from Cortés, the oidores set specific tribute rates for each of the Morelos encomiendas. Cortés and the principales of each of the area's towns were then ordered to honor these new tasaciones, which were dated May 21, 1534.[47]

Evidently the Marqués and his agents ignored the Audiencia's tasaciones and continued to collect the tribute and utilize the labor services of the peoples of Morelos as they had been doing since 1531. It was not until a number of new complaints were made and Viceroy Mendoza assumed the governorship of New Spain that the tasaciones were implemented. In the spring of 1536, Mendoza sent some of his lieutenants into the Morelos area to determine the amounts of tribute the Indians were paying and, if possible, the number of heads of households comprising each settlement. The information gathered was not too helpful in the matter of the heads of households, but it indicated that Cortés was collecting tributes in excess of the tasaciones of 1534 and that one of his mayordomos, Juan Zimbrón, had severely mistreated the Indians. Mendoza, acting with the Audiencia, then called Zimbrón to account for his activities and in March fined him 2,000 pesos de oro de minas.[48] In April the viceroy and the oidores ordered Cortés to collect only such tributes as were specified in the 1534 tasaciones and indicated that should he fail to do so he would be subjected to a heavy fine.[49] Thereafter, until 1544, Cortés and his agents seem to have followed the tasaciones in their Morelos operations.

The tasaciones of 1534 specified the composition—both types and quantities—of goods and the time schedule for delivery of the tributes the Morelos encomiendas were to pay. The cotton goods enumerated in the assessment were to be delivered in equal allotments four times each year, at the end of each of two 100-day periods and each of two 80-day periods. For the five towns these allotments were as follows: Cuernavaca, 234 cargas (4,680) of mantas, 4 cargas (80) of colchas, and 1 carga (20) of camisas and naguas; for Yautepec and Tepoztlan, 71 cargas (1,420) of mantas, 1 carga (20) of colchas, and 2 cargas (40) of camisas and naguas; for Oaxtepec, 96 cargas (1,920) of mantas, 1 carga (20) of colchas, and 2 cargas (40) of camisas and naguas; and for Acapistla, 45 cargas (900) of mantas, and 2 cargas (40) of camisas and naguas. Annually these tributes amounted to 1,784 cargas (35,680) of mantas, 24 cargas (480) of colchas, and 28 cargas (560) of camisas and naguas.[50]

The revenue value of these goods changed drastically between 1536 and 1544 as their market prices increased. Textile prices began to rise significantly about 1536 and did so steadily and without great variation until 1541 when a sharp upturn occurred, particularly in the case of mantas. Contributory to the increases, not only in the case of cottons but of other goods in New Spain's markets, were a number of factors hitherto not adequately defined. Among those commonly cited in contemporary accounts are several which appear valid. Cotton textiles for use as clothing by both the Spanish labor and Negro slave populations of the colony were increasingly in demand after 1530 as both segments of the society grew in numbers and importance. A parallel but much sharper decline in the Indian population of the colony—the result of a conglomerate of circumstances including the plagues noted previously and the similarly crippling epidemics and crop failures of 1538 (measles), 1541 (frosts), 1543 (drought and frosts), 1544 (frosts), and 1545–48 (an extremely vicious plague, perhaps typhus or yellow fever)—created a shortage of persons engaged in cotton production and textile weaving.[51] After the mid-1530s many surviving encomienda Indians sought and were able to earn their wages and pay their tribute assessments in money rather than in textiles and other goods. Some even began to buy the clothing they needed. Finally, New Spain's economy underwent a general inflation, beginning in the mid-1530s and continuing through several subsequent decades. A part of this inflation was escalation in the cost of living in the colony. Especially important with regard to the Morelos encomiendas were the population decline and the shift from tribute goods production to labor for wages on the part of the Indians. In addition, the Marqués and his agents forced improvement in the quality of the mantas and, to a lesser extent, the colchas, camisas, and naguas paid as tribute by the encomiendas in the early 1530s and again early in the next decade. The market value of those items was thereby increased.

The probable value of the mantas, camisas, and naguas delivered to the Marqués by the Indians of Morelos during the years 1536–44 is indicated in Table 2. That table illustrates the rise in annual revenue value of these cotton goods from 8,116 pesos de oro de minas in 1536–37 to 27,640 pesos de oro de minas in 1543–44.[52] The total value of these goods for the period 1536–44 was more than 138,826 pesos de oro de minas.[53]

The tasaciones of 1534 also enumerated the comida items which the Morelos encomiendas were to supply Cortés. These were considerably reduced in number and, in some instances, in quantities of items from those he procured before 1534. With one exception, all were to be taken to his household in Cuernavaca. On each of fifteen days in every month that town was to supply 8 turkeys except on fast (meatless) days when 100 each of frogs, small fish, and eggs were to be delivered. Oaxtepec was assigned five days, and Tepoztlan and Yautepec shared a like number every month on each of which 8 turkeys, or, in the case of fast days, 60 each of small fish, eggs, and frogs were supplied. Acapistla was an exceptional case in that it provided 8 turkeys or on fast days 60 frogs and 60 eggs on each of its four assigned days each month unless the Marqués was absent from Cuernavaca. If he was in Acapistla on those days it supplied him 2 turkeys there; otherwise, it fulfilled no comida requirements. The tasaciones made only Oaxtepec responsible for delivery of comida goods directly to Cortés' mayordomos or criados. Daily the Indians of that town were to give 1 turkey and 3 baskets (30 in each) of maize tortillas to a Spanish calpixque stationed there.[54] These comida items may have been valued at about 90 pesos de oro de minas per month for a total annual revenue equivalent to about 1,080 pesos de oro de minas.[55]

Despite sizable reductions in the quantity and number of tribute items required from the Morelos encomiendas as compared with what he had secured from them earlier, Cortés and his agents seem to have honored the arrangements specified in the tasaciones until after he left New Spain for the last time in 1539 or early 1540. Testimony of 1551 indicates that shortly after his departure Licenciado Altamirano, who was charged with the administration of the Marquesado in his absence, ordered the Indians to begin supplying undisclosed amounts of maize and tortillas to Cortés' palace in Cuernavaca and to supply the *ración de pan de castilla* or daily requirement of wheat flour bread needed by the Negro slaves, criados, and other persons residing there.[56] Altamirano's order was protested by the Indians as a violation of the 1534 tasaciones and the 1544 revisions thereof and forbidden by Viceroy Mendoza in a decree issued in January 1547, but it remained in effect until the early 1550s.[57]

The tasaciones of 1534 made no provision for the indios de servicio which had previously accompanied the daily comida tribute exacted from the Morelos towns. In fact, no labor services of any kind were included. This omission was consistent with crown policy, which, beginning in the early 1530s, intended to eliminate personal services by encomienda Indians and payment of wages to them for any labor performed for their encomenderos, since the wages could be applied to the tribute they were obliged to provide. Evidently Cortés received indios de servicio until 1536 but not later. The Morelos Indians who labored otherwise for him all apparently received wages or some form of compensation.[58]

The crown's intentions in this respect were reflected, at least in part, in Cortés' announcement late in 1539 that henceforth he would accept in moneys the value of the required tribute in mantas which the Morelos Indians could not deliver in kind. This announcement was also a response to repeated complaints from the Indians. They argued that it was impossible to produce the number of mantas specified in the tasaciones because their numbers had declined so markedly: a great many macehuales had died of diseases. Before Cortés left for Spain—according to testimony from some Indians, Andrés Díaz, and others—the Morelos encomiendas paid one of their quarterly tribute installments half in mantas and half in pesos de oro común. Andrés Díaz, who was responsible for collection of the Marquesado's tributes during Cortés' absence, received eight subsequent quarterly assessments from the Morelos encomiendas, all of which were paid the same way. In late 1541 or early 1542, Díaz informed the señores and principales of the encomiendas that those mantas which they did supply were thereafter to be of better quality, larger in size, and "*mejor tejidos y más delgado*" (more tightly and finely woven). He noted that if they could not deliver the mantas he would continue to accept their peso value but at a rate of ten *tomines* (a tomín was worth one-eighth of a peso) per manta or twenty-five pesos de oro común per carga rather than at the earlier rate of about half that amount. The Indians complied with these new stipulations until mid-1544, making two quarterly payments half in mantas and half in pesos, and eight in pesos only.[59]

Payment of cotton textile tribute assessments in moneys rather than kind was legalized for the Morelos encomiendas in June 1544 when the tasaciones of 1534 were revised by Licenciado Tello de Sandoval. Sandoval came to New Spain in the spring of 1544 as *visitador-general* (inspector general) to investigate the activities and policies of New Spain's governing officials—primarily Viceroy Mendoza and the members of the Audiencia of Mexico—and with special responsibility for introducing royal legislation of the years 1542–43, the so-called New Laws of 1542. Governmental reorganization was the purpose of some of this legislation, but much of it consisted of new statutes dealing with the status and treatment of the Indians.

The statutes lowered tribute assessments for the Indians of Morelos, providing legal recognition of practices that were already common. The tribute revisions made by Licenciado Sandoval did not alter the quantities of cotton goods specified in the tasaciones of 1534 with one minor exception: Oaxtepec was assessed an additional carga of colchas, to be paid in moneys rather than goods. A fixed value in pesos was established for these textiles with naguas, camisas, and mantas set at twenty pesos per carga, and colchas at twelve pesos per carga.[60] These values were significantly lower, except in the case of the colchas, than those met by the Indians in paying their tribute in moneys during the preceding three years (since 1541–42). The revisions reduced Cortés' annual Morelos textile tribute revenues from 27,640 pesos de oro de minas to 21,933 pesos de oro de minas, a sum he evidently received for each of the years 1544–45 and 1545–46.[61] Sandoval's rates were protested without success by Cortés' attorneys, who argued, with apparent justification, that they were inconsistent with current market price levels.

In 1546 Licenciado Altamirano evidently found it impossible to collect even the reduced amounts provided in Sandoval's revisions. On his orders Juan San Lázaro, a principal from the Marquesado town of Coyoacan, prepared a report on how much tribute could be collected from the Morelos encomiendas. After consideration of the San Lázaro report and consultation with his lieutenants in Marquesado administration, Altamirano agreed to accept about one-third of the stipulated tribute due from the Morelos towns for 1546–47.[62] During the last three years of his life (1544–47) Cortés received a total revenue of about 51,177 pesos de oro de minas from the cotton textile tribute paid by his Morelos encomiendas.[63]

Sandoval's revisions of the tasaciones of 1534 included a few relatively minor alterations in the number of fowl and eggs the towns were to deliver on their assigned comida tribute days each month and added only one other tribute requirement. Cuernavaca, Oaxtepec, Tepoztlan, and Yautepec were to supply a carga of yerba with each daily quota of comida tribute. For each carga of yerba Cortés was to pay one peso de oro común, however, so the Indians did not actually provide it as an additional tribute.[64] During the years 1544–47 the comida tribute Cortés received from his Morelos encomiendas remained, then, about the same as that he had received in the preceding decade, whose annual revenue equivalent— exclusive of the added, unstipulated items secured by Altamirano after 1539—was approximately 1,080 pesos de oro de minas.

4

Labor

The Morelos labor force, utilized by Cortés for a quarter of a century in the development of his properties there and elsewhere and in other Cortesian enterprises, was of considerable size and included wage earners, slaves, and unpaid encomienda laborers. It took form as he secured encomiendas and some lands in the area in 1522 but was of limited value to him during his ill-fated Honduras sojourn from late 1524 until mid-1526, and again from the time of the Second Audiencia's departure for New Spain in early 1528 until after its arrival there in 1531. First, members of the Cherino-Salazar, then the Estrada, and later the First Audiencia factions took, or tried to take and in the process denied him, this labor force as they did his properties, powers, and even some of his following.[1]

In this troubled first decade Cortés apparently used his Morelos encomienda workers to plant, cultivate, and harvest crops of maize, beans, wheat, and perhaps cotton on his lands in the area. These workers also dug some supporting irrigation canals, built fences, and tended small herds of cattle and horses. Some of them may have maintained the house and other buildings in Cuernavaca which he expropriated from local nobles. It is certain that they transported produce from his lands and tributes from his Morelos encomiendas to market outlets in Tenochtitlan-México and to his mining properties near that city, in Michoacán and near Taxco (see Table 3).[2] The number of encomienda laborers so employed remains unclear, but the tamemes, who were engaged in the transport of goods, probably constituted the largest number utilized in any given instance and throughout the decade. All labored not for wages but in fulfillment of the encomienda obligations of their communities, the cabecera and sujeto settlements of the area.

Cortés made vigorous, virtually uninterrupted use of his Morelos labor force after the formal recognition of his Marquesado grant by the Second Audiencia in May 1531 until his death in 1547. In the summer of 1531, encomienda Indians constructed his new residence in Cuernavaca, the materials for which they supplied in deliveries from the surrounding countryside. Other construction jobs followed in which they were similarly employed. Grist and fulling mills were built in Cuernavaca. Houses, stables, corrals, workshops, and storage sheds were erected there and in the area's four other cabecera towns as well as in several of their sujetos. For these structures the Indians used adobe, stone, lime, lumber, and other materials.[3]

Occasional references to these and other projects suggest that about one hundred Indians were consistently engaged in new or repair construction.[4] When large-scale works were undertaken, such as the Tlaltenango sugar mill built near Cuernavaca in 1535 and 1536, from five hundred to one thousand or more laborers from all five encomiendas were used. As the Tlaltenango mill was erected, Viceroy Mendoza ordered, and Cortés evidently provided, payment to the Indians for their labor and for the materials they supplied.[5]

Throughout the 1530s and the 1540s, encomienda laborers worked in Cortés' grain, cotton, sugar cane, and hemp fields as well as in his vegetable gardens, vineyards, orchards, and date palm and mulberry groves. They also tended his livestock and labored in his grist and sugar mills, in his iron and leather shops, and in his *obrajes* (textile factories). Others maintained his silkworms and served, at least until the late 1530s, as indios de servicio for his Cuernavaca and other households (see Table 3). As of 1535 the number of Indians engaged in these activities in the town of Cuernavaca and its environs was at least 170 and perhaps 200. In 1536 principales from Oaxtepec testified that, between 1532 and 1535, more than 400 men from that town and its sujetos had been continually busy with such tasks. Although accurate computation of the total number of Indians Cortés' Morelos encomiendas regularly provided to do these varied jobs is impossible, the cited references and others less specific suggest two thousand or more as a reasonable estimate. During the 1540s that number may have been reduced by one-third to one-half as the Indian population of Morelos decreased and the number of Cortés' Negro slaves increased.[6]

Even before the viceregal order of 1535–36, Cortés evidently paid wages to some of these macehuales, particularly those tending livestock and working either with silkworms or in mulberry groves (the Indians resented and resisted by neglect, destruction, and carelessness the worms and their supporting groves). In later years, Cortés paid wages to most and probably all of his encomienda workers. Conclusive data as to the value of these wages, unfortunately, are not available for either period. It does appear that payments were made on a job rather than a time basis.[7]

After 1531, Cortés utilized tamemes from the Morelos towns as he had before 1528. In the spring of 1532, the Second Audiencia, acting on instruction from the crown, fined him and ordered him not to do so in the future. Cortés promptly appealed this ruling, and the crown reacted favorably with decrees issued in October 1532 and February 1533. These cedulas instructed the Audiencia to return the fines it had collected from the Marqués and to permit use of encomienda Indians for transport of goods to ports on the Pacific Ocean (primarily Acapulco in the case of the Indians of Morelos) so long as they worked voluntarily, were treated well, and were paid wages.[8]

Following the crown's decision, Cortés used large numbers of his Morelos Indians as tamemes, paying wages initially only to those who made long trips but eventually to all of them. Their services were not limited to deliveries to Acapulco. They carried foodstuffs of all kinds, hemp, and other goods from the several towns and settlements of their area to his headquarters and household in Cuernavaca. They also transported large quantities of sugar cane from fields in all sections of the area to his Tlaltenango mill and to Antonio Serrano de Cardona's Atlacomulco mill, both situated near Cuernavaca. In 1536 principales from the five encomiendas reported that in recent months Cortés had employed from six hundred to seven hundred tamemes for local transport and one thousand or more to carry maize and lime to Tenochtitlan-México. They indicated that an additional one hundred and fifty or so were used every 30 days for delivery of foodstuffs to the Taxco mines.[9]

According to these leaders, in December 1535 some 780 to 840 tamemes—300 to 400 from Cuernavaca, 140 from Yautepec and Tepoztlan, 160 from Acapistla, and about 140 from Oaxtepec—carried foodstuffs and other goods to Acapulco. Licenciado Altamirano, acting in the name of the absent Marqués, enlisted these tamemes and paid them two mantas with a value of four tomines (one-half a peso de oro común) for the round trip.[10] Marquesado records maintained by Altamirano indicate that 1,940 tamemes under the supervision of 27 principales, all from the Morelos encomiendas, delivered sugar from the Tlaltenango mill in Cuernavaca to Juan Baptista de Marín's Tenochtitlan-México warehouses in May 1540. Each of the principales was paid one tomín and each tameme *tres cuartillos de plata* (three-fourths of a tomín or three thirty-seconds of a peso de oro común) for the trip.[11] Five years later, in April 1545, tamemes and principales of an equal number were used for the same task and paid the same amounts.[12]

Although an adequate, much less accurate, figure for the number of tamemes Cortés employed monthly or annually from 1531 to 1547 cannot be computed, these data suggest an annual one of between twelve and twenty-four thousand. Apparently after 1532 payment for their services was made on the basis of distance traveled. These and other data suggest a rate of about one tomín for approximately one hundred and forty-five miles.[13] That rate seems to have remained constant from 1535 through 1545 despite general inflation of prices and wages and a marked decrease in Indian population.[14]

Far less numerous than the encomienda Indians in Cortés' Morelos labor force but forming a valuable component of it were slaves, a majority of whom were Indians. During the conquest of the Aztec Confederacy large numbers of Indians were enslaved, some of whom became Cortés' personal property. Subsequently, as the Pánuco, Honduras, Guatemala, and other areas were subjugated, Indians were enslaved by Cortés and other conquistadores. In the years 1526–28, Cortés may have purchased slaves from Indian principales, received them as demanded tribute from his encomiendas, and purchased Indians who sold themselves into slavery. Perhaps he obtained some as children who were sold into slavery by their destitute parents or as Indians who were convicted of crimes by Spanish authorities and were auctioned into stated periods of enslavement.[15] For two or more years after he returned from Spain in 1530, Cortés received Indian slaves as tribute, but apparently not a large number and only upon a few occasions.[16] He secured a few others as he acquired mining and other properties which included slaves, and he probably purchased several at auction during the 1530s as he did in the subsequent decade. Such acquisitions, however, were not numerous.[17]

Sources of information concerning these slaves are few; the only major one is the inventory of Cortés' properties made in 1549.[18] Whether or not some of them comprised a part of his Morelos labor force before 1531 is not clear. Probably they did, particularly between 1526 and 1528 when he lived in Cuernavaca. They were a part of the force in 1531 and thereafter.[19]

In 1549, according to the inventory, they numbered 186 and were *naturales,* or natives, of various parts of New Spain including Tlaxcala, Soconusco, Colima, Tehuantepec, Pánuco, and Tenochtitlan-México (see Table 4).[20] Four areas of relatively early and, at least initially, bitterly contested conquest supplied the greatest number: Tlaxcala (21), Texcoco (13), Tepeaca (8) and Tenochtitlan-México (8). These were also areas subdued by forces under Cortés' direct command. At least 29 were natives of the Morelos area—primarily the town of Cuernavaca and its sujeto, Xiutepec (see Table 4), also an area of early, contested, and Cortesian-commanded conquest. A majority of the 96 male and 90 female slaves ranged from forty to fifty-nine years of age, and none were under age thirty (see Table 5). Few, if any, of the slaves were born of slave parents and most appear to have become slaves during the conquest.[21]

Employed in the Tlaltenango sugar mill were 165 of these slaves, 47 in positions of specialized skills: 11 were boiler workers; 16 were fullers and weavers of wool; 11 were oxen drivers; 1 was a cook; 1 a blacksmith; 1 a tiller; 1 a weaver of cotton mantas and sackcloth; and 5 were sugar-makers (see Tables 6 and 7). Sixteen worked in the headquarters and household in Cuernavaca; 2 each on the Tlaltizapan and Atelinca ranches; and 1 on the Atlicaca ranch (see Table 6). Of these 16, 4 were skilled workers—

a tailor, a gardener, a lace maker and a butcher located in Cuernavaca. Cortés also owned a one-seventh share of the 7 Indian slaves (including 2 identified as of convict-slave origins) employed in Serrano's Atlacomulco sugar mill (see Tables 8 and 9).[22]

Although Indian slaves were an important segment of the Morelos labor force (27 percent, all male, with specialized skills) and despite the fact that they outnumbered their Negro counterparts, they were valued at less and were generally regarded as inferior laborers.[23] Their number, as compared with that of the Negro slaves, decreased in the 1540s for several reasons including rather effective enforcement of crown legislation directed at terminating Indian enslavement. By 1556 there were no Indian slaves working in the Tlaltenango mill; they had been replaced by Negro slaves and Indian wage earners (probably from the Morelos encomiendas).[24]

Gonzalo Aguirre Beltrán and others have demonstrated that the Spanish conquistadores, including Cortés, took Negroes when they sailed from Cuba in 1519.[25] For several years thereafter Negroes were secured from Cuba and Santo Domingo and, beginning in the early 1530s, only directly from Africa or from Africa via Spain. During the first half of the sixteenth century, many Negro slaves were transported to the New World colonies by German and Genoese traders whose operations were licensed by the crown. Cortés may have dealt (and probably did) with some of these traders in the 1530s; he was doing so in 1540.[26]

In February 1542, Cortés entered into a contract with Leonardo Lomelín and Tomas de Marín, Genoese merchants of Sevilla, which provided for delivery to Veracruz of 500 Negro slaves, two-thirds of whom were to be males and one-third females. The slaves were to range from fifteen to twenty-six years in age, with a year more or less to be allowed in each case, and were to be in good health. For each slave, sugar in an amount of 76 *ducados* or 95 pesos de oro común was to be delivered to Lomelín's agents in Tenochtitlan-México.[27] Lomelín delivered 100 slaves to Cortés' agents in January 1544 but did not fully satisfy the agreement.[28] In 1542, in the same month Cortés arranged the Lomélin contract, one of his agents purchased a Negro slave for the Tlaltenango mill from Álvaro Hernández de Madrid of Tenochtitlan-México for 156 pesos, 1 tomín, and 4 granos (96 granos to the peso) de oro cumún.[29] Subsequently, in March 1547, Licenciado Altamirano purchased a male Negro, an experienced cartwright, for 370 pesos de oro de minas (555 pesos de oro común).[30]

Cortés was certainly using Negro slaves in Morelos as of 1542, and some data indicate that he began doing so at least as early as 1532.[31] Only the inventory of 1549 provides adequate information about the numbers, capacities, and locations in which they labored or about their ages and origins. Listed there are sixty males and forty-three females, not including Cortés' one-seventh share of the twenty-three employed in Serrano's Atlacomulco mill (see Tables 5 and 9). Ranging in age from a few months to over sixty years, ten of these slaves were in their twenties, fifty-three in their thirties and forties, and eleven in their fifties (see Table 5). Most of the slaves claimed origins in various parts of West Africa, the largest numbers citing Bran (twenty-one), Biafara (twelve), and Gelofe (eleven) as their homelands. For ten no origins were indicated, and one indicated that he was born in Portugal (see Table 10). Apparently few, if any, were among the slaves provided Cortés by Lomelín and Marín, although almost forty percent were not in the ladino, or Spanish-speaking, category (see Table 5).[32]

Eighty of the slaves, including seventeen children under nine years of age, were located at the Tlaltenango mill, and twenty-one, including seven children, in the headquarters and household in Cuernavaca. Two males worked on the estancias, or ranches, of Atelinca and Tlaltizapan (see Table 6). Twelve (about 11 percent) were skilled laborers. Five were oxen drivers; three were cartwrights; one was a blacksmith; and one was a master boiler-worker in the Tlaltenango mill. In Cuernavaca one was a miller, and one, a cook (see Table 7).[33]

In the Morelos labor force, in addition to the Negroes and their Indian counterparts, were five slaves otherwise classified. Three were mulatto children with Negro mothers in Cuernavaca; one was a male mulatto, the master sugar-maker in the Tlaltenango mill; and one, a vaquero, or ranch hand, on the Atelinca estancia, was a male morisco, probably of Spanish and mulatto parentage.[34]

Fewer in number than his slaves and encomienda laborers, but of considerable worth for their contributions to his endeavors in the Morelos area, were Cortés' Spanish employees. Several of these Spaniards occupied positions in his management organization (see Chap. 6), but others were a part of his labor force. For the years before 1531 little is known of those in the latter category, but it is clear that several, perhaps three or four, were employed as skilled and specialized laborers, particularly from 1526 through 1528, when Cortés resided more or less continuously in the area. They worked in construction and land development and performed personal services for the conqueror.[35]

An increased number of these Spanish employees were utilized in the Morelos area as Cortés established his household and the Marquesado headquarters in Cuernavaca and built the Tlaltenango sugar mill in a nearby community. During the 1530s and continuing into the 1540s, he regularly employed between seven and sixteen of them.[36] Although currently available data does not reveal the precise nature of the jobs performed by the Spaniards in the years 1531–47, they were probably similar to, if not the same as, those performed by the sixteen who were at work in the conqueror's several enterprises in the area at the time of his death in 1547.

Of the sixteen employed in 1547, ten were fairly consistently located in the headquarters and household establishment in Cuernavaca. In the household itself, Pedro de Mendano was employed as a *portero* (porter and gatekeeper), Francisco de Tordesillas as a *repostero* (butler), and Pedro de la Puente (perhaps, Fuente) as a *despensero* (steward). A woman named Lucía de Paz, one of Cortés' relatives, seems to belong among these wage earners, but she may have served only for her keep and the honor afforded her by the position she occupied, that of *camarera,* or, in this case, head maid and lady-in-waiting to the conqueror's wife, Doña Juana. Fr. Antonio de Zúñiga, a Dominican cleric and brother to Doña Juana, held the post of chaplain for the household-headquarters group and was the Marquesa's confessor. One other person—another relative, Ramiro de Arellano—appears to have served on the household staff, but his precise responsibilities are not known.[37]

Luis Hernández, Hernando Mirón, Juan Martín, and Francisco Ramírez were a part of the headquarters staff in 1547, the first two serving as *herrador* (blacksmith) and *caballerizo* (head groom), respectively, and the other two in unspecified positions. At Tlaltenango, Juan Zamorano was despensero for the mill; Pedro de Delgado, *maeso de azúcar* (master sugar-maker); and Lorenzo Yáñez, *cañavero* (cane master or head cane-cutter). Bartolomé Berguío and Maese Jerónimo were occupied with jobs in the Yautepec area. The specific nature of Berguío's tasks is not known, but Jerónimo was a *cirujano* (barber-surgeon).[38]

The Spanish laborers employed by Cortés in the Morelos area numbered but a few until 1531; thereafter, their number averaged about twelve. They filled skilled and personal or household service positions in the Morelos labor force. Frequently they were used to instruct, provide example for, and guide encomienda and slave laborers, but in several instances they performed individualized, special functions. No wage data for these laborers is now available, but most of them, like their counterparts of a decade later, probably contracted for an annual wage out of which they were expected to provide their own upkeep.[39] They appear to have been generally well paid and were especially valued by Cortés and his Marquesado administrators. A number of them were longtime criados, or employee-servant-followers—virtually retainers in the medieval sense—of the Marqués or the Marquesa or were members of their respective families.

The Morelos labor force utilized in Cortesian enterprise between 1522 and 1547 consisted mostly of encomienda Indians but included a number of slaves. All of the slaves and most of the encomienda laborers were occupied primarily with tasks related to the development of Marquesado properties in the immediate area. Some of the encomienda laborers—at times, a large number—were utilized in transport of goods and occasionally in performance of other services in support of Cortesian enterprise outside the area. The number of encomienda workers employed prior to 1531 cannot be adequately estimated, but thereafter for several years the daily average appears to have been between 2,133 and 2,166. In the late 1530s and the 1540s, that number may have been reduced by one-third to one-half.

A few of the encomienda workers were wage earners at least as early as 1531, and virtually all were after 1536. Wage amounts evidently were determined on a job rather than a time basis except for the tamemes for whom distance traveled was the determinant, with the rate apparently constant between 1535 and 1545.

Just after Cortés' death in 1547, slaves in the Morelos labor force included about 186 Indians and 103 Negroes, 1 morisco, and 4 mulattoes. Approximately 22 percent of these slaves were skilled workers including about 27 percent of the Indians, 11 percent of the Negroes, one of the mulattoes, and the morisco. A majority, some 246, worked in the Tlaltenango sugar mill. Cortés' headquarters and household employed most of the others (40) with a few (8) employed on Cortés' three estancias in the area. Cortés' share of the slaves serving in Serrano's Atlacomulco mill amounted to 4 (1 Indian and 3 Negroes). These slaves were of great value both in the services they performed and as property. A few purchase-price data suggest that all the 67 unskilled Negro adults together were probably worth between 6,365 and 10,386 pesos de oro común. The skilled adult Negroes (12), the morisco, and the mulatto were probably worth more than 7,770 pesos de oro común.[40] Property-worth data for the adult Indian slaves are inadequate, but in conjunction with Silvio Zavala's recent Indian slave sale-price computations they suggest that the 51 skilled slaves were worth approximately 2,040 pesos de oro de minas; the 135 unskilled slaves, about 2,700 pesos de oro de minas.[41] The Indians were, then, valued at considerably less than their Negro counterparts; the skilled, about 89 percent less; the unskilled, from 68 to 80 percent less.

Cortés' Morelos labor force was a large one, comprising at his death in 1547 at least 1,378 and perhaps 1,734 persons continuously employed in his many enterprises. Most numerous among these were wage-earning encomienda Indians from the Morelos towns, but important for their skills and property value and constituting from about 16.9 percent to about 21.3 percent of the total number were slaves. A few, less than 1 percent, were wage-earning Spaniards. Although given its initial form in the 1520s, this labor force was more fully formed and most useful to Cortés after 1531.

5

Land[1]

Acquisition

When Cortés and his followers established the villa of Veracruz in 1519 as a preliminary step in their conquest effort, they appropriated Indian lands, as they and the Spaniards who followed them to New Spain continued to do for decades thereafter. The lands taken then and later were either unoccupied by the Indians or, as was more often the case, were communal or private holdings. Communally owned properties comprised most of the land in use within the Aztec Confederacy in 1519, but private holdings were not uncommon and evidently had been increasing in number and extent for several decades. The apparent determinants in this change were (1) conversions of office lands to private property by many of the Indian nobles whose offices had become hereditary and (2) usurpation of communal lands by the state's ruling nobles whose powers and privileges had grown sufficiently to permit, if not encourage, such action.[2]

The Spanish took increasing amounts of land from the Indians after the defeat of Tenochtitlan but these holdings did not constitute a very large portion of the usable land in New Spain until well after 1532.[3] Land acquisition was generally a part of the founding of Spanish towns or accompanied the assignment of encomiendas during the years 1519–50. Loss of land to conquerors was not a desirable experience for the native peoples of New Spain, but neither was it a new one—particularly for those, like the peoples of Morelos, who had been incorporated into the Aztec Confederacy by force. Their losses to the Spanish did not go unprotested, especially as they became cognizant of the Spanish crown's intended recognition and confirmation of their legitimate claims to private and communal properties and as rival Spanish land claimants made use of these protests to discredit one another's claims.

In 1523 the Spanish crown authorized Cortés, as governor of New Spain, to make grants of land to deserving conquistadores and colonists. The size and value of each grant was to depend on the grantee's social status and the value of his services to the crown. The grants were to be located in and around the new Spanish towns in New Spain and were not to be made at the expense of Indian communities or Indian holders of private properties.[4] The crown, in effect, authorized what had previously taken place in the establishment of Veracruz, Segura de la Frontera, and Tenochtitlan-México but forbade the acquisition of land which was already taking place outside Spanish municipality areas and, particularly, in encomienda provinces and towns. For the most part, acquisitions in the latter case were, therefore, of extralegal character: lands taken from Indians without formal crown approval in what amounted to forceful seizures of one kind or another. Often, the Indians were "persuaded" by their encomenderos to provide land in lieu of tribute or to sell (actually exchange) parcels for goods which could be utilized in tribute payments. Most of the land obtained in this fashion was eventually recognized as the legal property of Spanish possessors but only after numerous lengthy legal disputes. Many of these contests, some involving rival Spanish as well as Spanish and Indian claimants, were concluded with awards of damages to the Indians as individuals or communities.

Presently available title-records for land transactions in New Spain do not include assignments Cortés made to himself, but it is obvious that in Morelos he assumed ownership of portions, if not all, of the private property formerly held by Moctezuma II. He seems to have done so in 1522 when he secured the area's five major encomiendas—Cuernavaca, Yautepec, Tepoztlan, Oaxtepec, and Acapistla—for himself.[5] He had also acquired by 1526, and probably in 1523 or 1524, the properties (and tribute rights) of Yoatzin, señor of Cuernavaca at the time of the arrival of the Spanish. Evidently Yoatzin died, and Cortés named himself guardian for Don Hernando, the señor's heir and successor, who was still a minor. These properties, located in the town of Cuernavaca and its surrounding sujetos, included a considerable amount of land worked by macehuales and Yoatzin's mayeques and slaves, as well as several undescribed houses and other buildings.[6]

As acting señor, Cortés may have generally reorganized Cuernavaca's political, social, and economic life just after Yoatzin's death, reassigning lands, local administrative offices, and the like, as later described in the *Códice Municipal de Cuernavaca*.[7] Perhaps he did so following his unfortunate Honduras trek and eighteen-month absence from New Spain. All of the Morelos encomiendas were taken from him during that absence, but upon his return in the spring of 1526 he resumed control of three of them, apparently permitting Diego de Ordaz to retain the two—Tepoztlan and Yautepec—recently granted him.[8] Cortés probably participated in the erection of the Franciscan mission-monastery there in the fall of 1526 while he was resident in Cuernavaca. He evidently supplied funds, encomienda laborers, and construction materials, as well as land taken from Yoatzin's holdings or from the town's communal properties, for the project.[9] There is no evidence that he or any other Spaniard except Ordaz secured other properties in the Morelos area until he departed for Spain in 1528.

While he was in Spain and before the end of 1529, Cortés gained title to a piece of land comprising some seventeen acres and located about one-half league or one and one-half miles outside the town of Yautepec (see Table 11). The acreage was planted with citrus and other fruit trees and was purchased, according to both Spanish and Indian witnesses testifying in 1551, by Ordaz from the town of Yautepec in 1526 or 1527 for an undisclosed amount.[10] It passed to Cortés in a personal exchange of encomiendas, Huejotzingo for Tepoztlan and Yautepec, arranged between him and Ordaz. The exchange was only a paper one until 1531, however, as action by New Spain's new governing body, the First Audiencia, denied both Cortés and Ordaz all of their holdings in Morelos.[11]

When he returned to New Spain in the summer of 1530, Cortés found that a rival had established himself as encomendero of Cuernavaca (the same rival who had managed to do so during his Honduras sojourn) and as a landowner in the area. Antonio Serrano de Cardona, whose claim to the encomienda of Cuernavaca, although hotly contested by the conqueror's attorneys, was recognized by the First Audiencia in April 1529, was in the process of developing a profitable sugar plantation on some 789 acres of land located in Cuernavaca's barrio-sujetos of Tetela and Iztayaca (see Table 11). In October 1529, Serrano purchased this property from the señores and principales of the town and its two barrios for some 320 to 360 mantas valued at from 80 to 90 pesos de oro común. Serrano's purchase price, in terms of the pesos then in use, amounted to about 38 maravedís an acre.[12] On some of these lands, Serrano built several houses, barns, and other structures, and his Atlacomulco mill. He planted an orchard near the mill and sugarcane on most of the remaining acreage. By 1531 he was producing sugar in the Atlacomulco mill from cane grown in nearby fields, some of which were also used to supply his slave workers in the mill with wheat and other foodstuffs (see Table 9).[13]

Cortés was unable to assume full possession of any of his holdings in New Spain until May 1531, when the Second Audiencia formally recognized the royal decree of 1529 which provided him with title to (and extensive rights over) some twenty-three encomiendas in the colony including the five he had originally secured in Morelos.[14] Immediately after the Audiencia's action, Cortés undertook the redevelopment of his holdings in Morelos as a part of his new Marquesado.

When he replaced Serrano as encomendero of Cuernavaca, the conqueror took steps intended to force this dangerous rival to abandon his landholdings in the area. Serrano responded with a suit brought before the Audiencia in late May 1531. He charged that agents of the new Marqués had cut off the water supply to his cane fields and orchard and were denying his millworkers procurement of firewood and lumber, both essential to the operation of the mill. He also insisted that Cortés' agents were destroying his cane fields and persuading the Indians of the area not to work for him or to supply the foodstuffs needed by his laborers. Attorneys for Cortés answered these charges with arguments based upon the civil and criminal jurisdiction over the towns in Morelos granted their client in the royal order of 1529. Cortés, according to the attorneys, was protecting the rights and interests of the Indians of those towns by preventing the deforestation of the hillsides around Cuernavaca and the diminution of the water and land resources required for the production of essential foodstuffs.[15] The Audiencia rightly did not regard Cortés' efforts as altogether altruistic and ruled in Serrano's favor in spite of the arguments of Cortés' attorney. It made this ruling in 1531 and was forced by continuing complaints from Serrano to reassert it in 1532 and 1533. The Council of the Indies, meanwhile, heard the case on appeal initiated by Cortés and in 1534 upheld the Audiencia's decision. Even after he received word of the high court's action, the conqueror persisted in his attempt to inhibit Serrano's Morelos enterprise.

Finally, in an attempt to end their harassment, Serrano's agents concluded an agreement with Licenciado Altamirano, the administrator of the Marquesado, by the terms of which Cortés was given a one-seventh interest in the Atlacomulco mill and its surrounding orchard and sugarcane and wheat fields (see Table 11).[16] This agreement reduced friction for a few years, but in 1546 Isabel de Ojeda, Serrano's widow and only heir, brought a suit against Cortés which essentially repeated the charges made by her husband in 1531.[17] Again, the Audiencia heard the suit and ordered Cortés to stop interfering in the operations of the Atlacomulco establishment, and again the Council of the Indies upheld the Audiencia's order, this time in 1547, the year of the conqueror's death. Still the dispute was not ended; it was continued for three decades thereafter by Doña Isabel and her business associates and Don Martín Cortés, the conqueror's son and heir.[18]

In 1531, Cortés evidently reclaimed most of the property in Morelos which he had controlled prior to 1529 and began securing additional land for crop and livestock production. Although Don Hernando, Yoatzin's successor in the señorío of Cuernavaca, reached adulthood in 1528 or 1529, Cortés relinquished to him only some of the lands which had belonged to his father.[19] Cortés planted sugarcane and grapevines in a number of the fields which had belonged to the señor and were not passed on to his son, and on the land in Cuernavaca occupied by some of Yoatzin's houses and gardens, he began building a house, corrals, and other structures. Then, in 1533, the properties which had been provided Don Hernando as inheritance from his father were confiscated by Cortés' agents. This action was taken, or so the agents reported later, because Don Hernando scandalously took a female Indian named Inés, who was part of Cortés' household, and fled with her to Mexico City where he went into hiding in some houses left to him by his father.[20]

The particulars of the above incident are not recorded, but in 1536 Don Hernando brought suit against the Marqués in an attempt to regain the confiscated properties as well as the others held by Cortés which had belonged to his father. Cortés' attorneys tried to discredit Don Hernando's claims by suggesting that the lands held by Yoatzin were not private properties but were part of the señorío or lordship of Cuernavaca. The attorneys argued, further, and Don Hernando denied, that the señorío was not hereditary but was held at Moctezuma's—and subsequently, by virtue of the Marquesado grant—Cortés' pleasure (with the concurrence of the principales of Cuernavaca). The newly appointed Viceroy Mendoza and the Audiencia considered the case and decided to investigate not only Don Hernando's property claims but also his tribute claims, as well as Marquesado use and collection of encomienda dues, both tribute and labor, in the Morelos area. After the investigation, Cortés was ordered to return some lands to Don Hernando, to pay him a specified sum (unhappily not recorded) for the remainder, and to allow him, as señor of Cuernavaca, to collect tribute from the macehuales of certain of Cuernavaca's barrios and sujeto settlements.[21] Cortés evidently paid Don Hernando the required sum for the lands on which he had constructed his palatial residence and other buildings in Cuernavaca, for those on which he had constructed his own Tlaltenango sugar mill—already a productive enterprise—for some of the more than seven hundred acres in and around Cuernavaca which he had planted with sugarcane and grapevines, and for the seventeen acres near Acatliquipa (one of Cuernavaca's sujetos) where he had planted a mulberry grove (see Table 11).

The several pieces of land Cortés acquired near Yautepec and others not far from Oaxtepec had belonged to Moctezuma.[22] During the 1530s and the 1540s, he seems to have secured some additional land from Don Hernando and either purchased or simply appropriated certain plots of land from both the communal and private holdings of the Indians of all five of his Morelos encomiendas.[23] At least six and one-half acres apparently so obtained in the Cuernavaca barrio of Amanalco were given to Bernaldino del Castillo in exchange for Coyoacan property (see Table 11). There and on acreage rented from the Indians of Cuernavaca (for which he was forced by the Audiencia to pay back-dated rent in 1550) Castillo developed a small sugar operation.[24]

Cortés' Morelos lands were inventoried in 1549, two years after his death, at 1,402.1 acres (see Table 11). The inventory of 1549 revealed that another 119 acres in the area were used by the Marquesado as mulberry groves for support of the already unsuccessful silk industry. These acres belonged to the Indian communities of Tlaquiltenango, Zacatepec, Tetecala, Temimilcingo, and Tetelpa, sujetos to Cuernavaca located in the southern part of the Cuernavaca valley.[25] In some instances, these lands were rented or leased; in others, the communities were given a share of the silk produced by Marquesado worms commensurate with the quantity of leaves supplied by the trees on their lands.[26] Over the years 1531–47, the acreage utilized by Cortés for various purposes no doubt varied from time to time, but it probably averaged annually about what he was using at the time of his death: over 1,500 acres.

Cortés' sometime employee, Bernaldino del Castillo, owned about 6½ acres in Morelos in 1549 and was using an additional rented area comprising perhaps as much as 315 acres (see Table 11).[27] The conqueror's only Spanish entrepreneurial rival in the area, Isabel de Ojeda, successor to Antonio Serrano de Cardona, owned 676.8 acres in 1549.[28] She and her husband may have rented additional lands in the years 1529–31, but after 1531 they were probably limited to using what they owned.

Development

Cortés began the agricultural development of his estate in New Spain in 1522 when he demanded tribute from his newly acquired encomienda Indians in foodstuffs and other agrarian goods of the kinds which they had been producing for decades, if not centuries. At about the same time he apparently had these Indians plant some of the land he had appropriated with maize, frijoles, and cotton, all native American plants with which they were familiar.[29] A year later, following receipt of seeds, plant cuttings, and livestock which he had requested from the Spanish crown, Cortés evidently introduced his encomienda Indians to livestock care and breeding and to the cultivation of wheat, sugarcane, fruit and perhaps mulberry trees, and other European plants.[30] By 1529 his landholdings, worked by both encomienda laborers and slaves, were producing maize, frijoles, cotton, wheat, sugarcane, and grapes, and were supporting chickens and herds of cattle, horses, and sheep.[31] In the spring of that year Cortés lost control of these lands and was unable to regain it until 1531. Thereafter, however, he vigorously pursued the agricultural development of his properties, including those in Morelos, until his death in 1547.

The ample water supply, fertile soils, and climatic conditions of Morelos were ideal for various agrarian pursuits, including those normally undertaken in both temperate and subtropical regions. During the years

1522–29 Cortés probably improved and extended the area's preconquest irrigation system in order to provide more water for his fields.[32] After 1531 he acquired additional lands all over the area and concentrated his efforts on the production of fruits of various kinds, grapes for wine-making, mulberry leaves for his silkworms, wheat, and sugarcane, and on the raising of livestock. From then on he apparently depended on his encomienda tribute for most of the maize, frijoles, and cotton which he used to support his establishment in Morelos and for sale purposes.

In 1531 Cortés took over the Tlalhuitongo orchard which had been the property of Diego de Ordaz.[33] The orchard (see Table 11) comprised seventeen acres in 1549 and by that date had been producing oranges, limes, lemons, citron, and other fruits "de Castilla" (from Spain), for more than twenty years. Elsewhere in Morelos, between 1531 and 1547, Cortés developed orchards on about thirty-five acres of his land (see Table 11) which produced pomegranates, quinces, figs, apples, pears, citrus of various kinds, dates, and the fruit of the native American zapote tree.[34] One of these orchards, the huerta de Chinampa, located near Acapistla, was also planted with 1,000 grape vines. Fifteen years earlier the Marqués had owned a vineyard and wine press in Yautepec, but by 1547 he had, in addition to the Chinampa vines, only one vineyard, of eleven and seven-tenths acres.[35]

The least successful of the Cortesian agrarian enterprises undertaken in Morelos was silk production. As early as 1523 Cortés may have secured some mulberry cuttings and silkworms from Spain, but he evidently did not succeed in cultivating either plants or worms effectively until after his return to New Spain as Marqués del Valle de Oaxaca in 1530. Even then, although he planted mulberry trees in the Morelos area and apparently raised a few silkworms in Yautepec, he was unable to produce satisfactory amounts of silk and within a few years gave up the effort.[36] Cortés undoubtedly authorized the last attempt at silk production in Morelos as he prepared for his final trip to Spain in 1539. Just after his departure, Licenciado Altamirano, administrator of the Marquesado, began utilizing encomienda laborers in the effort and by 1545 had planted about 32,000 mulberry trees on lands owned or rented by Cortés (see Table 11) and constructed a breeding house for worms just outside Yautepec.[37] In 1546 and for a few years thereafter the Yautepec worms produced some silk (at one point noted as nearly thirty pounds), but by 1549 the enterprise was again on the wane.[38] The inventory taken of Cortés' properties that year revealed that only 25 percent of the mulberry trees planted by Altamirano were in usable condition and that more than 50 percent were dying for want of water and proper cultivation.[39] Apparently Indian resistance to the enterprise was the primary reason for the successive failures in its development. Encomienda laborers neglected both the trees on Indian lands and those on Cortés' acreage and evidently only worked with the silkworms when they were compelled to do so.[40]

Unlike his silk production effort, the sugar industry Cortés developed in Morelos was a most profitable success. During his residence in Cuba the conqueror was evidently associated with some sugar-making businesses, and in 1522 or 1523 he introduced the industry into New Spain. He established a small mill in Tuxtla, a town located in the southern part of the present state of Veracruz, and was profitably producing sugar there by 1524. His sugar business was probably concentrated in that area until his departure for Spain in 1528, following which the First Audiencia seized the mill and its surrounding cane fields.[41] During his absence, Antonio Serrano de Cardona established his Atlacomulco mill in one of Cuernavaca's barrio-sujetos.[42] Almost immediately after Cortés returned and was able to regain control of the Morelos encomiendas, he challenged Serrano's right to the Atlacomulco mill and its supporting fields. He was apparently determined to make the Morelos area economically as well as politically his. Serrano had already proven himself a dangerously able political and economic rival and therefore had to be eliminated from the area.[43] Doubtless Cortés was also intent on regaining a major share of the colony's sugar business, and, as he had not yet recovered his Tuxtla operation, he turned to Morelos as an area already proven useful for that purpose.

Sugar production required ample supplies of water, wood or charcoal, fertile soil, and semitropical climate conditions for growing the cane, and an abundant labor force, all of which the Cuernavaca area was providing Serrano. In 1532, as his first attempt to induce Serrano to abandon his Atlacomulco mill failed, Cortés planted some of his lands in Morelos with sugarcane and evidently established a small horse- or oxen-powered mill not far from Serrano's larger water-powered operation.[44] Subsequently he secured more land for cane cultivation (partly at the expense of the señor of Cuernavaca) and began producing sugar. Meanwhile he continued to harass his competitor, and, although he was unable to force Serrano from the area, he managed in 1539 to secure a one-seventh interest in the Atlacomulco mill and lands.[45]

Even before he acquired an interest in the Atlacomulco enterprise, Cortés had established himself as New Spain's largest sugar producer, a status he enjoyed until his death in 1547. He had regained control and improved the facilities of his Tuxtla mill and had developed a sugar operation in Morelos that was huge by the standards of the time. In 1537 or 1538 the construction, begun two or three years earlier, of a sugar mill located not far from Cuernavaca in Tlaltenango, one of that town's sujetos, was completed. The Tlaltenango mill consisted of a large two-

story stone and mortar building, in which water-powered machinery was
installed, and a number of small adobe buildings used as shops and
housing for mill workers. Surrounding the mill were cane fields owned by
Cortés. The fields probably encompassed between 600 and 700 acres by
1539.[46] Although records of the quantities of sugar produced by Cortés'
Morelos properties during the 1530s are not presently available, on the
basis of such data for the 1540s it is possible to suggest that by 1538–39
his Tlaltenango mill was producing annually about 5,000 arrobas or
125,000 pounds of sugar, which he was selling both in New Spain and in
Spain.[47]

As he prepared for his second and final journey to Spain in 1539, the
Marqués organized a company with García de Morón, a merchant of
Mexico City, to handle the sale, both local and export, of his sugar. For a
period of three years beginning January 1, 1540, agents were to deliver
the sugar formed at Tlaltenango and Tuxtla to Morón in Mexico City.
Morón was to sell the sugar in New Spain or in Spain, providing the
necessary transportation in the latter case. After the handling expenses
incurred by Morón were deducted, he and Cortés were to share equally
the amount set as the sale price of the sugar, approximately 3 pesos per
arroba.[48] The sugar supplied to Morón from the Tlaltenango mill
averaged about 5,155 arrobas (128,875 pounds) per year. The annual
gross income shared by Morón and Cortés amounted to about 6,595 pesos
de oro de minas.

On May 11, 1542, a little over seven months before the contract with
Morón was to expire, the Marqués entered into an agreement whereby
the sugar produced by his Tlaltenango and Tuxtla mills was to be supplied to Tomás de Marín and Leonardo Lomelín, Genoese traders of
Sevilla, as payment for Negro slaves which were to be delivered to Veracruz.[49] An amount of sugar—valued at 550 maravedís (1 2/9 pesos de oro
de minas) per arroba for refined white and lesser amounts for inferior
grades—equal to 47,500 pesos de oro común, the price specified for 500
Negro slaves, was to be delivered to Lomelín-Marín agents in New Spain.[50]
The Genoese traders apparently failed to fulfill their share of the agreement, and in 1548 the conqueror's heir, Don Martín, initiated a suit
against them in an attempt to recover the value of most of the sugar
delivered.[51] The suit indicated that about 6,490 arrobas of sugar worth
5,636 pesos de oro de minas were received by Lomelín's agents each year
for four years beginning September 1, 1544. Probably about 5,155 of these
arrobas (worth about 4,696 pesos de oro de minas of net revenue) were
the annual output of the Tlaltenango mill.[52] At the time of his death in
1547, then, Cortés' Morelos sugar industry comprised the Tlaltenango
mill, its supporting 769 acres of cane fields (see Table 11), and a one-
seventh share in the Atlacomulco operation. The industry was producing

about 5,798 arrobas of sugar for him each year: about 5,155 formed at Tlaltenango and one-seventh of the estimated 4,500 formed at Atlacomulco.[53]

The acreage near Yautepec used by Cortés for growing sugarcane before he concentrated his sugar operation in Tlaltenango (1536–48) was planted in wheat at the time of his death.[54] In 1547, as Table 11 indicates, some 300 of his acres were wheat fields, and his share of the Atlacomulco lands similarly utilized amounted to 9 acres. Throughout the 1530s and the early 1540s Cortés harvested considerable quantities of wheat on his Morelos lands. Evidently some of the grain was sold in Mexico City markets, but most of it was used to supply his slaves and employees in the area with bread and other products. From time to time the Marqués apparently grew hemp, muskmelons, cantaloupes, and other crops on this acreage, but his wheat fields seldom comprised fewer than 250 acres.[55]

More important than his wheat production in terms of investment and revenues was the livestock the Marqués raised on his estancias in Morelos.[56] From the 1520s onward, herds of horses, cattle, sheep, oxen, and hogs were tended by encomienda laborers and slaves on these estancias. As of 1547, Cortés had a herd of 429 cattle, including bulls, yearlings, and mature cows, on his Atelinca estancia. At Tlaltenango he had 164 oxen, and his share in the Atlacomulco mill included 2 more of those beasts as well as 2 goats and 3 sheep.[57] At Tlaltenango and his headquarters in Cuernavaca he had 163 pigs and 130 sheep. The horses he pastured in Morelos, including numerous colts, breeding mares, and stallions, numbered 257 at the time of his death. With the horses, which were corraled at five different places, as indicated in Table 11, were 27 mules, 1 male ass, and 1 burro. Many of these animals were used in various kinds of work in the Morelos area, and others were slaughtered there for food. Some, however, such as his carefully bred colts, were evidently sold from time to time in Mexico City or elsewhere in New Spain.

It is apparent that Cortés used his landholdings in Morelos to develop numerous agricultural enterprises, most of which were quite successful. These various enterprises netted him some revenues and supplied much of the food required by his slaves and employees not only in the Morelos area but in other areas as well. His sugar industry and livestock breeding were particularly successful and produced revenues which increased gradually for many years after his death. The sum total of his effort in the development of Morelos lands was the foundation of a prosperous agricultural estate.

6

Management and Revenues

Management

As he acquired encomiendas and secured his first landholdings in New
Spain in the years 1522–29, Cortés apparently developed the administrative organization which he employed thereafter in the management of
his properties and interests. As the years passed this organization became
an extensive two-level one in which the conqueror's authority was always
evident but over which he exercised less and less direct supervision. It
effected the economic utilization and political administration (as a part
of New Spain's governing structure) of encomienda towns and the development of lands and business enterprises. It also facilitated pursuit of the
conqueror's political ambitions, including his exploratory activities and
other endeavors.

The first, extralocal level of the organization consisted of administrators and their assistants to whom responsibility for policy formation, general management, and the supervision of lesser officials was assigned. The
duties of these officials varied from time to time but were predominantly
part of large-scale commercial transactions including the movement and
sale of large quantities of goods, judicial proceedings—especially involving encomienda tribute and labor disputes—and administration of Indian
towns. The second, local level of the organization comprised lesser officials
entrusted with specific duties in three general categories: the governing
of encomienda towns, the administration of encomienda dues, and the
management of various particular enterprises and establishments. Although the responsibilities of these lesser officials frequently overlapped—
as, for instance, in the case of tribute collection and encomienda labor
usage—few serious intraorganizational problems seem to have developed.
There were, however, endless disputes between the organization and New
Spain's colonial bureaucracy after Cortés relinquished his dominant position in the latter. After 1532 these problems were particularly difficult for
several of the organization's local administrators and some of their
superiors inasmuch as they were also officeholders in the bureaucracy and
thereby subordinate to the colony's ranking royal officials.

In the years 1522–24 the first-level positions in the organization were evidently occupied by the conqueror, his relatives Rodrigo de Paz and Fray Diego Altamirano, and several of his conquest companions-in-arms, including García de Llerena. Assigned to perform second-level functions during these years were some who had served as soldiers in the conquest, such as Francisco de Santa Cruz, Carbano Bejarano, and possibly Francisco de la Peña, who has not as yet been clearly identified. The first two of these were tribute collectors and labor overseers in the Morelos area, and the last may have been the alcalde mayor or principal governing official for the encomienda towns there.[1] Assisting and serving as lieutenants to these officers were the area's Indian señores and principales.

As he had in developing the encomienda system generally, Cortés dealt with his encomienda towns by continuing, with some modifications, the governing, tribute, and labor service systems that existed at the time of the conquest. In Morelos, he replaced the Aztec Confederacy's two calpixques, or tribute collectors and labor supervisors (one stationed in Cuernavaca, the other in Oaxtepec), with his agents, Bejarano and Santa Cruz. With some individual exceptions, the roles of the area's Indian señores, principales, and macehuales in the collection and payment of tribute, the assignment and performance of labor services, and local political and judicial administration remained much the same as those they had fulfilled in preconquest times.[2] In this early period, or after he returned from Honduras in 1526, Cortés apparently met with the area's principales in order to confirm, as was the case in most instances, or to deny their claims as local native nobles to lands and to governing authority over the macehuales of their communities and to initiate some changes in these matters of officeholding and landholding.[3] When he did so he evidently assumed the señorío of the town of Cuernavaca himself, possibly selecting one of the town's principales as native leader of that ruling group.[4] At the same time he probably appointed de la Peña alcalde mayor of Cuernavaca and charged him with supervision of the native nobility in the governing of that and the other towns and settlements in the area.[5]

Prior to his departure for Honduras in 1524, Cortés authorized Rodrigo de Paz to act during his absence as the administrator of his properties in New Spain. Evidently Fray Diego Altamirano, Llerena, Bejarano, and Santa Cruz continued in the positions earlier assigned to them, with Santa Cruz also acting as mayordomo or manager of Cortés' developing household-headquarters in Cuernavaca. The four exercised their several functions under Paz's supervision until Salazar and Cherino put him to death and seized the conqueror's properties in 1525–26.[6] After Cortés returned to New Spain in May 1526 they again assumed their duties and were joined by Hernán López Dávila who became Cortés' contador.[7] Subsequently Cortés employed Francisco Terrazas, Diego de Ocampo,

Francisco de Herrera, Francisco de las Casas, Andrés de Barrios, Licenciado Juan Altamirano, Pedro Gallego, Pedro Núñez de Maldonado, Francisco Sánchez de Toledo, Luis Canzado Pareba, and Francisco Sánchez y Castro, the first five as mayordomos of agricultural and business enterprises and the others as attorneys and business negotiators.[8] Later, in the spring of 1528 as he prepared to leave for Spain, the Conqueror entrusted three of these, Altamirano, Ocampo, and Gallego, with primary responsibility in the administration of his properties and interests. To assist them he named Francisco de Herrera successor to Dávila as contador and García de Llerena and Pedro Núñez de Maldonado chief attorneys and debt negotiators. He also engaged Gonzalo Herrados as alguacil (constable or sheriff) in Cuernavaca.[9] Within a year after his departure, these administrators and their subordinates were left virtually unemployed save in the pursuance of legal protests as the First Audiencia deprived their employer of all his properties in New Spain.[10]

Not until May 1531, almost a year after his return to New Spain, was Cortés able to regain control of some of the properties he had accumulated prior to 1529 and to begin acquiring others.[11] He again formed an administrative organization through which he could provide for the development and management of these properties, now collectively known as the Marquesado, and his other interests (see Table 12). Evidently he initially secured tribute collectors and labor supervisors and sent them to the encomienda towns included in his Marquesado grant. They made arrangements for collecting the quarterly tribute payments due him and began employing encomienda labor in various construction projects and in planting crops on his lands.[12] Among these officials were Domingo Martín and Martín Sánchez, the first assigned as the collector of tribute for Cuernavaca and its sujetos and the second in the same capacity for the towns of Oaxtepec, Yautepec, Tepoztlan, possibly Acapistla, and their sujetos.[13] Apparently these two were accompanied by Bernaldino del Castillo and Hernán Rodríguez, both of whom were to serve as labor supervisors and to perform other unspecified duties.[14]

Very soon after he arranged for the handling of the tribute and labor services due him from the Indians of the Morelos area, Cortés selected Licenciado Altamirano to serve as alcalde mayor for the area. At about the same time he appointed Altamirano *teniente de justicia* (his deputy or lieutenant in the administration of justice) for the entire Marquesado.[15] In June or July of 1531 Altamirano, accompanied by his recently appointed subordinates—Francisco de Triana, alguacil for the Morelos area; two notaries, Alonso Díaz de Gibraleón and Alonso de Mata; and others—went to Cuernavaca. There they established an audiencia and a jail for the Marquesado.[16] Their efforts reflected Cortés' decision to establish a headquarters for the Marquesado in Cuernavaca. He joined them there sometime in early July in order to oversee their work and to take charge, at least temporarily, of the campaign (begun earlier for him by Bernaldino del Castillo and Hernán Rodríguez) to wrest control of the Atlacomulco sugar mill from Antonio Serrano de Cardona. In that unsuccessful effort both force and persuasion were employed by Cortés, Altamirano, Triana, Castillo, and those who assisted them. While he was engaged in harassing Serrano, the Marqués also supervised the construction in Cuernavaca of a palatial residence and other buildings required for his headquarters.[17]

In the fall of 1531 Cortés moved his household from Tenochtitlan-México to Cuernavaca and centralized the administrative machinery of the Marquesado in that town.[18] From that time until September 1534 the Marqués acted as governor, or chief administrative officer, for the Marquesado, with Licenciado Altamirano serving as his first deputy. In addition to supervising the administration of justice and the governing of the encomienda towns within the Marquesado, Altamirano appears to have been responsible for overseeing the work of the Marquesado's legal staff. That staff—on which García de Llerena and Diego Pizarro held prominent positions and to which Juan de Villanueva, Alonso de Paredes, and Francisco de Esquivel were appointed—was occupied with numerous lawsuits over Cortés' encomienda holdings, including the matter of the counting of his 23,000 vassals, the seizure of his properties by the First Audiencia, and his long-delayed residencia. Among the other first-level administrators employed by Cortés were Francisco de Herrera, who discharged the duties of contador for at least a year or two after 1531, and Gonzalo de Herrera, who served as procurador.[19]

Among the lesser officials who were active in the management of the Marquesado between 1531 and 1534, in addition to those previously mentioned, were Pedro de Arteaga, Sebastián Cerezo, Bartolomé Cáceres, Francisco de Hinojosa, Antón García, and Francisco Terrazas. All of these men were employed in the Morelos area: Arteaga, as a notary; Cerezo, as a calpixque or supervisor of encomienda laborers; Cáceres, as a winemaker and apparently supervisor of the Marqués' wine enterprise; and Hinojosa, García, and Terrazas, as supervisors of land cultivation, the construction of barns, shops, and other structures, and the shipment of goods to Tenochtitlan-México, Acapulco, and elsewhere.[20] Jorge Cerón de Saavedra and Francisco de Santa Cruz were mayordomos of Cortés' agricultural enterprises outside the Morelos area, and Juan de Salamanca and Juan de la Mercader Zarza apparently were responsible for some of the Marquesado's business transactions in Mexico City.[21]

The establishment of business enterprises, the development of lands and the formulation of management procedures were the principal concerns of most of the Marquesado's administrators in the years 1531–34.[22]

Considerable effort was expended, for instance, in providing for the sale of the cotton goods paid as tribute by the Indians of the Morelos encomiendas. In 1531 and 1532, Cortés and Altamirano agreed to sell the goods to a group of itinerant merchants, at least three of whom were Morelos Indians, two from Xoloztoc and one from Acapistla. These merchants were to buy the textiles in Cuernavaca and to absorb the expenses of transporting them elsewhere for resale.[23] Subsequently, in 1533 or 1534, other means for the handling of the tribute cottons were arranged in a contract agreement with Juan Marín, a merchant whose headquarters were in Tenochtitlan-México. The goods were to be sold to Marín after delivery to his warehouses in the capital city by Cortés' agents.[24] After major alterations in the Marquesado administrative organization, the contract with Marín was dropped in 1535 in favor of one which drew loud and unsettling protests from the textile retailers of the colony.[25]

Despite continuous involvement in the many enterprises he designed for the Marquesado, Cortés had time for numerous other endeavors in the years 1531–34. Even before he went to Spain in 1528 he had pursued exploratory activities in the Mar del Sur, and from the time of his return to the colony until he set out on his last transatlantic journey in 1540 he spent considerable time in the Tehuantepec and Acapulco areas building and outfitting ships, some of which he loaded with supplies and trade goods and dispatched southward to the developing Spanish enterprise in Peru. Most of his vessels were sent northward along New Spain's Pacific coast in explorations for which he enjoyed formal crown authorization as of 1531. His exploratory efforts were not encouraged, however, by the Second Audiencia and were overtly opposed by Nuño de Guzmán. Guzmán, as one of Cortés' longtime adversaries, was determined to keep the conqueror out of the area then under his control, the northern coastal region of New Spain, essentially the province of Nueva Galicia, much of which is now included in the Mexican states of Jalisco, Nayarit, and Sinaloa.[26] In the fall of 1534, frustrated by repeated failures involving heavy shipping and manpower losses, some sustained in defense against attacks by Guzmán's forces, Cortés decided to organize another, larger, two-pronged (by sea and land) expeditionary group, one part of which he would personally lead overland through Guzman's Nueva Galicia. In the winter of 1534–35 he assumed direct command of the group and again set out in pursuit of conquest and exploratory success.[27] On the eve of his departure he elevated Licenciado Altamirano to the governorship of the Marquesado and consigned to him complete authority in all matters relating to its administration.

The power-of-attorney authorizing Altamirano to assume the governorship of the Marquesado was promulgated on September 8, 1534. He was instructed to take:

. . . possession and lordship, actual and physical, of the villas,
pueblos, and jurisdiction which I [Cortés] have and hold and [which]
belong to me, according to that included in the concession from his
majesty [Charles V] by which I have been entrusted with civil and
criminal jurisdiction [including] the sovereign power to decide civil
cases and to impose and effect punishments with cognizance of cause,
and with the offices, taxes, laws and tributes of the said pueblos;
and in order that over it and that which depends upon or is joined
to or connected to it you can take those measures which correspond
[are suitable] and appear necessary . . .[28]

Altamirano was more explicitly charged with assumption of the responsibility for: (1) judicial administration of the Marquesado's towns,
determining what crimes had been committed and by whom after having
heard argumentation and having evaluated evidence, and issuing appropriate sentences; (2) appointment, instruction, and supervision of the
Marquesado's alcaldes mayores, alguaciles, *escribanos* (notaries), and
justicias ordinarias (justices of the peace), and for conducting residencias
of these officials, replacing them if necessary; (3) formulation of policies
and issuance of orders necessary for the administration of the Marquesado; (4) collection of all tributes, taxes, and other dues (such as labor
services) owed to the Marqués by the *vecinos* (citizens) of his towns; (5)
supervision of the management of the haciendas, mines, shops, inns, and
funds of the Marquesado; (6) collection and payment of debts owed to
and by the Marqués; (7) purchase and sale of properties for the Marquesado; (8) conduct of trade in which the Marquesado was involved, whether
in New Spain, Spain, or elsewhere; (9) employment and dismissal of the
employees of the Marquesado; and (10) handling all legal matters involving the Marqués and the Marquesado, including lawsuits tried before
either the Audiencia of México or the Council of the Indies, contracts for
the sale of tribute goods and other items, and the borrowing and lending
of money.[29]

Altamirano made one immediate personnel change in the administrative organization (see Table 12) of the Marquesado; he removed himself
as alcalde mayor for the Morelos area and named Juan Zimbrón to the
position.[30] That change brought Zimbrón into the judicial proceedings of
1533–34 that were conducted against the señor of Cuernavaca, Don
Hernando. The proceedings resulted in Don Hernando's replacement, at
least for a time, in the Indian lordship and rule of Cuernavaca and the
seizure of some of his properties. Subsequently, Zimbrón acted both as
alcalde mayor and mayordomo of Cortés' headquarters-household in
Cuernavaca. In 1536 he was fined by the Viceroy and Audiencia for
having mistreated the Indians of the Morelos area in his capacity

as mayordomo.[31] A part of this affair may have been the imprisonment of some of the principales of Cuernavaca and its sujeto settlements. Apparently the imprisonment was intended to encourage cooperation from the Indian leaders in the implementation of tribute assessment and collection changes which were attempted at this time.[32] Shortly after he was fined, Zimbrón was probably replaced by Francisco Sánchez de Toledo, who was mayordomo in Cuernavaca by late 1537 or early 1538, and by Altamirano, who seems to have reassumed the duties of alcalde mayor in Cuernavaca after 1536.[33]

In January of 1535 Altamirano arranged to transfer the sale of the cotton textiles paid the Marquesado by the Indians of Morelos from Juan Marín to a company in which García de Llerena, Alonso de Paladiñas (both of whom were on the Marquesado's legal staff), and Altamirano, representing Cortés, each held a one-third interest.[34] The company was to buy the cotton textiles at stated wholesale prices and to resell them at retail prices reflecting a 50 percent markup. The profits derived were to be split among the partners on an equal basis. Llerena and Paladiñas, who were responsible for the retail sale of the goods in Mexico City, immediately became embroiled in a legal hassle with other retailers as they violated a cabildo ordinance which required merchants to register their tribute textile purchases and the prices paid for them with a city official before offering them for resale. The ordinance allowed a stipulated time period after such registration during which the city's population could buy the textiles for household and personal use at the amount paid for them by the merchants.[35] The entrepreneurs who brought suit against the partners cited the ordinance violation and charged them with an attempt to defraud the city's retailers, arguing that Altamirano was attempting to guarantee control for the Marquesado of both the wholesale and retail sale of its tribute textiles. The angry tradesmen may well have been right, in that Llerena and Paladiñas were probably partners in name only, without investment or profit rights, and the company was therefore a Marquesado enterprise. Certainly the company's wholesale-cost prices and therefore its retail-sale prices could be managed so as to undercut competitors. The cabildo reacted to the dispute by ordering the company to observe the ordinance in future transactions.[36]

During the suit over the textile company's operations and before Cortés returned from Nueva Galicia, Altamirano evidently moved the Marquesado's headquarters to Mexico City, locating its offices in one of Cortés' buildings there. In 1536, when he returned to the City, Cortés resumed governorship of the Marquesado, but he evidently did not relieve Altamirano of all the responsibilities assigned to him two years earlier. In fact, Altamirano seems to have been cogovernor of the Marquesado for the next three years. The only important change in the administrative organization or management of the Marquesado during those three years was the appointment of Francisco de Santa Cruz to the mayordomoship of the recently completed Tlaltenango sugar mill.[37] On November 7, 1539, as he prepared to depart for Spain, Cortés again entrusted Altamirano with the governorship of his estate and charged him with the additional responsibility of supervising, as teniente to the Captain-General of New Spain (Cortés' one remaining official title), the exploratory activity still in process in the Mar del Sur.[38] Thereafter for about a decade Altamirano administered the affairs of the Marquesado as its governor and justicia mayor, doing so for a time after Cortés' death in 1547 in the employ of the conqueror's son and principal heir, Don Martín.

The first-level administrators employed by Licenciado Altamirano in the Marquesado organization (see Table 12) for the years 1539–47 included Andrés Díaz and Diego de Guinea, chief tribute collectors charged with particular responsibility for the Morelos and Oaxaca areas respectively; Álvaro Ruiz, who seems to have served as principal attorney or procurador for the estate; and Juan Altamirano (another of Cortés' relatives, not to be confused with the licenciado-governor, to whom he was indirectly, if at all, related), who acted as contador.[39] Among those assisting these administrators were Pedro de Alcalá, Diego Muñoz, and Rodrigo de Baeza, payment officers and registrars of gold and silver shipments, the last also a notary; Alvaro Hernández de Madrid and Alonso de Villaseca, buyers and sales agents, the first also employed in tribute collection; Diego de Coria, a tribute collector; and Juan San Lázaro, an Indian principal of Coyoacan, Alonso Lucero, and Domingo Martín, *tasadores* (assessors, in this case of tribute payments) and investigators employed in the several tribute and labor-services disputes and reassessments of the 1540s. Among the local or second-level officials for the Marquesado in these years were Francisco Sánchez de Toledo, who served as mayordomo of the Morelos encomiendas and perhaps of the subordinate headquarters (but still principal household-residence) in Cuernavaca; Francisco de Santa Cruz, mayordomo of the Tlaltenango sugar mill; Juan de Carasa, alcalde mayor for the Morelos area; Martín Sánchez, calpixque in Oaxtepec; and Bernaldino del Castillo, now a resident and sugar producer in the Cuernavaca area who served as a sometime lieutenant to Sánchez de Toledo, Carasa, and Santa Cruz.[40]

These administrators were occupied with numerous management and other problems during the years 1539–47. In all they were in frequent correspondence with the absent Cortés, from whom they sought approval for their principal decisions, although the approval requested was generally after the fact, as Altamirano, usually in consultation with his first-level administrators and at times with the Marquesa Doña Juana, made and effected policy. Before he reassumed the governorship of the Marquesado in 1539, Altamirano entered into negotiations arranged and presided over by Viceroy Mendoza to settle the longtime Serrano-Cortés dispute over the Atlacomulco sugar mill. In March of that year he met with Juan de Burgos, onetime encomendero of Oaxtepec and now agent for Antonio Serrano de Cardona, and the viceroy. The negotiations produced Altamirano's pledge that the mill's operations would not henceforth be hampered by interference from the employees and officials of the Marquesado, in return for which Serrano agreed to grant the Marqués a one-seventh interest in the mill and its supporting lands.[41]

Immediately after Cortés reappointed him to the governorship of the estate, in December 1539, Altamirano concluded an agreement with one of New Spain's merchants, García de Morón, whereby the sale of the Marquesado's tribute textiles and the sugar produced by its Tlaltenango and Tuxtla (Veracruz area) mills were to be handled by Morón for a three-year period beginning January 1, 1540.[42] Morón was a major handler of New Spain's textile, sugar, and other products. Among his suppliers in addition to the Marquesado were the two other Morelos entrepreneurs, Bernaldino del Castillo and Antonio Serrano de Cardona, and the Mexico City merchant and sometime agent for the Marquesado, Álvaro Hernández de Madrid. Morón was also a handler of Negro slaves, some of which he provided his suppliers in exchange for shipments of sugar and cottons. The Marquesado acquired some of these slaves, most of whom were doubtless assigned to the Tlaltenango and Tuxtla mills.[43] The abandonment of the Llerena, Paladiñas, and Cortés partnership company in favor of the Morón arrangement represented, in part, a move for the Marquesado from wholesale and retail operations in New Spain to wholesale participation in export trade. The new arrangement was also an attempt to provide more adequately for the sale of the ever larger amounts of sugar the estate was producing and to facilitate the procurement of Negro slaves as a labor replacement for the declining numbers of Indian slaves and encomienda workers.

In the spring of 1542, before the Morón agreement expired, Cortés entered into a contract, drawn in Valladolid, Spain, which obligated his administrators to deliver all the sugar produced by the Marquesado to the agents of Leonardo Lomelín, a Genoese slave trader whose headquarters was located in Sevilla. This new agreement involved a barter of sugar for Negro slaves. Subsequently, in the fall of 1543, Altamirano and the mayordomos of the Tuxtla and Tlaltenango mills began making the specified deliveries of sugar to Lomelín's warehouses in Veracruz. Apparently their early deliveries included sugar goods accumulated since early 1543 as well as more recently produced sugar. In time the shipments to Lomelín's agents also included sugar purchased by the Marquesado

from Bernaldino del Castillo, from Serrano's Atlacomulco mill (exclusive
of Cortés' one-seventh share of its production, which had been a part of
the shipments from the beginning), and probably from others among
New Spain's producers. Deliveries to Lomelín were continued until 1548,
at which time Altamirano and the Marquesado's legal staff brought suit
against the Genoese trader and his partners and agents in the colony,
charging that they had failed to fulfill properly their part of the
contract.[44]

Even before the Cortés-Morón agreement was terminated, the Marquesado was phased out of the textile trade, as encomienda tributes in
cotton were replaced by money payments. In early 1540, Altamirano,
Andrés Díaz, and Francisco Sánchez de Toledo conferred and agreed to
receive money equivalents from the Indians of the Morelos towns and
settlements, who had previously supplied most (and the best quality) of
the Marquesado's textiles. Cortés concurred in the administrators' decision following correspondence from them which explained the Indians'
increasing inability or unwillingness to meet their manta assessments and
the related, rapidly inflating textile prices in the colony.[45] This change
coincided with similarly developing royal policy and received formal
crown approval in the new tasaciones of 1544, which also reduced the
amounts of the tribute payments the Morelos Indians were to make.[46]

The assignment of the new tasaciones and related developments embroiled Sánchez, Díaz, Altamirano, the Marquesado's attorneys, and the
alcalde mayor of Cuernavaca, Juan de Carasa, in serious difficulties with
the Morelos Indians over tribute payments, labor service demands, and
land ownership. In one instance the alcalde mayor, following the unsuccessful and unfortunate example of his predecessor, Zimbrón, imprisoned
some of the area's principales in an equally unsuccessful attempt to force
acceptance of Marquesado desires.[47] These difficulties, which began in
1544, were a local result of (1) the drastically debilitating plagues and
other misfortunes of the 1530s and the early 1540s, which produced a
general deterioration, in numbers and circumstance, of the colony's
Indian population, and (2) the attempted implementation of the crown's
response thereto, the New Laws of 1542. Several lawsuits, some of which
served as a sort of prelude to those initiated by the Morelos Indians
during the adjustment period immediately following Cortés' death, and
another reduction in the amounts of tribute due the Marquesado, made at
official insistence in 1546–47, were an outgrowth of the difficulties.[48]

Licenciado Altamirano and those associated with him in the administrative organization of the Marquesado during the years 1539–47 were
concerned not only with these affairs but with the purchase and sale of
livestock, the refining of minerals, the management of shops, the day-to-
day provision of food, shelter, and the other needs of an army of laborers,

both slave and free, and other activities. Most of them had been in the employ of the Marqués since the early 1520s and had assisted him in the development of his properties in New Spain for almost three decades. Many of them aided his son and heir in establishing himself as the Marqués del Valle de Oaxaca after 1547. By the early 1550s, however, the Marquesado organization had undergone major modification, and they had been replaced in it by new men who, with the young Marqués, were seeking new methods of producing revenues from the properties and enterprises of the Marquesado.[49]

The administrative organization (see Table 12) developed by Fernando Cortés to provide for management of his properties and interests in New Spain was large and complex by the time of his death. It included managers of sugar mills and trading establishments, shop foremen, overseers of farming and stock-raising enterprises, mine operators, accountants, auditors, inspectors, notaries, tribute collectors, legal and governing officials for his encomienda towns, lawyers, chaplains, and military officers. In 1547 all of these administrators were following procedures and policies formulated during the previous twenty-five years by Cortés and his estate governor, Licenciado Juan Altamirano. Beginning in 1539 Licenciado Altamirano assumed a primary role in the affairs of the estate and made most of the decisions regarding its management, consulting Cortés only when major changes were to be effected. It was Cortés, however, who developed his estate's administrative machinery, incorporating into it traditional forms of Spanish provincial government and business management and some of the tribute collection, labor usage, and governing practices employed in preconquest times by the Aztec Confederacy and local Indian rulers.

After his properties in New Spain were given formal recognition and definition by the Spanish crown and thereby became the Marquesado, Cortés attempted to make of them a feudal state within the colony of New Spain. As he saw it, the grants given him by the crown in 1529 and 1530 provided the necessary physical and legal basis for the creation of such a state, i.e., specified encomienda towns (to include their subject areas) over which he was to enjoy señorial rights (taxation, appointment, and other privileges) and a considerable measure of civil and criminal jurisdiction.[50] The conqueror apparently envisioned his state as separate and apart from, in effect cut out of, the colony of New Spain—a special entity within the developing Spanish empire. He saw it as constituting a personal *provincia* over which he, or one he appointed, would govern as both administrative (governor) and judicial (justicia mayor) head. As such, his state and its officials would enjoy equal status with the other provinces of the colonial empire—New Spain proper, Pánuco, Yucatán, and the developing Nueva Galicia—and would not, therefore, be subject to the administrative or judicial authority and supervision of any local colonial governing agencies but would answer only to the Council of the Indies and, of course, the crown.[51] Like the colony's other provinces, his would be organized into major and minor subdivisions or administrative and judicial units: alcaldías, corregimientos, villas, and pueblos. The appropriate officers for the subordinate jurisdictions of his state would exercise the same functions as their counterparts elsewhere but would receive their appointments not from the crown but from him and would serve not at the crown's pleasure but at his, for he was not only the provincia's governor but also its señor.[52]

Even before he left Spain in 1530, Cortés sought to begin establishing the Marquesado as the special entity he envisioned. There is evidence of his attempts, for instance, in the petition which he forwarded to the Pope requesting patronage privileges within the territories of the Marquesado not unlike those his king enjoyed in other parts of the Spanish empire.[53] Considering the rewarding quality of the services he had rendered the crown, the traditional means of rewarding such service (employed at least in some degree in the treatment of contemporaries only a few years earlier), and the general nature and, to a very considerable extent, even the wording of his grants of 1529–30, Cortés' ambitions for the Marquesado were not entirely without validity. The crown, however, obviously did not find his visions consistent with its immediate intent or its long-range interests. In this case, as some men previously rewarded for exploits in the Indies had discovered and as still others would discover in their cases, the crown regretted and went on to deny, in part or in full, sooner or later, that which it had granted, particularly in the areas of territorial privilege and political power. The conqueror might well have anticipated as much, as he had earlier experienced and was, for that matter, then being denied privilege and power he had previously enjoyed.

The crown very quickly made it clear that Cortés' privileges and powers as Marqués del Valle de Oaxaca and holder of the Marquesado were not to be what he envisioned. The extensive patronage rights he had successfully obtained from the papacy were effectively denied him, and in matters germane to the Marquesado he was immediately subjected to the authority of New Spain's governing agencies, initially the Second Audiencia.[54] Within a short time he also lost his powers of civil and criminal jurisdiction over several of the towns included in his Marquesado grant, retaining in those cases only his encomendero privileges.[55] The personal provincia, the state within a state, which he envisioned for the Marquesado, was never realized, but he was able to make at least one part of it, and perhaps only one, something resembling a feudal estate over which he exercised a considerable measure of the extensive political and judicial power he had sought for the whole. That one part comprised his holdings in Morelos.

Revenues

Fernando Cortés' properties in Morelos produced revenues which, for the most part, can only be estimated, as presently available documentation treating income produced and expenses incurred is scant indeed. Particularly scarce are cost records. Existing information does suggest that gross encomienda and agricultural enterprise revenues from the area increased steadily during the years 1522–47. From the beginning, the greatest portion of these revenues was derived from the sale of goods received as tribute from the towns of Cuernavaca, Oaxtepec, Yautepec, Tepoztlan, and Acapistla, and their sujetos. Second in importance after 1531 were the profits secured from the sale of sugar. Supplementing these two primary income-producers were grain, livestock, and foodstuff sales.

For the years 1522–25 the gross tribute revenues provided Cortés by his Morelos towns evidently amounted annually to about 7,000 pesos de oro de minas.[56] The gross annual income derived from his Morelos agricultural enterprises during the same period may be reasonably estimated at about 350 pesos de oro de minas. His properties in Morelos yielded, therefore, a gross yearly income of about 7,350 pesos de oro de minas (see Table 13). During the years 1526–29 this income was reduced (see Table 13), and for about one of the seven years in this early period and for the two immediately following, 1529–31, Cortés did not receive any revenues from his Morelos interests.[57] For five years after he resumed control of them, 1531–36, they netted him an average gross annual income of 10,752 1/10 pesos de oro de minas. Of that amount 6,642 pesos were profits from the sale of tribute textiles; 3,106 were secured from other tribute and labor dues; and 1,004 1/10 pesos were accumulated in the sale of agricultural goods produced on his lands (see Table 13).[58]

Beginning in 1536 and continuing through most of 1544, annual gross revenues from the Marquesado in Morelos probably averaged about 22,499 1/8 pesos de oro de minas including 18,433 1/4 pesos, tribute income; 2,769 3/8, sugar income; and 1,296 1/2, income from agricultural enterprises other than sugar production (see Table 13).[59] During the last three years of his life, the Marqués' gross annual income from his Morelos estate was 26,358 pesos de oro de minas, a sum derived from tribute payments of 18,139 pesos, sugar sales of 5,396 pesos, and agricultural, other than sugar, revenues of 2,823 pesos (see Table 13).[60]

The increased gross revenues produced by Cortés' Morelos properties during the years 1531–36, as compared with earlier years, reflect the concentrated attention given these properties, especially the area's encomiendas, as they became a part of the new Marquesado as it was defined and developed. Indians and others complained that then and later the Marqués and his agents began collecting more and better quality (in the case of cotton mantas) tribute, in some instances taking the tributes which had been paid to members of the local Indian nobility such as Don Hernando of Cuernavaca and apparently others. In addition they began acquiring and utilizing more lands, also evidently taken in most instances from the Indian nobility, with Don Hernando again a case in point.[61] Increasing market demand for cotton and other goods in New Spain, with accompanying inflated prices and profits, also contributed to the growth of the conqueror's Morelos revenues.

The inflationary trend in New Spain's overall economic development that was observable in the years 1531–36 continued more or less through the years 1536–47 and, in combination with sharply decreasing cotton textile production on the part of those Indians who had traditionally provided it, pushed textile prices and profits higher and higher. That circumstance, together with the completion of the Tlaltenango sugar mill, the acquisition of an ownership share in the Atlacomulco mill, and particularly the maturation of the livestock and other agrarian enterprises begun earlier, netted the Marquesado in Morelos ever greater gross revenues.[62] Another factor of contributory significance was the Marquesado's full-fledged entry into the colony's export trade.

Of particular interest in the composition of the revenues secured by the Marqués from his Morelos holdings in the years 1522–47 were those provided by the tributes from his encomiendas. In 1522–23 tribute income comprised over 95 percent of estimated gross revenues; in 1531–32, over 91 percent; in 1537–38, over 69.9 percent; and in 1547, over 50.5 percent.[63] The peso value of these tribute revenues increased by some 401 percent between 1522 and 1544, and then began declining rapidly. The agrarian goods which supplemented tribute income in the Marqués' gross revenues from his Morelos properties rose from about 4.8 percent of the total during the early years to about 49.4 percent in 1547. Of these products, those other than sugar rose from about 4.8 percent to just over 16.9 percent with an increase in peso value of an astonishing 806 percent, while sugar, added in the years 1537–38, netted about 21.4 percent of gross revenues in 1531 and over 32.4 percent in 1547, with an increase in peso value of more than 170 percent between 1537 and 1547.

A large share of the gross revenues produced by Cortés' Morelos properties during the early years of his utilization of them probably constituted net income, as that utilization seems to have entailed little expense. His labor costs, for instance, were few, if any, as he depended heavily, if not exclusively, upon encomienda workers to whom wages were not paid. His net profits, therefore, may well have comprised as much as 80 percent and perhaps more of his gross revenues. Subsequently in the years 1531–36 he invested heavily in the area in the construction of a number of works and the development of his silk, sugar, livestock, orchard, and other enterprises. His expenses also rose rapidly as, for instance, he began paying wages to his encomienda laborers, employing Spanish craftsmen, and using large numbers of slaves. Actual profits in this period may have been whittled down to a few pesos.[64]

In the years which followed and until 1540, Cortés' investment in the Morelos area apparently slowed somewhat, and his expenses seemingly remained constant even as his gross revenues increased significantly. After he went to Spain again in 1540, Negro slave purchases, the unsuccessful redevelopment of his silk industry, and other endeavors again produced sizeable investments and expenses in his operations in Morelos. His net income probably averaged between 6 percent and 12 percent of gross revenues in these years, with the larger figure more applicable to the years 1536–40; thereafter, the lower. By the early 1550s (for which reasonably accurate and fairly complete records are available) Marquesado profits, after investments as well as expenses, were averaging about 6 percent of gross revenues and were considered less than desirable.[65]

The estimated average annual revenues produced by Cortés' Morelos estate during the years 1522–47, excepting about three of those years— 1525–26 and 1529–31—amounted to more than 16,005.7 pesos de oro de minas of which an average of over 11.3 percent, or more than 1,808.6 pesos de oro de minas, may well have been net profit.[66] The value of this income, which was only a part (probably averaging between 50 and 53 percent especially after 1531) of that produced by the entire Marquesado, is suggested by comparing it with the annual salary paid New Spain's highest ranking official (after 1535), Viceroy Mendoza, and the 1546 gross income enjoyed by one of Spain's wealthiest and most prominent figures, Francisco de Los Cobos, secretary to the Emperor Charles V and holder of a multitude of income-producing positions, grants, privileges, pensions, properties, and tax and other monopolies.[67] Mendoza received an annual salary of 8,000 ducados (3,000 as viceroy and governor of New Spain; 3,000 as president of the Audiencia; and 2,000 as an expense account) or 6,666 2/3 pesos de oro de minas.[68] Cortés' probable net revenues from his Morelos properties, then, were equal to about 27.1 percent of the viceroy's total annual salary. Los Cobos' total gross income for 1546 amounted to 44,202 pesos de oro de minas.[69] The estimated gross revenues (31,232 pesos de oro de minas) produced by the Marquesado in Morelos that year were equal to about 70.6 percent of the secretary's total gross income. The conqueror, therefore, consistently received very handsome revenues, for the time and place, from his encomiendas, lands, and enterprises in Morelos.

7

The Morelos Marquesado in 1547

The properties that Fernando Cortés owned in the Morelos area at the time of his death in 1547 included encomiendas, slaves, and an elaborate headquarters-household establishment. The towns of Cuernavaca, Yautepec, Tepoztlan, Oaxtepec, and Acapistla, each with numerous sujeto settlements—many traditionally sujeto and others assigned by Cortés and crown officials—comprised his five encomiendas in the area. Collectively these towns probably boasted a tributary vassal population numbering about 25,400 and were inhabited by a total population of some 82,000 Indians plus other persons.[1] The internal political and judicial administration of the towns and their sujetos was the responsibility of the native nobility—the señores and principales—of each, as was the collection of the tribute and the assignment of the labor service dues owed by them to Cortés. Supervising the Indian officials in the performance of their duties were Spaniards employed by Cortés as administrative officers for the area. One, Juan de Carasa, served as alcalde mayor and was headquartered with his several deputies and assistants—an alguacil, a notary, and other lesser officers—in Cuernavaca. Another, Francisco Sánchez de Toledo, exercised the duties of mayordomo for the properties in Cuernavaca and was assisted by several tribute collectors and labor service supervisors. Ministering to the spiritual needs of the Indians in their several towns and settlements, as well as to the Spaniards who lived and worked among them, were Franciscan, Dominican, and Augustinian missionary priests. During the preceding quarter-century these friars, often using funds supplied by Cortés and always assisted physically and materially by his encomienda Indians, had established large permanent monasteries and churches in the cabecera towns of Cuernavaca, Yautepec, Oaxtepec, and Acapistla and in the larger sujeto communities of Tlaltenango and Zacualpan de Amilpas as well as in nearby Totolapan and Ocuituco, Morelos towns excluded from the Marquesado. In most of the area's other larger settlements they had established temporary churches and were at work, in 1547, on more permanent structures in several.

Marquesado landholdings in the Morelos area consisted of 1,402 fertile acres, most of which supported crops of sugarcane and wheat, orchards of mulberry and fruit trees, vineyards, and herds of livestock. Of these lands more than two-thirds were located in the town of Cuernavaca or its sujeto area, as were the additional 119 acres rented by Cortés from the Indians for the purpose of growing mulberry trees. More than half of the remainder were in or around the town of Oaxtepec. Occupying a small part of these landholdings but of great value among his properties were the buildings which housed Cortés' craft enterprises, his slaves and employees, his livestock, his tools, equipment, supplies, and sale goods, and his household and headquarters establishment. A large breeding-house for silkworms, a threshing shed, and a wheat storage barn, all adobe, were located on his lands in Yautepec, and in his nearby Tlalhuitongo orchard were two adobe houses.[2] In Tlacomulco, one of Yautepec's sujetos, his buildings included a stone threshing-shed and wheat storage barn, and on his ranch in Tlaltizapan, another of the settlements sujeto to Yautepec, were two stone houses and a large stone corral and stable. On his ranch lands in Texcalpa, one of Oaxtepec's sujetos, Cortés had a large stone house, two large adobe wheat storage barns, and a stone corral and stable, and on his acreage in Acapistla he had two adobe houses.

The remainder of Cortés' buildings, like most of his landholdings, were either in the town of Cuernavaca or in its sujeto area. In the southern part of this sujeto area, in the vicinity of the settlements of Mazatepec and Miacatlan, were two of Cortés' ranches, those of Atelinca and Atlicaca, on each of which he had built stone houses (two at Atelinca and three at Atlicaca), stone corrals, and stables. Besides the Atlacomulco sugar mill buildings, in which he had a one-seventh interest, the other buildings owned by Cortés either housed his Tlaltenango sugar mill or his household and headquarters establishment in Cuernavaca. The buildings which were used in the Tlaltenango sugar manufacturing operation included the large two-story stone *casa del purgar,* or refinery; a number of straw-roofed adobe houses where the employees and slaves who worked in the mill lived; an adobe building where woolen cloth was woven; and two rather flimsy structures of wooden poles and straw. In one of the last, woolen cloth was fulled, and in the other, iron tools, machinery, and other items were forged and repaired.

In the main room on the first floor of the Tlaltenango casa del purgar were the imported mill machinery; numerous copper caldrons, buckets, sieves, pumps, boilers, kettles, and other items; and iron wedges, hoops, hammers, knives, pickaxes, cart and mill axles, bolts, bearings for the mill machinery, and fetters and shackles used in disciplining new or uncooperative slaves. In a smaller room on the first floor were more iron and copper tools, including axes, saws, chisels, sickles, a carpenter's plane, and hoes; a large wooden chest with a lock and key, which contained the vestments and utensils necessary for celebration of mass, including a silver chalice, lead vials, a damask chasuble, several altar cloths of coarse material, a fine altar frontal piece of white damask and blue velvet, several linen cloths, a used missal, and a maniple, stole, and amice, the first of white linen and the last two of blue velvet and flesh-colored calico; and a sizeable quantity of sugar in various stages of manufacture.

Upstairs in the casa del purgar were two rooms, the contents of which included more iron and copper tools and equipment; several arrobas of citron, orange, and lemon juice in large earthen jars; several arrobas of citron preserves also in large earthen containers; a huge vat or tank containing forty arrobas of honey; eight arrobas of iron bars; several plowshares, a metal mathematical compass; several adzes and augers; and a scale, knives, and machetes used for butchering. Just outside the casa were twenty-two long wooden carts with iron axles used for the hauling of sugar cane. In the cloth-weaving and fulling buildings were looms; spinning wheels and spindles; a number of arrobas of raw and carded wool and several arrobas of balls of woolen thread; and about one hundred large woolen mantas, designed to be worn by the Negro slaves working in the mill. In the forge building were bellows, several large and small iron anvils, iron hammers, chisels, punches, files, tongs, spikes, and nails.

On the five acres of land which he evidently took from the holdings of the señor of Cuernavaca, Cortés built the two-story stone fortresslike house which his household, including his wife, Doña Juana de Zúñiga, occupied in 1547. Surrounding this palatial residence were several other buildings used as repair shops, storage sheds, and quarters by the slaves and employees who lived and worked in the main house; a grist mill; and an orchard and garden. The main house evidently consisted of a grand sala of immense size, a kitchen and dining room, a chapel, and a number of other rooms, most of which were used as bedrooms. It had two Arabic-style porches, one on the first floor and one immediately above on the second floor, and a courtyard patio immediately in front of the lower porch. Throughout the house, but particularly in the grand sala, hung rich tapestries, twenty-one in number, which varied in size and quality. The largest and most elaborate was thirteen feet long and twenty-two feet wide and was described as decorated with several figures, including one in its center of a male nude in a blue cape and three others, representing three winds, at his feet. The smallest and least elaborate was one eight and one-quarter feet square, which had as its center decoration two parrots in a cage. The floors of the grand sala and perhaps those of some of the bedrooms were covered with finely woven rugs, the largest of which was twenty feet long and five and one-half feet wide. This rug was violet, decorated with white stars and bordered by lions and monsters which were yellow, green, and black. The smallest of the fourteen rugs was eight and one-fourth feet long, seven and one-half feet wide, decorated with orange and blue circles on a background of the same colors and bordered by bands of green, yellow, and red.

The walls of the many bedrooms of the palace and perhaps those of the grand sala were also hung with Moorish leather tapestries, most of which were embossed with silver or gold. There were fifteen of these leather wall-hangings, varying in size from one which was sixteen and one-half feet long and a little over twelve and one-quarter feet wide to two which were eleven and four-fifths feet wide and eleven feet long. At the doors of these bedrooms were eight heavy curtains which ranged from eight and one-quarter feet long and six and five-sixths feet wide to six and one-sixth feet square in size. These curtains were decorated with various designs usually worked in dyed silk, one of which depicted two horses, one bay and the other white. In one bedroom, perhaps the one used by Cortés when he was in Cuernavaca, were an encased shield; an elaborate set of horse trappings, some items of flesh-colored leather decorated with pearls, silk tassels, and velvet linings, and others of gilded iron and embossed leather; a knapsack of velvet; a single-edged sword and leather scabbard; a single-edged cutlass with an enameled blue and green handle and a belt of red and blue silk garnished with gold thread; a bed with blue taffeta and flesh-colored silk furnishings; and a table covered with a cloth of scarlet and silver lace.

The other bedrooms of the house were furnished with four canopied beds, richly decorated sheets and spreads, three trunks, two high-backed chairs with velvet backs and seat cushions, and several tables covered with velvet and satin embroidered cloths. Typical of the canopies was one described as made of silver lace and blue silk bordered with brocade, scarlet satin, and a fringe of silver thread, and lined with finely glazed black and tawny buckram. On the beds were coverlets of various kinds, one of which was grey damask and scarlet velvet. One of the trunks in these rooms was just over four feet square and was described as arched and made in Flanders.

The chapel, which was apparently located on the first floor of the house, contained a number of items required for the celebration of mass. Among these were several wine vessels, a bell, a wafer box, a chalice, and a small plate, all of solid silver, the wafer box weighing enough to be worth 156 pesos de oro de minas. Also stored in the chapel were eight sets of priestly vestments, all of expensive materials and ornamented with gold and silver thread; two altar frontal pieces, one of scarlet velvet and the other of white damask and blue velvet; a missal adorned with blue velvet; and seven psalm and music books with covers of vellum and embossed, gilded leather.

The dining room of the house was evidently furnished with a large dining table on which utensils of solid silver were used, including plates, cups and goblets, water pitchers, serving dishes, spoons, and four candle-holders, and around the table were a number of high-backed chairs.[3] On the wall, perhaps along with some tapestries like those hung elsewhere in the palace, was a silver, partially gilded crucifix, reportedly made by the Indians of the Cuernavaca area. The cooking utensils required by the household were stored in a sort of annex to the main building, perhaps just off the dining room. Among these utensils were iron frying-pans, cups, pots, a grater, and grates; copper pans, caldrons, and a sifter; a mortar (for pulverizing foods) and a large basin made of brass; and several reed baskets.

Outside the palace in the garden and orchard which surrounded it were several buildings, one of which was used as an armory and for the storage of tools and other equipment; another, as a blacksmith shop. Spanish lances, shields, harquebuses, crossbows, swords, and body armor as well as Mexican cotton-quilted armor and shields were stored in the armory-warehouse. With these armaments were trunks of iron arrowheads and balls of lead, sacks of gunpowder (the total weight of which was 400 pounds), cannon barrels and balls, sail canvas, and drums. Elsewhere in this building were tools much like those used in the Tlaltenango sugar mill as well as some saddles and a number of brass and iron wheel hoops. The blacksmith shop was equipped with about the same kinds of tools as were in use in the Tlaltenango repair shop, although hanging on its walls were some particular items such as branding irons (seven of them) and iron hooks used in the treatment of mange. Beyond the armory-ware-house and blacksmith shop, evidently bordering on one edge of the garden-orchard, was a large stone stable and corral which housed the horses and mules used by members of the household, and some saddles, bridles, and other riding gear. Elsewhere in the garden-orchard were houses used by the slaves and employees of the palace, a gristmill, and perhaps the buildings, including a rundown jail, used by the officials of the Marquesado who were stationed in Cuernavaca.

Macehuales from the Morelos encomiendas worked in the various enter-prises which were housed in all of these buildings and on the lands which supported them. They also delivered wood, hay, and perhaps some quan-tities of foodstuffs to the palace in Cuernavaca and to some of the houses used by Cortés' tribute collectors in the other towns of the area. Their coworkers in some places, particularly at the Tlaltenango sugar mill and in the Cuernavaca palace, were slaves owned by Cortés and a few salaried Spaniards. The slaves, numbering 294, of which 186 were Indians, 103 Negroes, 4 mulattoes, and 1 Morisco, also constituted a valuable part of Cortés' Morelos properties. Overseeing all of these laborers and responsible for the day-to-day management of the Morelos Marquesado were Spaniards like Carasa and Sánchez de Toledo as well as others like Francisco de Santa Cruz, mayordomo of the Tlaltenango mill, who were concerned with enterprises not directly a part of the administration of the area's encomienda towns.

Each year these properties supported the peoples who lived and worked upon them, providing the necessities of life, food, drink, and clothing that they required and producing a sizeable amount of revenue for Cortés. For 1547 the gross total of that revenue amounted to some 16,610 pesos de oro de minas of which about 6 percent was net profit. As Licenciado Juan Altamirano, governor of the Marquesado, Andrés Díaz, chief collector of tribute revenue for the Morelos area, and Juan Altamirano, contador for the Marquesado—the men responsible for receiving that revenue, accounting for it in Cortés' interest, and disbursing some of it to cover the expenses of the Marquesado—were completing their work for 1547, they found they were no longer employed by the conqueror but by his son, the second Marqués del Valle de Oaxaca.

On December 2, 1547, in the village of Castilleja de la Cuesta, not far from Seville, Fernando Cortés died. Two months earlier (October 1), realizing that he was near death, the older soldier drew up his last will and testament, which he signed on October 11.[4] That document named his fifteen-year-old son, Don Martín, heir to the title Marqués del Valle de Oaxaca and to the properties in New Spain known as the Marquesado; provided ample dowries for his daughters, legitimate and illegitimate; and adequate income for his illegitimate sons, Don Luis and Don Martín. In addition, endowments were provided for several religious institutions he had founded in New Spain and for others which the young Marqués and his guardians were ordered to construct. Most of the funds set aside for these purposes were to be drawn from the revenues produced by the Marquesado. The will named two sets of curators and administrators for the Marquesado and called upon the individuals named to serve as Don Martín's guardians until he reached his majority. That majority was set at age twenty-five, but the will stipulated that the young Marqués was to begin receiving full benefit of the Marquesado's revenues at age twenty. In the first group named were Don Juan Alonso de Guzmán, Duque de Medina Sidonia; Don Pedro Álvarez Osorio, Marqués de Astorga; and Don Pedro de Arellano, Conde de Aguilar, all ranking members of the Spanish nobility and resident in Spain. The second group, all of whom resided in New Spain, included Doña Juana, the conqueror's wife; Fray Juan de Zumárraga, longtime Bishop and recently appointed Archbishop of Mexico; Fray Domingo de Betanzos, senior ranking member of the Dominican missionary organization in the colony; and Licenciado Juan Altamirano, governor of the Marquesado.[5]

Cortés included three provisions in his will in order, as he expressed it, to clear his conscience and that of his young heir with regard to the acquisition and utilization of the properties of the Marquesado. He charged Don Martín and his guardians with the execution of these provisions, which provided for investigation into the methods employed in acquiring the landholdings, Indian slaves, and encomiendas of the Marquesado and in the collection of dues from the Indians of the encomiendas. If the investigation revealed that illegal or unfair methods had been used in the acquisition of these properties or in the collection of tribute and labor dues, those who had been taken advantage of were to be compensated for their losses: land claimants were to be paid the value of the lands taken from them plus an amount equal to the revenues produced by those lands during the period when they were illegally a part of the Marquesado; Indians illegally enslaved were to be freed and paid an amount equal to the earnings they might have received during the years of their enslavement; those who had justifiable claims to the Marquesado's encomiendas were to be paid an amount equal to the value of the dues they might have received during the period when the encomiendas were illegally held by the conqueror; and an amount equal to the value of any excessive encomienda dues collected from the Marquesado's Indians was to be paid to them.[6] Once they were publicly known, these provisions prompted many who felt they had complaints of the sort enumerated—particularly the Indians of the Marquesado's encomienda towns including those of the Morelos area—to initiate official demands upon and lawsuits against the second Marqués.

Even as Cortés was making his will, the Marquesado's attorneys in New Spain were embroiled in two legal disputes over the management of his Morelos properties. One of these, begun in February 1547, was initiated by the Indians of the town of Cuernavaca, who charged that Cortés' alcalde mayor for the Morelos area, Juan de Carasa, was collecting encomienda dues in excess of the tasaciones of 1544 and was mistreating them in other ways.[7] Isabel de Ojeda and Antonio de la Cadena, owners with Cortés of the Atlacomulco sugar mill, instigated the other lawsuits with renewed accusations that Cortés' agents were interfering in the operations of the mill.[8] The Ojeda-Cadena-Cortés dispute was partially settled in 1553 as de la Cadena sold his three-sevenths interest in the Atlacomulco properties to the new Marqués, but litigation with Isabel de Ojeda over the ownership and management of the mill continued for more than a decade.[9]

The suit involving Carasa and one initiated three years earlier, in 1544, by the fiscal of the Audiencia of Mexico, which charged Cortés with mistreatment of the Indians of the Morelos area, were merged with the numerous other complaints—many encouraged by the provisions of the conqueror's will—which the Indians of the Marquesado began presenting the Audiencia in 1548.[10] Most of these complaints—which took the form, in time, of lawsuits—were not entirely satisfied until the early 1560s, and some were carried over into the 1570s.

Among the complaints made and the lawsuits which resulted were a number which originated with the Indians of the Morelos area. By December 1, 1549, the crown and council in Spain had received, evidently via the Audiencia of Mexico, reports of the following grievances suffered by these Indians: (1) the Indians of Oaxtepec were being forced to pay tribute in excess of their capabilities, they were being required to tend an estancia of horses belonging to the Marqués without pay and the horses were harming their fields by grazing in them, and four estancias belonging to the señor of the towns had been seized by the Marqués, on the lands of one of which a gristmill had been constructed; (2) the Indians of Cuernavaca were being required to perform personal services for the members of the Marqués' household and his Tlaltenango mill workers, and some of the lands of the señor of that town had been seized by the Marqués; (3) the Indians of Yautepec were forcibly prevented from appearing before the Audiencia with their complaints by Andrés Díaz and others in Cortés' employ; and (4) all of the Indians of the area were required to work as tamemes against their will, for which the payment of wages was made to the señores and principales of the area, who failed to recompense the macehual tamemes. They were also required to support one of the Marqués' establishments, located in a town two leagues from Mexico, with foodstuffs, firewood, and hay without pay and in addition to their assessed encomienda dues, and they were all physically mistreated by the Marqués' agents.[11] The response to these complaints was a crown-ordered inspection of the Marquesado by Doctor Antonio Rodríguez de Quesada in early 1550. His instructions, dated December 31, 1549, were as follows: (1) he was to determine whether the tribute and services required by the Marqués were in excess of the tasaciones set by Licenciado Sandoval for the Marquesado encomiendas in 1544, and if they were he was to see that the Indians from whom they were required were compensated by the Marqués; (2) he was to adjust the tasaciones of 1544, if necessary, to assure that the tribute and services assessed the Indians were not in excess of what they were able to pay; and (3) he was to see that agents, if any, of the Marqués who had mistreated the Indians were punished and that the Indians so abused were properly compensated.[12]

The results of the inspection prompted Quesada to set new, greatly lowered tasaciones for the Morelos encomienda towns (based essentially on a new census made of those towns) and to order that the Marquesado surrender several pieces of land to the Indians of the area. His stipulations were promptly appealed by the attorneys for the Marquesado, and, at the same time, the Indians requested through lawsuits four in the case of the Indians of Cuernavaca; two involving tribute, and two, land—that the stipulations be upheld by the crown.[13] This litigation was not concluded for more than ten years and, like that pursued by Licenciado Juan Altamirano which sought fulfillment of the provisions of the conquerer's will, encumbered the revenues of the Marquesado for a number of years.

In 1549, Don Martín, acting with the Conde de Aguilar, one of his guardians, granted Licenciado Altamirano's request for release from the duties and responsibilities of the governorship of the Marquesado. Altamirano was replaced first by Pedro de Ahumada Sámano and then in 1551 by Don Tristán de Arellano. As Arellano assumed the governorship of the estate, Altamirano introduced a lawsuit against the young Marqués, the Conde de Aguilar, Ahumada, and Arellano charging them with neglect of the financial obligations assigned to them by the conqueror in his will. Altamirano's suit carried over into the late 1560s, lasting even until after the licenciado's death and the crown's sequestration of the Marquesado properties and interests in the wake of the so-called Cortés-Avila Conspiracy.[14]

Despite these difficulties and others created by changes in the administration of the estate, throughout the late 1540s and into the 1550s the Morelos properties produced considerable revenues for the second Marqués, exceeding those produced for his father by several thousand pesos de oro de minas. For the years 1550–52, for instance, the Morelos area yielded gross revenues of between 63,866.8 and 65,224 pesos de oro de minas for an annual average of between 31,933.4 and 32,612 pesos de oro de minas of which, even though heavy expenses were incurred, between 6 and 7 percent was net profit.[15] Of the total gross revenues the second Marqués collected from his Marquesado properties and interests in this two year period, the Morelos share constituted some 53.6 percent.[16] After 1547, then, the Morelos Marquesado comprised a very valuable property, the proceeds from which continued to increase much as they had during the preceding quarter century.

8

Coda

What is now the Mexican state of Morelos comprised two rich and important provinces within the Aztec Confederacy when Spanish forces penetrated it for the first time in March 1521. For 8,000 years or longer, Tlahuica and Xochimilca peoples and their predecessors had dominated its numerous settlements and fertile, well-watered, volcanic soils in valleys surrounded by mountains, producing large quantities of valuable agricultural products and other goods. The laborers among them—the commoners or macehuales, the serflike, soil-bound mayeques, and the slaves— used valleys in the high-altitude north, whose climate ranged from temperate to semitropical and semi-arid, and in the less elevated, tropically hot and humid south to grow maize, beans, chile, tomatoes, peppers, squashes, some fruits, chia, huautli (amaranth), cotton and, perhaps cacao.

On their valley lands, these working folk also raised turkeys for meat, eggs, and feathers and dug clay for pottery-making. In the streams, lakes, and rivers, some of which supported their fields with irrigation waters, they collected fish and frogs. From the surrounding mountains and plateaus, they secured various fruits including the hog plum and aguacate; a variety of herbs; maguey for making pulque and fiber ropes, bark from the amaquavitl tree for making paper; animals and birds such as quail and rabbits for meat, fur, and feathers; and construction stone and lime. Their efforts in the lands of Morelos yielded quantities of these items sufficient to their needs and to the tribute demands of their nobility and their Aztecan overlords.

Most of the fields worked by the macehuales were theirs by individual use-right as community members. They hunted, gathered, and quarried together in upland areas, many of which were likewise the communal properties of their settlements. These commoners also performed required labor services on "office" and institutional lands set aside for the support of the nobility and religious establishments of their towns as well as for locally resident Confederacy bureaucrats. At times they were also employed on lands worked primarily by the mayeques and slaves, the private holdings of some local and Confederacy nobles, including the ruler of the Aztecs, Moctezuma II.

The Spanish returned to Morelos a second and decisive time in April 1521. Led this time by their determined commander, Fernando Cortés, the invaders effected military conquest of an important part of the area. The following year, more of the Morelos settlements were brought under Spanish domination in "mop-up" and expansion operations after the defeat of Tenochtitlan. Morelos was economically subjugated by the conqueror in that year, 1522, as its several towns were divided into encomienda districts. All its communities except northeastern Tetela del Volcán, Hueyapan, and their sujetos were initially included in five Cortesian-defined encomiendas. They remained, with one exception made in the early 1530s, as defined by the conqueror throughout the sixteenth century. The exception was the subtraction by New Spain's Second Audiencia of the northern town of Totolapan and its sujetos from the encomienda of Acapistla.

Cortés reserved the five newly created Morelos encomiendas for one of the most worthy conquistadores—himself—and held them without interruption from 1522 through early 1525. Thereafter until 1531 (following the crown's provision of his Marquesado grant and its formal recognition by New Spain's governing officials) other Spaniards enjoyed intervals of service and tribute provided by the peoples of Morelos. Among these were two, Antonio Serrano de Cardona and Diego de Ordaz, who, like Cortés, secured and made use of lands in the area. Few other Spaniards except the missionary clergy appear to have acquired land in Morelos between 1522 and 1547. Franciscans, Dominicans, and Augustinians built mission-churches and conventos on plots apparently limited to the requirements of that and related construction and to the minimal maintenance of resident friars. It is clear that in the mid-1530s Cortés provided Bernaldino del Castillo, his follower-in-arms and criado, with some of his acreage in exchange for properties near Coyoacan, but he and Serrano were the principal, and probably the only, other Spanish land developers in the area after 1529.

The lands of Morelos produced profitable quantities of a variety of goods for these Spaniards in the years 1522–47. Most important among these goods were sugarcane, livestock (cattle, horses, hogs, sheep, and oxen), wheat, citrus, and other European, as opposed to native American, fruits, including dates, figs and grapes, mulberry leaves, and fodder. These goods were utilized in three principal new enterprises developed in the area by the Spanish: the very successful sugar and livestock and the unsuccessful silk industries.

In the development of Morelos as a conquered province, the Spanish altered, through the introduction of new items and industries, but also encouraged and even demanded, through tribute and market requirements, the traditional uses of its lands. Throughout the years 1522–47, the area's native peoples produced most of the kinds of goods—although in several instances in increasingly smaller amounts—that they had produced before the Spanish arrived. They added, at the same time, such items as sugarcane, wheat, mulberry trees, European fruits, and fodder-grasses. They also added hogs, an occasional cow or sheep, and chickens to the turkeys they had long raised. Together with their Spanish conquerors, the Indians made new demands, along with the older ones, on the waters and highlands of Morelos in the years 1522–47. They did so with increased irrigation, establishment of water-powered mills, procurement of large amounts of fuel, firewood, and especially charcoal for the sugar and other enterprises, and considerably increased use of lumber, stone, and lime in construction work.

As they did not discontinue but rather altered land use in goods production, so the Spanish in their first quarter-century of occupation did not discontinue but altered landholding practices in Morelos. In 1547 most of the land in Morelos was held by Indian communities, as it had been when the Spanish arrived, but then, as before, some of it was held by individual Indians. The amount of land held by individual Indians probably continued to increase in these years as it had before the Spanish arrived; but, as Charles Gibson has so admirably demonstrated was true for most of the Aztecan area, many "office" and institutional lands of the preconquest period disappeared.[1] The Spanish created "institutional"—church, crown, and municipality—lands in Morelos as they did elsewhere, and they joined the Indian nobility as landowners.

The holdings of the Spanish landowners in Morelos in 1547 totaled some 2,085.4 acres; their rented properties, perhaps another 434 acres. The largest blocks of these holdings, about 1,000 of Cortés' acres and all those of Serrano-Ojeda, were concentrated in and around the town of Cuernavaca; the remainder were scattered, generally small plots, located in northern and central Morelos. None seem to have been located in the southern, hot, humid Cuautla Valley, and few in the southernmost reaches of the Cuernavaca Valley, both areas evidently also largely unoccupied by Indians.

These three Spaniards indirectly utilized other acreage in Morelos as they encouraged Indians to raise sugarcane, in particular, but also other items which they purchased for use in their enterprises. Their actual holdings were about as described, however. The present state of Morelos comprises more than a million and a quarter acres of which just over half is now crop-pasture land.[2] Even allowing for increases in crop-pasture acreage brought about as new technologies have been applied to land-use in the region, it is clear that the original Spanish occupiers of Morelos took but a small fraction of its lands as their own. Certainly, no

great haciendas were created in Morelos during the quarter-century
following the conquest.

The productive estate developed by Fernando Cortés on his lands in
the Morelos area during the years 1522–47 was comprised of various enterprises which in their several stages of development were representative
not only of the other properties and interests of the conqueror in New
Spain, collectively known as the Marquesado, but also of the general
economic development of the colony during the first quarter-century after
the conquest of the Aztec Confederacy. Throughout these years Cortés
was an initiator of economic endeavors which were copied by his contemporaries, and at the same time he often subscribed to ideas developed
by others engaged in manufacturing, agricultural, and other business
pursuits in New Spain.

For almost a decade after 1522 the conqueror was involved in legal
disputes with other Spanish colonists and royal officials over the control
of the encomienda towns of the Morelos area which he attempted to make
his personal property and the foundation of his estate there. During that
ten-year period his fluctuating income from the area was derived for the
most part from the encomienda dues paid to him by the five cabecera
towns of Cuernavaca, Yautepec, Tepoztlan, Oaxtepec, and Acapistla,
and their sujetos. He did not develop many other enterprises in the area,
although he did acquire some lands there on which he planted and
harvested certain crops and raised livestock. In 1531, after he received his
Marquesado grant from the crown and again gained effective control over
the five Morelos encomienda towns, he began to diversify and to expand
the properties of his Morelos Marquesado.

Beginning in 1531 and continuing until he left for Spain in early 1540,
Cortés secured numerous tracts of land in the Morelos area, where he
built a palatial house, the Tlaltenango sugar mill, several gristmills,
ranch houses, corrals, and barns, and on which he planted sugarcane and
wheat, fruit, and vegetables. He also took the first steps toward introducing silk production in the area. After he departed for Spain, the
governor of the Marquesado, Licenciado Juan Altamirano, sought to
expand the silk industry, but this phase of the economic development of
the Morelos Marquesado failed to achieve lasting success. During the
1520s and 1530s the conqueror relied heavily on his Cuernavaca encomienda towns for the labor which was necessary in the development of
his estate properties. The Indian laborers provided by these towns were,
as a rule, paid wages after 1534–35, and together with his Indian slaves
they constituted the greater part of his labor force. After 1540 he supplemented these Indian workers with large numbers of Negro slaves.

From 1522 onward Cortés enjoyed an annual income from his Morelos

Marquesado which increased steadily until just before his death in 1547, when it tapered off sharply. For more than a decade (1522–33) that income was derived almost entirely from the sale of tribute goods paid to him by his Morelos encomiendas; thereafter the sale of sugar, livestock, and grains produced an increasingly significant part of it. This income supported, in part, his explorations during the 1520s and 1530s, the development of his other properties in New Spain, the maintenance of his households in Mexico City and Cuernavaca, his last trip to Spain, and his residence there during the 1540s.

Although Cortés' Morelos properties did not include any mines, they were otherwise quite similar in composition, organization, and productivity to the remainder of the Marquesado and to estates of other Spanish colonists in New Spain. The Marquesado was unique, however, in that it was a great estate developed with crown acquiescence by a conqueror-explorer in the area that he had made a part of the Spanish Empire and that he and his heirs were to hold during the entire colonial period. Unlike many, if not most, of his great contemporaries of the late fifteenth and early sixteenth centuries, Cortés, although not given the political recognition he desired, did secure very substantial rewards for his efforts in behalf of the Spanish crown. He died in 1547, a wealthy and respected figure, leaving his son and heir the noble title of Marqués del Valle de Oaxaca and a great estate, the Marquesado, the richest and most important part of which comprised properties and interests in Morelos.

Appendix 1

The Cuernavaca Area in 1519:
Provinces, Towns, and Tribute

The content of this appendix is taken from the published edition of the *Códice Mendocino* edited by Francisco del Paso y Troncoso, the *Matrícula de Tributos* edited by Antonio Peñafiel and published as *Monumentos del arte mexicana antigua,* the *Información sobre los tributos que los indios pagaban a Moctezuma, Año de 1554,* published by France V. Scholes and Eleanor B. Adams as Volume Four of their *Documentos para la historia del México colonial,* and some pre-conquest tribute data gleaned from the manuscript sources used in determining the tribute paid by the Indians of the Cuernavaca area to their postconquest encomenderos (see Chapter 3). R. H. Barlow's *The Extent of the Empire of the Culhua Mexica* and *The Aboriginal Population of Central Mexico on the Eve of the Spanish Conquest* by Woodrow W. Borah and Sherburne F. Cook were also consulted.

I. Province of Quauhnahuac (Cuernavaca) [1]
   A. Towns

1. Quauhnauhuac	(Cuernavaca)
2. Teocalçinco	(Tzocalzingo, Guerrero)
3. Chimalco	(Panchimalco)
4. Huiçilapa	(Huitzilac)
5. Xochitepec	(Xochitepec)
6. Acatlycpac	(Acatlipa)
7. Miacatla	(Miacatlan)
8. Coatlan	(Coatlan del Río)
9. Xiuhtepec	(Xiutepec)
10. Xoxoutla	(Jojutla)
11. Amacoztitla	(Amacuzac)
12. Iztla	(Puente de Ixtla)
13. Ocpayuca[2]	
14. Atlicholoayan	(Atlacholoaya)
15. Molotla	(See n. 2)
16. Yztepec	(See n. 2)
17. Atlpoyecan	(Alpuyeca) [3]
18. Maçatepec	(Mazatepec)
19. Tlaquiltenanco	(Tlaquiltenango)
20. Cacatepec	(Zacatepec)

B. Tribute Paid to the Empire
  1. Paid four times each year[4]
    a) Cotton Goods
        2,000 white mantas (mantles possibly of two sizes)
        1,200 colored and/or decorated mantas
        400 loin cloths
        400 huipiles and naguas (skirts and blouses)
    b) Other Goods
        8,000 sheets of paper
        2,000 bowls (either gourd or pottery)
  2. Paid once each year
    a) War Goods
        8 rich warriors' costumes
        8 rich feather shields
    b) Foodstuff
        1 *troje* (granary) of maize[5]
        1 troje of frijoles
        1 troje of chia (species of sage)[6]
        1 troje of huautli (amaranth)[7]

II. Province of Huaxtepec (Oaxtepec)
  A. Towns

1. Huaxtepec	(Oaxtepec)
2. Xochimilçacinco[8]	
3. Quanhtlan	(Cuautla Morelos)
4. Ahuehuepan	(See n. 8)
5. Anenecuilco	(Anenecuilco)
6. Olintepec	(Olintepec)
7. Quahuitlyxco	(Cuautlixco)
8. Çompanco[9]	
9. Huiçilan	(Huitzila)
10. Tlalticapa	(Tlatizapan)
11. Coacalco	(Ocalco)
12. Yzamatitla	(Itzamatitlan)
13. Tepoztla	(See n. 9)
14. Yauhtepec	(Yautepec)
15. Yacapichtla	(Acapistla)
16. Tlayacapa	(Tlayacapan)
17. Xoloztoc	(Joloxtoc)
18. Tecpaçinco	(Tepaltcingo)
19. Ayoxochapa	(Axochiapan)
20. Tlayacac	(Tlayecac)
21. Tehuizco	(See n. 9)
22. Nepopoalco	(Nepopualco)
23. Atlatlanca	(Atlatlahuacan)
24. Totolapa	(Totolapan)

25. Amilçinco	(Amilcingo)
26. Atlhuelic	(See n. 9)
27. Hueyapan	(Hueyapan)[10]
28. Ocopetlayuca	(Ocopetlayuca)
29. Tetela [del Volcán]	(Tetela del Volcán)

B. Tribute Paid to the Empire
  1. Paid four times each year
     a) Cotton Goods
        2,000 white mantas
        1,200 colored and/or decorated mantas
        400 loin cloths
        400 huipiles and naguas
     b) Other Goods
        8,000 sheets of paper
        2,000 bowls (either gourd or pottery and possibly of two sizes)
  2. Paid once each year
     a) War Goods
        6 rich warriors' costumes
        6 rich feather shields
        40 common warriors' costumes
        40 common feather shields
     b) Foodstuff
        1 troje of maize
        1 troje of frijoles
        1 troje of chia
        1 troje of huautli

Both the province of Oaxtepec and that of Cuernavaca probably also supplied sizeable quantities of *gallinas de tierra* (turkeys), *huevos* (eggs), *aji* (chile), *tomatl* (tomatoes), *pepitas* (small peppers), *ollas* (jars), *tinajas* (large jars), *cantaros* (pitchers), *escudillas* (large plates), *lebrillos* (basins or small tubs), *leña* (wood), *ocote* (pitch pine), and *sal* (salt) as well as macehual servants and laborers, both men and women, to the rulers of the Empire and, perhaps, to their tribute-collecting representatives stationed in Cuernavaca and Oaxtepec. The two provinces may also have supplied cotton products, slaves for sacrifice, and various items of gold and featherwork to the rulers of the Empire for each of five fiestas, or religious ceremonies, which took place during the months of Panquetzaliztli, Tlacaxipeualiztli, Tecuilhuitontli, Etzalqualiztli, and Ochpaniztli.[11]

Appendix 2

Document sur la fondacion de la Villa de Cuernavaca[1]
(Códice Municipal de Cuernavaca)[2]

Aquí asentamos y ponemos la verdad en esta villa de Cuernavaca, de como entró la fé y como entraron los Padres a componer esta Villa. Primeramente se hizo la Iglesia, y empezó la doctrina, y se juntaron todos los cristianos a oir el sermón que fué en nuestra presencia. D. Toribio de San Martín Cortés y todos los principales que fué delante de nosotros como se hizo la iglesia, que fué en medio de cuatro lomas donde está, que fué la que nos endonó el Rey Ntro. Señor y para que hicieramos estas armas para nuestra fuerza y para defensa nuestra y librarnos de los Españoles para que no nos pierdan el respeto, nos quiten algo, o nuestros benditos Padres no nos maltraten, que sea esto para nuestro favor y amparo, pues no lo ordenó y le recibimos con la fé Santo Bautismo cuando entró el Sr. Cortés á esta tierra donde ganamos el Cacicazgo, y Señorío por haber trabajado y ayudado. Y así ponemos aquí todos nosotros dos Principales como nos hizo el favor y merced el Rey Ntro. Sr. de no ir al servicio de Tazco, porque esperamos lo enviase y recibimos y esperamos a los soldados y a todo aquello que se ofreciere de servicio real y lo obedecemos.

Cuando entró en esta Villa de Cuernavaca el Rey Ntro. Sr., se llamaba D. Felipe, y el primer Guardián se llamaba fray Pedro García. Y cuando entró el primer Alcalde Mayor a esta Villa fué el 30 de enero y vino a componer dicha Villa: se llamaba D. Francisco de la Peña y cuando se empezó el primer día de feria pusieron una silla en la mitad de la plaza y delante de dicho Alcalde mayor se trataba y contrataba y se vendían todos géneros y daba fé de los almades y medida de vara, y la que no era de verdad la quebraba para que no engañaran con el peso y medida, y tenía cuidado de todo, así del chile; como sal y otras cosas el mismo Alcalde mayor Sr. D. Francisco de la Peña y tenía este cuidado cada día de feria y tenía su derecho y un topile de su servicio.

Y en cada fiesta titular de esta Villa tiene obligación de venir a aderezar y a adornar el convento y el palacio los pueblos siguientes: Tetlaman, Cohuentepec, Miacatlan, Zonexco, San Francisco Cohuatlan, Mazatepe, San Miguel Quauhtlan, Quauhchichinola, Huaxintlan, Ahuehuetzinco, Acatlicpac, Xochitepec, Alpoyecan, Xoxocotla, Tetelpan, Panchimalco, Tlatenchi, Huitzilac, Quauhxomolco, Ocotepec, Chienmilpas, Santa María Tetelan, Tlaltenanco. Cien cruces pusieron todos los principales y Caciques para acordarse que en ella padeció Jesucristo Redentor Nuestro.

Teliucan donde concuerda el ojo de agua de Chapultepec, Señalaron los

Principales y Caciques treinta y dos caminos de entradas y salidas a esta villa que no las desbaraten los dichos Principales.

Dn. Bernabel Tequitzin ayudé en todo a la República y a la villa y a la Santa Madre Iglesia y fuí mayordomo de la Cofradía del Santísimo Sacramento. Mi casa se llamaba Pochtlan: mis tierras están en Acatlan y en San Diego, que aquí se echará de ver, cuando se fabricó la Iglesia de Tlaltenanco de Sn. José y San Gerónimo, ayudé en la fábrica y la del Molino y que no entre justicia en él por ser hijos del Marqués y están reservados del servicio del Real y minas de Taxco, y primero se hizo una procesión y el agua que es suya nadie se la pueda quitar y es dada de merced del Sr. Marqués.

Ustedes los caciques y principales que dispusieron que el agua de Cocotzingo entre a esta villa para servicio de ella y de donde nace está una piedra agujerada y un palo de copal que sirve de lindero que allí se hallará quando se buscare en el pueblo de Sta. María Ahuehuetitlán donde se hallará una pila donde nace el agua que allí los principales cortaban tule del barrio de Tecpan y Xalan, Panchimalco y Tepecacalco, lindero de Olac, y está un camino encima a raíz del cerro y se llamaba Tepemalpan y hay cuatro barranquillas y cuatro caminos, uno sale de donde nace el agua, de Zoquitzingo, otro que va a Olac y dos al camino de en medio que va a Huitzilac.

El barrio de Iztlitleocan, barrio de Texacalpan, barrio de Ocotenco, el Calvario donde está el Santo Intierro, Panchimalco, Tetella, Chiamilpa, Coyocalco Sta. María.

Año de 1232 (así el original debe ser a lo que parece 1532) entonces se trajo a Ntra. Sra. de la Asunción de Xochimilco y la fueron a traer todos los principales Caciques.

El lindero de Tepetonco de las tierras linda con las tierras de Jacinto y se midieron en presencia de D. Mateo de Sta. María, y a donde está el ojo de agua está una pared que sirve de lindero.

Quando vino el marqués á esta tierra se sitió en Huitzilac donde descansó y comió, y trujo dos hombres, el uno se llamaba D. Pedro Gregorio y el otro Antonio Gregorio, y no sabían comer carne Los principales y caciques vivían en Tequac que eran sitios de merced, y es por la parte de donde sale el sol, delante de un caño grande por la parte de donde se mete el sol que hay se verá quando lo busquen los Principales.

Aquí asentamos quando fué el eclipse del sol que fué en el mes de Octubre.

Aquí ponemos como se repartían las tierras de los Caciques. Tres mancebos que eran primero se daban las mejores tierras y se medían con un cordel y después se medían con la vara, y se reconocían qué tanto tenían, y con buenas razones las daba el un mozo, que no desearan nada, y luego les enseñaba una cerca de ortiga, que allí había de estar siempre que aunque se pudiera la habían de reparar siempre.

San Miguel Acampantzinco. D. Miguel también trabajó en la república en todos los oficios y sirvió al Santísimo Sacramento.

Aquí comienza el pueblo de Quetzallotla donde está la pluma y donde está la pared vieja donde se había de de haber formado la Villa de Cuernavaca y por no haber agua, no se fundó, y en el pueblo de Acapantzinco vivían los Principales y caciques que aquí echará de ver.

St. María Sra. Ntra. en Sta. Clara está un lindero de una piedra enterrada junto a la iglesia en donde dos lomas, una de Quauhtecpan y allí vivían los principales y hoy se hallará.

San Bernabé. En Mazatepetongo que es un cerro en el cual está un venado que era pueblo entonces, y al pie de está una cuevecita al pie de un fresno donde nace agua.

Oztotoltzingo. Donde está una iglesia entre dos lomas donde vivía el cacique.

Barrio de Tzipitlan son las tierras de Tzipil S. Antonio Tepexic, Xayacapechco Huitzilaque, Quauhxomulco, Xalloztoc, Acatonco, Zayulan, Atlancholoayan Tecpanapan, Atrapulco Olactzinco, Tepetenco donde está la cruz, S. Diego, S. Pablo, Jerusalen, Sto. Christo, San Francisco, San Pedro, Sta. Catalina, San Juan, S. Miguel, Sta. Cruz, Cohuacalco, Calvario Niño Jesús, Tlaltenanco, Tetela, S. Gerónimo Cocotzinco, Sta. María Zoquitzinco, Ocotenco, Calvario, Sto. Entierro, Chiamilpan, Ocotepec, Ahuatepec.

S. Pablo tiene tierras en S. Juan y severan los linderos y mojoneras de las tierras de esta villa que los vean los hijos y los Principales y Gobernadores donde aquí se señala.

Don Toribio de Sandoval S. Martín y Cortés y mi esposa Doña María Salomé, y mi hijo D. Diego Toribio digo que trabajamos y servimos al Smo. Sacramento y a nuestro padre S. Francisco, y a nto. Rey en toda servicio e hicimos un altar de ntro. padre S. Francisco y se le ha de hacer la fiesta cada año, y tengo una huerta que se nombra Axomulco, la cual les dejo a los principales de esta Villa para que la cuiden y reparen con una tierra que está en Copalhuancan y las tierras de Tepetenchi donde está un temazcal, el cual les dejo a mis parientes, el uno se llama D. Pedro y el otro Juan Martínez que en ningún tiempo nadie se los quite; y una casa que está en la esquina de la huerta y enfrente está otra que concuerda con está dicha. En Tezicapan estan cinco tierras que son de la Iglesia, en la esquina está una cruz junto a un puente a piedra linda con una casa grande donde está una cerca de espinas, y allí confinan las tierras de D. Felipe Martines que son tierras de cacicazgo que ninguno las puede quitar. Donde comienzan las tierras desde la puente que llaman Acachuihtla, y cogen derecho por la loma donde está una piedra grande que se pasa por delante de ella para ir á Acatlán. Y encima de otra loma donde están tres piedras grandes y un árbol de Quauhtecomate, cogen derecho a raíz de la barranca donde está el es otro lindero donde está el ojo de agua, y allí comienza la barranca que llaman Zacatzonac, y allí se encuentra otra barranca llamada Tlapitzaco, que todo es mío, y las tierras de Callan donde era un Xiloxochitl por lindero, y está un jongo de piedra junto a la barranca donde está un temazcal y un árbol de Quauhlote, y al fin de la barranca está otro Temazcal, donde se encuentra el río grande donde está una loma cuesta arriba que se llama Chiltepec todas son tierras de Callan todo se hallará conforme acá se va diciendo. Y como también para el mantenimiento de los padres y servicio suyo les dí un fiscal, dos mayores, un topile, un tepixque, un sacristan y digo que en muriendo mis parientes les dejo a S. Francisco las tierras y la casa.

Barrio de S. Antonio Callan. El camino de Tepetlapan señala con una cruz la calle de Tlauhtenco, otra cruz otra casa que viene de S. Antonio á la Iglesia sobre una piedra: otra cruz la calle que va á Teliuhcan: otra cruz la calle que va á Xuchitenco y á Molotlan; otra cruz á Panchimalco Tetzontitlan; otra cruz la calle que va á Chilpan, otra cruz la calle que va de Atliyacan, otra cruz la calle que va á Huitzilac, donde esta un Temazcal, Tzicotlan, Tzicapan, Atecomulco se señala con una cruz.

Las casas de Dn. Toribio son dos llamadas Acaxtenco, Tepayeccan Techinantitlan, Apanticpan, Zoyacalco Choloapa detras de la capilla Xuchitlan la huerta, meson, Oaltenco donde está el amacahuite, los Jarreros o cantarreros la cruz de Guanalan y Xalan, Quauhnahuacazingo, Quauhtexco, Tequixquipan, Xalancalco, Tlacuilocan, Temamatlan, Tlacatecpan, Tepetlatitlan, Acolco, Tecuac, S. Lucas, Pochtlan, Atzompan, Acxotlan Sta. Catalina cruz Tepeticpac, Ycotla, Capilla Caltitlan cruz, el hospital donde se encuentran a nuestro Señor delante de la Iglesia, la puente de Xopetlac Zoyacaltipac, Tlapala, Olac, Aticpac, el salto del agua, Nochtla, Tepetenchi aquí está una cruz, Tepotzpizca, Zacatepec, Atxompan, Tecpantzinco, Texihuacan, Jeroselen, Tlalchichilpa, Tlalnahuac, Nochtlacatzinco, Acachiuhtlan puente. Catipotlan, Calpolixpan, Tzonmolco, Quecholac, Ahuacatla, Tepanahuayan, Xochimilcapan, Calnacazco cruz, Ahueyhuetitlan, Chiapan, Totlan, Colhuacatzinco cruz, Comluilican, Tlapecho, Zacanco cruz, Tocalpan, Yztlahuacan, Huaxtla, Ameyalticpan, Texcacohuac cruz, Coyocalco, Tetla, Tetzicapan, Mayecapan, Otlipan cruz, Atlitilcaxtitlan, Acatlatenco, Atolpan, Tlayecac, Tepexic, Analco, San Antonio, Tlayccac, Cruztitlan, Tzapotitlan, Quauhxincan, Acxotlan, Xocotitlan, Quatla cruz, (cruz de caña de maíz verde), Cohuacalco Tzitzintitlan, Teopanquiahuac, Oxnotitlan cruz, Tlalcahuapan, Iluexotitlan cruz, S. Miguel Calyecac, y aquí se verá como es el nombre de las puentes, la puente de Tetela se llama Techalotl cruz, Telpochhuehueco donde está un puente la cruz de Hueycihuac está una puente donde brincó el cavallo rucio del Sr. Marqués a las tres de la tarde que allí ha de estar en Aquauhtitlan (Aquauhyotl caño de agua) donde nace el agua, donde trabajan los de esta Villa que se llama Tlilcohuac Chimamalpan donde se divide el agua que va á Acapatzinco, que allí empiezan las tierras de Atenantla y bajan á Teopanzolco y Zayolla, y á Zoquiapa Huxotla Quauhtetelco, Axomulco, Quauhtepetonco, las casas de Acatlán, Ytzintli, Itzcuintzin, Tzipitlan, y Tloac donde está un puente de piedra, S. Miguel Acapatzinco, S. Diego; todos estos son nombres de los barrios.

Aquí ponemos que en nuestro entero juicio vimos el primer Nexcuitili y exemplo porque el demonio tentava a los cristianos, y entonces lo conjuraron porque no se apoderara de las almas, así haveis de hacer vosotros los que quedais en el mundo, y par que nos acordemos de la Pasión de Christo Señor nuestro, que no es juguete, lo ponemos aquí para acordarnos de como murió Christo y así se ha de ir continuando en lo de adelante y para que sepais como se puso la estrella que guió a los Reyes Magos quando fueron a visitar á nuestro Redentor. Y como se hizo la primera Iglesia, que es donde está el colateral de San José, y tenía el campanario y despues se desvararartó; y trabajaron en el todos los Principales, para que lo sepais los que vivis, que haveis de trabajar y cuidar la casa de Dios de día y de noche.

Y para que sepais como se aparecieron las santísimas cruces, que fué a una

Cihuapile que se llamaba Doña María Salomé, que mando cortar una planta de Zapote prieto, donde partiéndolo por la mitad se aparecieron dentro de las dos santas cruces y luego envió a avisarle al fiscal de la iglesia, el cual vino a dar fé y avio a los Padres, los cuales fueron a traer en compañia de todos los españoles y los trajeron á la Iglesia, y los Principales le señalaron el sitio donde le fabricaron una capilla a su costa.

Don Sebastián de San Martín fué quien juntó las limosnas de las tierras que le endonaron á las dichas Santas Cruces y todos los que tenían mulas daban limosna á la Santa Cruz, y donde está dicha capilla se llama Oztotonco, y el sitio coge donde tuerce el caña de agua que baja de Cocotzinco se pone aquí para que lo sepan los principales.

Aquí ponemos quando entró el Señor Marqués á esta Villa y los nombres de los benditos Padres que vinieron a introducir la Santa Fé del Santo Bautismo en nosotros: Fray Martín Silva, Fray Francisco Martínez, Fray Ortiz, Fray Luis, Fray Juan de Serva, Fray Francisco de Soto, Fray Andrés de Córdova, Fray García de Ceros (Cisneros), Fray Martín de Jesús (Coruña), Fray Juan Juares, Fray Juan Motolinía, año 1524.

El pimer fiscal de la Sta. Iglesia se llamo Baltazar Valeriano, y trabajó en la Sta. Iglesia y serví al Santísimo Sacramento y a ntra. Sra. de la Asunción, y tenía cuidado de los altares y les hacía cargo a los sacristanes que con unas plumas limpiaran los dichos altares, y mandaba yo a todos los oficiales cantores, campaneros porteros y los Domingos remudaban los frontales de los altares y en cada año en las misas de aguinaldo hacía yo a los cantores que encendieran hartas luces delante del Santo Cristo que está en el coro que siendo yo fiscal tenía cuidado de todo lo dicho, y les hacía a los cantores que no faltaran a todo lo que es de su obligación, y les hacía los Domingos de quaresma hacer exemplos (Mexcuitiles), para abrirles en entendimiento a todos y les mandaba yo todos los días de fiesta del año a uno que tenía solo este cargo que no faltaran flores en la Iglesia en todos los altares y quando alguno caía en algun pecado lo traian delante del fiscal, y despues de haberles dado muy buenos consejos le mandaba á su topile quantos azotes la habían de dar para que tuvieran miedo y el solo condenaba, y mandaba á el que iba errado en algo, y no lo azotaban él mismo por no perder su señorío y cacicazgo y así se ha de observar en esta Villa de Cuernavaca.

En Tixhuacan vivía el fiscal, su casa estaba enfrente de la Iglesia de Jerusalen, y tenía un pedazo de tierra donde llaman Tepetonco, y allí está un corral que le sirve de cerca. En Telyucan está una casa a raíz del caño frontero del patio de la Iglesia que coge hasta la puente redondo de piedra, y de allí para abajo coge hasta la puerta de la Iglesia, y de parte de donde se mete el sol llega hasta donde está la cruz sobre la piedra de parte de la barranca y sirve de lindero, y por parte, de arriba coge hasta donde está un ojo, o cueva que hace frontero de S. Pedro, digo que es mío, yo Don Juan Papatzin, lo cual le dexo a la República por tierra de cacicazgo, y en lo que las arguilaren en todo tiempo se la aplico a nuestro padre San Antonio para que se celebre la fiesta de cada año, y digo que ayudé en todo lo fué necesario en la Sta. Iglesia y se hizo delante de mi.

Yo, Don Gaspar de S. Martín digo que trabajo y ayudé a esta república en todo y a la Sta. Iglesia, qu ndo se fabricó, fué en mi presencia. Y mi casa está en Telyucan frontero de la Iglesia de S. Pedro, de parte de donde se pone el sol delante de la cerca de D. Felipe Martínez, que allí llegan mis tierras de parte de la barranca para que sepan los Principales que es mío y son tierras de cacicazgo.

D. Felipe Martínez digo que ayudé y trabajo en la república y fabrica de la Iglesia y pongo aquí que tengo una casa y tierras enfrente de S. Pedro por donde se mete el sol junto á la calle Real, junto á la cerca de D. Toribio que es tierra de cacicazgo y la dejo a la República y el censo a nuestro Padre San Pedro.

Don José Axayacatzin digo que trabajé e la República y en la fabrica de la Iglesia personalmente, y digo que tengo una casa y tierras donde llaman Xayacapechco, donde confina una barranca grande que allí hize una puente por donde pasaban a las lomas que son de nuestro Padre San Juan que allí está un cueva donde se empezó la Iglesia y las dos lomas está una canoa por donde pasa el agua que viene de San Antonio y á tres lomas junto á la loma cerrada esta un peñasco por lindero, y á cuatro lomas junto á la dicha loma cerrada del camino tiene por lindero dos cercas de piedra, junto á la otra cerca se topa el camino que va á Tlatempa llamado Oztontzinco, allí vivían los Señores y Principales, que allí estaba una Iglesia cuando había mucha gente en esta Villa, y porque se sepa que es de nuestro P. S. Antonio.

D. Jacinto Chilpan digo que trabajé en la república, y fabrica de la Santa Iglesia y en mi presencia entró la fé del Santísimo Bautismo en nosotros, y tenía yo mi casa y morada donde llaman Chiltepec, y allí tengo un pedazo de tierra en la loma, que lo circulian unos cerritos junto á la barranca grande por donde se pone el sol y subiendo por la loma de arriba de parte de donde sale el sol, confina donde hace una barranquilla frente á la huerta de la Iglesia, la cual de dexo al barrio de S. Antonio, que ellos saben lo que determinaran de ello.

Dn. Melchor de la Cueva digo que trabajé en la República y fabrica de la Santa Iglesia que en mi presencia se acabó vivía yo en la loma que llaman Quauhlotitlán donde acaba la cueva, que allí estaba un temazcal llamado Tepetlacalco, subiendo por la mitad de la loma a caer á la barranca está una cueva donde está un temazcal de donde sale el sol, donde confina esta barranca es frontero de la huerta de la Iglesia donde llaman Apanticpan, y porque es verdad todo esto, que todo esto nos endonó ntro. Rey cuando nos bautizaron, y por entonces ganamos el Señorío y Cacicazgo cuando recibimos la fé, nos señaló y sitio donde pusimos el lindero en la loma que llaman Quauhlotitlá, lo qual les dexo a la del barrio de San Antonio que ellos saben lo que determinarán de ello.

Dn. Pedro Quauhximatzin digo que serví y trabajé en la república y fabrica de la Santa Iglesia y servir al Santísmo Sacramento cuando entro la fé en nosotros y vivía yo entonces con los Principales en una loma que llaman del Xiloxochitl y mis tierras de merced están donde confinan dos barrancas grandes y una chica está por donde sale el sol, y la grande por donde se mete y cuesta arriba llegan á donde tuerce el camino que va á Tlapala, que estas señas hallarán cuando se busquen: los linderos son tres piedras grandes frontero de donde llaman Tecocopan, junto á un árbol de Quauhtecomate.

Dn. Nicolás Zacatzin digo que serví y trabajé en la república y en la fabrica de la Santa Iglesia y en el Santísimo Sacramento y vivía yo donde llaman

Tzcomolco, y mis tierras de merced llegan á donde llaman Zacatzonac, y de anchas llegan á mitad de la loma que está enfrente de la puente por donde sale el sol y la otra llega á donde está la barranca junto al camino real por donde se mete el sol, como se hallará estas señas, que la república sabe lo que determinará de ello.

Dn. Lázaro de San Martín digo que trabajé y serví a la República y fabrica de la Sta. Iglesia y el Santísimo Sacramento, mi casa y morada estaba junto al camino real donde llaman Tezcocohuac y tengo dos tierras grandes de merced que se llaman Tezcocohuac, y otras dos en Acatlán, que se alquilan a diez reales, los cuales le dejo á nuestro Padre San Francisco.

Dn. Lorenzo de Mendoza digo que trabajé y serví al Santísimo Sacramento y a la República y fabrica de la Sta. Iglesia. Mis casas están junto á la Iglesia de mi padre San Francisco, y la tierra á donde está la iglesia es suya del santo, y otra que esta enfrente por donde se pone el sol que allí está un Xilosochitl la qual se alquila en diez reales, y es del santo con otras que se alquila en un peso que está en la misma parte frontero del Puchiote, todas son de San Francisco, aquí lo asiento como lo saben los del barrio.

Dn. Juan Coyotzin digo que serví al Santísimo Sacramento y a la República y fabrica de la Santa Iglesia y mi casa es donde llaman Coyocalco, y tengo tres pedazos de tierra de merced de parte a donde de se mete el sol junto al caño grande, y son de San Antonio.

Dn. Bartolomé Martínez digo que trabajé en la República y en la fabrica de la Santa Iglesia y serví al Santísimo Sacramento mi casa esta donde llaman Tetlicapan, mis tierras de merced estan á orillas del camino por donde rodea la procesión de San Francisco y estan divididas donde llaman Tlalcoztli como se verá.

Dn. Lázaro de Aquino digo que serví Santísimo Sacramento y a esta República y fabrica de la Sta. Iglesia, mi casa está donde llaman Tetla y tengo un temazcal debajo de la escalera y esta tierra donde esta fundado no es todo mío, es de la República, y lo de al rededor de mi casa de parte de abajo le hago donación á San Francisco de ello, le se dan cuatro reales de alquiler, son del santo; por parte de donde se mete el sol esta otro pedazo de tierra, la mitad es del santo y la otra mitad mío, la República sabe que hará de ello.

D. Domingo de Santiago digo que serví a nuestra Señora de la Asunción y a la República y fabrica de la Iglesia mi casa está donde llaman Tocalpa, a raiz del camino real por donde sale sol, y mi merced de tierras donde está fundada mi casa; por la parte de abajo esta un pedazo de tierra mío con otras dos que estan en Acatlán, los cuales le dejo á mis hijos que no se los quite nadie.

D. Diego de Santiago digo que serví al Santísimo Sacramento y trabajé en la República y la fabrica de la Sta. Iglesia y yo vivía en Zacanco en el camino real, la tierra por donde está mi casa es de los principales, y un pedazo de tierra que está en Zoquiapa en la orilla, y otro que está en Acatlán al pie del cerrito la cual se la dexo á mis hijos.

D. Miguel Ambrosio digo que serví al Santísimo Sacramento y a la República y en la fabrica de la Iglesia y se hizo a mi costa el altar de Transito, yo vivía en Tlapechco donde era mi casa y mis tierras de merced, y tengo un pedazo de tierra en Ocotepec junto al camino real y otro en Zoyula al pie de cerro los cuales dejo á mis hijos.

D. Lorenzo Díaz Sandoval digo que serví a la República y a la fabrica de la Sta. Iglesia, para abajo; mis tierras son cacicazgo y cogen hasta el puente de piedra llaman Xopetla, y tengo dos pedazos de tierra en Chiamilpa donde llaman Tepechco que allí está una cruz, y otro pedazo de tierra tengo en Ocotepec en el mismo camino donde confina un corral de parte donde se pone el sol, otro pedazo de tierra tengo en Ahuatepec donde se topan los caminos que son de Santo Domingo.

Dn. Francisco de Molina digo que serví a la República de Juez, y estaba yo empadronado en el barrio de San Antonio y vivía donde llaman Atlauhtenco, que allí tengo mis casas y tierras, y tengo otro pedazo de tierra en Azoquiapa frontero de un fresno grande que allí está y tengo otro pedazo de tierra eriasa en una joya en el barrio de San Antonio, las quales dexo á mis hijos que ninguno pueda quitarselas.

Dña. Juana Ximénez, Dña. María Ximénez, Dña. Catalina vivían donde está Ximénez, que allí tenían sus casas propias y se las feriaron los señores caciques por otras que están en el camino.

Dn. Gaspar de Santiago digo que serví al Santísimo Sacramento y trabajé en la República y en la fabrica de la Santa Iglesia y vivía yo donde llaman Acaxtenco, y mis tierras son de merced y cacicazgo y nos las ordenó ntro. Rey por haberle ayudado, tengo un pedazo de tierra donde llaman Tezcacohuac, y otro pedazo en Tepanahuayan en la cual está una casa, y otras dos en Azoquiapan, y otras quatro en Acatlán que son de mis hijos.

Don Antonio Ambrosio digo que serví al Santísimo Sacramento y trabajé a la República, y a la fabrica de la Iglesia: mi casa esta a la orilla del caño frontero de la pared, donde nace agua, la casa y tierra que estan en Acatlán donde mi cacicazgo, las quales dexo á mis hijos.

Tecpan San Pedro, donde vivía el Gobernador D. Lucas de Sn. Martín y Sandoval que en dicha casa se juntaban todos los principales a celebrar las fiestas, y donde disponían danzas a el son del teponaztli de donde solían a ir por el acalde mayor á Palacio para traerlo a misa y bolverlo a lleven: la dicha casa tenía muchos arcos de piedra que en dicha puerta era donde topavan al Niño-Dios y la pared linda con la Iglesia de S. Pedro, y tuerze á el camino real por donde se pone el Sol, y por la otra parte por frente de la casa de D. Toribio donde está una cruz que serví de lindero, con más una casa grande que divide esta mesma toda de arqueria y de boveda a raiz del caño grande por donde sale el sol, y tuerze por el norte á espaldas de la hermitia de S. Pedro, y por parte del Sur confina frontero de la Iglesia está la casa grande llamaban Hospital donde guardaban los ornamentos de la Iglesia.

Aquí empiezan las tierra de merced y cacicazgos de dicho Gobernador donde llaman Atliyacan está una tierra, en Quanalan otra tierra, en Molotlan otra tierra, por el camino que sube al pueblo de Chiamilpa otra tierra, en Tlayecapa otra tierra, todas son de S. Pedro que de ellas sale para su fiesta; y para que se eche de ver que está en varias partes lo explico aquí, con mas otra que está en Sta. María, y donde llaman Acxotla en el mismo camino esta una piedra grande, la cual serví de lindero á raiz del caño de Xuchitlan, todos son de los Principales de Tecpan.

D. Antonio Bautista Gobernador de esta villa vivía donde llaman Tepeticpac, donde está un Amacahuite donde tengo mi cacicazgo y trabajé en la República y fabrica de la Iglesia, y en mi presencia se hizo el Palacio casa de los Alcaldes Mayores y fabricamos un molino en el costado del Palacio en el qual se molió trigo en ese tiempo y donde juntabamos los reales tributos era una casa grande de boveda llamada Tepeticpac, y luego de allí se iban á la plaza donde llaman los Virreyes donde, paran los soldados, y se sentaban los Señores Caciques a hacer Audiencia, donde determinaban las causas da los reos y luego llamaban á un mayor para que los doctrinaran con azotes á los que tenían causa y dicho Gobernador y Alcaldes estaban en su tribunal, y si uno de estos azotara á los reos perdía de ser Principal y cacique que no hacían más que justificar, y tener cuidado de sus hijos, que no perdieran el respeto unos a otros, y así se ha de ir observando esto como va aquí impreso.

D. Pedro Bautista digo que serví al Smo. Sacramento y trabajé en la República y fabrica de la Iglesia mis casas estan donde llaman Aticpac, las cuales eran de altos y arqueria con corredores y ventanas que caían á la huerta del Sr. Marqués: mis tierras de cacicazgo son grandes las cuales estan en Acatlán al pie de un cerrito, y la otra en Olactzinco donde está el camino que va para abajo por donde se pone el sol, y la otra enfrente de los paredones que están encima de la loma donde están un terremoto y un Xiloxochitl, y otra en Quauhlotitlan y otra en Chiltepec donde está el lindero de están tres piedras grandes, y un Quauhtecomate a orillas de la barranca y el otro lindero está en Tecocozpa que coge de parte de arriba hasta donde está una cruz, que allí comió el Marqués y allí sitió una casa como lo veran en buscando estas señas.

D. Salvador de Sandoval y Roxas digo que serví a la República y trabajé en la fabrica de la Iglesia y serví á los benditos Padres quando entró en nosotros la fé del santo bautismo, mis casas están donde llaman Tecpantzinco Calnepantla, y mis tierras cacicazgas son grandes y están en Acatlán junto á una cerca grande de piedra, y otras tengo en San Pablo donde está una cruz por la parte de abajo de la barranca, y otra tierra tengo grande a raiz de la barranca de Quauhtepetongo, que bien se los linderos que tiene en Tecocozpan donde están tres piedras, y un palo de Quauhtecomate, que allí lo hallarán en buscándolo los Principales.

Dn. Antonio de Santiago y Cortés, Gobernador de esta Villa digo que serví al Santísimo Sacramento y trabajé en la fabrica de la Santa Iglesia y por haber servido al Rey, me dió la merced de Cacique y principal de esta Villa, y por haber recibido la fé del Sto. Bautismo, mis tierras cacicazgas y mi morada está donde llaman Totlan, y otras tierras tengo en Acatlán que son quatro y otra en Quecholac á orillas del caño de parte de donde sale el sol, y tiene un árbol de zapote prieto que serví de lindero, y tengo otra tierra de labor en Chiamilpa, en Olactzinco á raiz de la barranca por donde se pone el sol, y se la dejo a mi hijo Dn. Francisco de Santiago y Cortés.

Dn. Antonio de Santiago y Cortés digo que se quantas tierras tiene esta Villa de Cuernavaca y que tiene nueve barrios de donde confinan todos los linderos y que se midieron delante de mi, y sí mañana, y ese día fuese Dios Nuestro Señor servido de llevarme, le dejo á mi hijo enseñado y señalado donde conbinan todas las tierras para que el las enseñe á los que quadren, el dicho mi hijo se llama Dn. Francisco de Santiago y Cortés.

Dn. Bartolome Juyas Gobernador de esta Villa digo que serví al Santísimo Sacramento y a la República en todos los cargos, y que delante de mi se hizo la Iglesia: mis casas están en el barrio de San Francisco donde está un Ahuehuete, mis tierras cacicasgas empiezan donde mi casa, y confinan con las de Coyocalco, y tengo otro pedazo de tierra grande donde llaman Huexotla á orilla de la barranca, y entrente otra pedazo de tierra de mi cacicazgo, las quales dejo á mis hijos que ninguno pueda quitar; y el barrio de San Pablo en la esquina de la hermita que divide el camino de parte de la barranca tengo otro pedazo de tierra que llega hasta el peñazco de á orilla de la barranca; el qual pedazo de tierra tiene siete partes, el qual es de mi Padre Sn. Francisco: en Ocotepec tengo otra tierra que hace una loma entera y una joya en Olactzinco y otra loma en Chapultepec que empiera desde donde esta una piedra partida por la mitad, y va a acabar donde está un corral y los peñazcos de la orilla del pueblo, estas se hallarán manaña, y es otro día.

Dn. Juan Piltintli digo que serví al Santísimo Sacramento y trabajé en la República en todos cargos y que ayudé a hacer la hermita del Niño Jesús digo que tengo mis casas y tierras de mi cacicasgo en la puerta de dicha hermita, y otro pedazo de tierra de parte de donde se pone el sol, y el arrendamiento de dichas tierras se lo endonó al Niño Jesús para misas cada año, y así lo han de ir observando mis Venideros.

Dn. Lucas de Santiago y San Martín digo que serví al Santísimo Sacramento y á la Santa Iglesia, mi casa está en San Antonio, yo era el demandatario de las limosnas que daban los hijos de barrio que era de dos reales cada uño para la celebración de su fiesta, y mi cacicazgo estaba en las tierras brutas las quales, me endonó el Señor Marqués, para que las rompiéramos y labraramos, para en ellas sembrar para nuestro mantenimiento, y limosna de nuestro Padre San Antonio.

Appendix 3

*The Encomiendas Held by Fernando Cortés
and the Estimated Value of the Tribute and Services
Paid Annually by Them, 1524–1525*[1]

Towns and/or Provinces	*Tribute and Estimated Annual Value in Pesos de Oro de Minas*
I. In the vicinity of Tenochtitlan-México:	
A. Coyoacan, Tacuba, and Tlacubaya	Gold, cloth (cotton), grains, and services; 2,000 pesos.
B. Province of Chalco-Tlalmanalco and sujetos	Gold, cloth, grains, and services; 2,000 pesos.
C. Texcoco, Guatinchan, Tepetlaoztoc and sujetos	Gold, cloth, grains, and services; 1,500 pesos.
D. Toluca, Calimaya, Tenango, and Metepec with other towns in the Valle de Matalcingo	Gold, cloth, and livestock; 2,000 pesos.
E. Cuernavaca, Oaxtepec, Acapistla, Yautepec, Tepoztlan, and sujetos	Gold, cloth, grains, and services; 6,000 pesos.
F. Huejotzinco	(nothing listed)
G. Atotonilco and sujetos	Gold, cloth, grains, foodstuffs, and services; 800 pesos.
H. Otumba, Tepeapulco, and sujetos	Gold, cloth, maize, and services; 2,000 pesos.
II. In Michoacán:	
A. Uchichila (Tzinzuntzan), Tamazula, and sujetos	Gold, silver, foodstuffs, livestock, grains, and services; 2,000 pesos.
B. Tuxpan, Amula, Zapotlan, and Guaniqueo	Gold, silver, foodstuffs, cloth, grains, and services; 2,500 pesos.
III. In Oaxaca:	
A. Oaxaca, Cuilapa, Etla, and sujetos	Gold, foodstuffs, grains, and services; 5,000 pesos.

IV. In Pánuco:
  A. One-half of Tamohi and the　　　Gold, cloth, slaves, and services; 5,000
     Province of Oxitipa　　　　　　　pesos.

V. In the vicinity of Veracruz:
  A. Cotaxtla, La Rinconada,　　　　(no listing); 2,000 pesos.
     Mizantla, and sujetos

VI. Other Areas:
  A. The Province of Tututepec　　　Gold; 2,000 pesos.
  B. Tlapa, Ayacastla, and sujetos　Gold; 3,000 pesos.
  C. Tehuantepec, Nexapa,　　　　　Gold, grains, and services; 3,000 pesos.
     Xalapa, and sujetos
  D. Soconusco and sujetos　　　　　Gold and cacao; 2,000 pesos.

Appendix 4

The Cuernavaca Encomienda Towns and Their Sujetos as Reported in 1531–1532[1]

I. Quaonavac (Quauhnahuca)[2]
    Acatliquipaque (Acatlycpac)
    Suchitepeque (Xochitepec)
    Alpuxeca (Atlpoyecan)
    Miacatlan (Miacatla)
    Coatlan (Coatlan)
    Çacatepeque (Cacatepec)
    Maçatepeque (Maçatepec)
    Ocopayuca (Ocapayuca)
    Yztla (Iztla)
    Xuxucutlan (Xoxoutla)
    Teocalcingo (Teocalçingo)
    Tlaquiltenango (Tlaquiltenanco)
    Xiutepeque (Xiuhtepec)
    Temimilcingo
    Guachichimula
    Amatetlan
    Teuiztlan
    Teçivca
    Tequisquitengo
        (Atlacholoayan)
        (Molotla)
        (Amacoztitla)
        (Chilmalco)
        (Huiçilapa)
        (Iztepec)

II. Tepuztlan (Tepoztla)
    Ciertas caserías que estan
    pobladas hacia la sierra

III. Yautepeque (Yauhtepec)
    Tlalticapan (Tlalticapa)
    Aviléca (Atlhuelic)
    Uichichila (Huiçilan?)
    Amatepeque
    Ticoma

IV. Yaxapicstla (Yacapichtla)
    Tlayacaque (Tlayacac)
    Tetela (Tetela)
    Xoloztoque (Xoloztoc)
    Tecpançingo (Tecpaçinco)
    Axuchapa (Ayoxochapā)
    Atlatavco (Atlatlanca)
    Totolapa (Totolapā)
    Totonilco
    Xunacatepeque
    Cantetelco
    Amaycan
    Guaçocango

V. Guastepeque (Huaxtepec)
    Çumpango (Çompanco)
    Quautlisco (Quahuitlyxco)
    Suchimilcacingo (Xochmilçacinco)
    Quautla (Quanhtlan)
    Anenecuicuilco (Aneneicuilco)
    Olintepeque (Olintepec)
    Avevepa (Ahuehuepan)
    Tlayacapan (Tlayacapa)
    Yçamatitlan (Yzamatitla)
    Suchilmilcapa
    Quevyztla
    Tlacuba
    Tlatalucapa
    Ayutlycha
    Chiameca
    Tecivaque
    Yzcatepeque
    Quluacalcingo
    Mexicatçingo
    Tutulapa
        (Tehuizco)
        (Amilçinco)
        (Nepopoalco)
        (Coacalco)
        (Hueyapan)
        (Ocopetlayuca)

Appendix 5

List of Abbreviations Used in Notes

AGI	Archivo General de Indias, Seville,
Just.	Papeles de Justicia,
Patron.	Patronato.
AGN	Archivo General de la Nación, Mexico,
HJ	Ramo de Hospital de Jesús.
Bancroft	Bancroft, Hubert Howe. *History of Mexico.* 6 vols. San Francisco, 1883-1888.
Ced. Cort.	Arteaga Garza, Beatriz, y Guadalupe Pérez San Vicente, eds., *Cedulario Cortesiano.* Mexico, 1949.
Cortés, *Cartas*	Cortés, Hernán. *Cartas de Relación.* Mexico, 1960.
DII	*Colección de documentos inéditos relativos al descubrimiento, conquista, y organización de las antiguas posesiones españoles de América y Oceania.* 42 vols. Madrid, 1864-1884.
DIU	*Colección de documentos inéditos relativos al descubrimiento, conquista, y organización de las antiguas posesiones españoles de Ultramar.* Segunda serie. 25 vols. Madrid, 1885-1932.
Doc. inéd.	*Documentos inéditos relativos a Hernán Cortés y su familia.* Mexico, 1935.
ENE	Paso y Troncoso, Francisco del, ed. *Epistolario de Nueva España, 1505-1818.* 16 vols. Mexico, 1939-1942.
LC	Library of Congress. Washington, D.C.
Hark.	Harkness Collection of Spanish Manuscrips Concerning Mexico.
PNE	Paso y Troncoso, Francisco del, ed. *Papeles de Nueva España.* 9 vols. Madrid, 1905-1948.

Notes

Chapter 1: Introduction

1. Jorge L. Tamayo, *Geografía general de México,* 4 vols. (Mexico, 1962), 1:221–31.
2. Ibid., 1:452–54, 2:429–47.
3. Ibid., 1:452–54.
4. Jesús Galindo y Villa, *Geografía de México* (Mexico, 1950), pp. 54–68.
5. Cortés, *Cartas,* p. 105 (*See* Appendix 5): "Aquella noche dormimos en aquel pueblo [Cuernavaca] y por la mañana seguimos nuestro camino por una tierra de pinales, despoblada y sin ninguna agua, la qual y un puerto pasamos con grandisimo trabajo y sin beber; tanto, que muchas de los indios que iban con nosotros perecieran de sed . . ."
6. Alfonso Luis Velasco, *Geografía y estadística de la República Mexicana,* 13 vols. (Mexico, 1889–93), 8:24–26.
7. Proceso de la villa de Cuernavaca contra el Marqués del Valle sobre que no pueden complir [con sus tributos], 1551, AGN, HJ, leg 289, exp. 102 (*See* Appendix 5).
8. Joaquín García Icazbalceta, ed., *Códice franciscano* (Mexico, 1940), p. 19.
9. Luis García Pimentel, ed., *Relación de los obispados de Tlaxcala, Michoacan, Oaxaca y otros lugares en el siglo XVI* (Mexico, 1904), p. 115.
10. For this and succeeding paragraphs the works of Florencia Müller, George C. Vaillant, Jorge A. Vivo, Wigberto Jiménez Moreno, Eduardo Noguera, and Francisco Plancarte y Navarette (all listed in the Bibliography) were utilized.
11. *Códice Chimalpopoca* (Mexico, 1945), p. 35; and Florencia Müller, *Historia antigua del Valle de Morelos* (Mexico, 1945), p. 37.
12. Müller, pp. 37–39.
13. George C. Vaillant, *The Aztecs of México* (Baltimore, 1966), pp. 112, 116–17. Apparently for a time after Moctezuma I's conquest in the Morelos area the Xochimilca towns there and some of the Tlahuica settlements in the Cuernavaca Valley, including the cabecera town of the same name, paid their tributes directly to the rulers of Texcoco, more specifically to Nezahualcoyotl. Following Nezahualcoyotl's death in the early 1570s and the assumption of primacy in Confederacy affairs by the Mexica chieftains, tributes from the Morelos towns were paid into Confederacy coffers through agents stationed in the area (as is noted in paragraphs following). See Charles Gibson, "Llamamiento general, repartimiento and the Empire of Acolhuacan," *Hispanic American Historical Review,* 36, no. 1 (1956): 1–27.
14. ENE, 10:121 (*See* Appendix 5).
15. Eduardo Noguera, *Zonas arqueológicas del Estado de Morelos* (Mexico, 1960), p. 6.
16. Cortés, *Cartas,* p. 104: ". . . y a las diez del día llegamos a Gustepeque [Oaxtepec], de que arriba he hecho mención, y en la casa de una huerta del señor de allí nos aposentamos todas, la cual huerta es la mayor y más hermosa y fresca que nunca se vió, porque tiene dos leguas de circuito, y por medio de ella va una muy gentil ribera de agua, y de trecho a trecho, cantidad de dos tiros de ballesta, hay aposentamientos y jardines muy frescas, e infinitos árboles de diversas frutas, y muchas hierbas y flores olorosas, que cierto es cosa de admiración ver la grandeza de toda esta huerta."

17. Diego de Durán, *Historia de las indias de Nueva España e islas de tierra firme*, 2 vols. (Mexico, 1867–80), 1:316.

18. Ibid., 1:252–53.

19. Noguera, p. 6.

20. Müller, p. 40.

21. This estimate is based upon the data and methods set forth in Woodrow Borah and Sherburne F. Cook, *The Aboriginal Population of Central Mexico on the Eve of the Spanish Conquest* (Berkeley and Los Angeles, 1963). Commentary thereon follows in Chapter 7.

22. R. H. Barlow, *The Extent of the Empire of the Culhua Mexica* (Berkeley and Los Angeles, 1949), pp. 73–81. Barlow describes the tributary provinces of the Aztec Confederacy and lists the major towns (cabeceras) in each. The major sources he utilized were the *Codex Mendoza* in the Bodleian Library of Oxford University and the *Matrícula de Tributos* in the Museo Nacional de Etnología e Historia, Mexico City. (More specific information as to these pictographic manuscripts is included in Appendix 1.) Barlow's contention as to the northern Xochimilca towns (Totolapan, Tlayacapan, Atlatlahuacan and Nepopoalco) exclusive of Tepoztlan seems well taken. Supplementary and generally substantiating argumentation is recorded in, El gobernador y principales del pueblo de Totolapa con los gobernadores, concejos e indios vecinos de los pueblos de Nepopoalco y Tlayacapan y Atlatlauca [Atlatlahuacan], 1556, AGI, Just. (*See* Appendix 5), leg. 156, no. 1; and Los indios de los pueblos de Atlatlauca y Tlayacapa con los indios del pueblo de Totolapa sobre quererse estos segregar de su jurisdicción y declarar pueblos de cabezera, 1570, AGI, Just., leg. 176, no. 2. He probably erred, however, in the case of Tepoztlan which appears to have been included in the province of which Oaxtepec was the administrative center. That error has been suggested by Oscar Lewis, *Life in a Mexican Village: Tepoztlán Revisited* (Urbana, Illinois, 1963), p. 88, n. 23; and convincingly demonstrated by Charles Gibson, *The Aztecs Under Spanish Rule* (Stanford, Calif., 1964), p. 479, n. 69, chap. 3.

23. Fernando de Alva Ixlilxochitl, *Obras Históricas,* 2 vols. (Mexico, 1952), 2:309; *Códice Chimalpopoca*, pp. 59–61; and Proceso de Don Hernando, indio de Cuernavaca contra el Marqués del Valle [sobre tierras], 1536, AGN, HJ, leg. 293, exp. 144.

24. These generalized statements are based upon a variety of printed and manuscript sources. Particularly useful among these secondary sources was Gibson, *The Aztecs.*

25. Lewis, p. 90; and Pedro Carrasco, "Tres libros de tributos del Museo Nacional de México y su importancia para los estudios demográficos," in Congreso Internacional de Americanistas, 35, Mexico, 1962, *Actas y Memorias,* 3 (1964): pp. 373–79.

26. This general treatment is based upon the excellent definitive discussion of Aztecan pre- (and post-) conquest landholding practices in Gibson, *The Aztecs,* pp. 257–99 and on items from various manuscript sources. Additional commentary follows in Chapter 5.

27. For the well-known events in New Spain's early history which had no direct bearing on developments in the Morelos area and which are summarized in this and subsequent chapters, no specific citations have been made. The standard modern histories of William H. Prescott, Hubert H. Bancroft, Manuel Orozco y Berra, Henry R. Wagner, and others, as well as the contemporary accounts of Bernal Díaz, Fernando Cortés, Francisco López de Gómara, and their sixteenth-century fellows, were employed as reference sources and are listed in the Bibliography.

28. Müller, p. 40; *Códice Chimalpopoca*, p. 61; and the testimony of Don Hernando, son of Yoatzin, lord (señor) of Cuernavaca at the time of the conquest, in AGN, HJ, leg. 293, exp. 144.

29. Exact dating for this period in the conquest has not been determined, as the

major contemporary accounts, those of Bernal Díaz and Cortés, are anything but definite in date references. Henry R. Wagner placed these events in February but noted that Díaz reported otherwise in his confused dating. Orozco y Berra, with whom I am most in agreement, placed them in March.

30. Bernal Díaz del Castillo, *Historia verdadera de la conquista de la Nueva España*, 2 vols. (Mexico, 1939), chap. 142: ". . . dos cientos soldados y veinte de a cavallo, y diez o doce ballesteros y otros tantos escopeteros, y nuestros amigos, los de Tlaxcala y otra capitanía de los de Texcoco . . ." In his account of the incident Cortés differed with Díaz in citing 300 as the number of infantry involved (Cortés, *Cartas*, p. 101).

31. Ibid., chap. 142: ". . . Y desde que el capitán Sandoval se vió libre de aquellas refriegas dió muchas gracias a Dios y se fué a reposar y dormir a una huerta, que había en aquel pueblo, la más hermosa y de mayores edificios y cosa mucho de mirar, que se había visto en la Nueva España (I), y tenía tantas cosas de mirar, que cosa admirable y ciertamente era huerta para un gran principe, y aun no se acabó de andar por entonces toda, porque tenía mas de un cuarto de legua de largo . . ." The (I) in the quotation refers to a note made to the content in the edition cited. I have included it here as follows: "I.—Tachado en el original: Así del gran concierto de la diversidad de árboles de todo género de fruta de la tierra, y otras de muchas rosas y olores; pues los conciertos que en ella había, por donde venía el agua de un río que en ella entraba; pues los rico aposentos y las labores dellos, y la madera tan olorosa de cedros y otros árboles preciados, salas y cenadores y baños, y muchas cosas que en ella había, todas encaladas y hermoseadas de mil pinturas; pues los pescaderos y el entretejer de unas ranas con otras, y a parte de hierbas melicinales [sic], y otras legumbres que entrellos son buenas de comer." This note was evidently taken from Díaz's manuscript and included in this edition by the annotator, Joaquín Ramírez Cabañas. These gardens were obviously those of the Mexican rulers established by Moctezuma I a half-century before Sandoval saw them.

32. Cortés, *Cartas*, pp. 101-2: ". . . y este pueblo era muy fuerte y puesto en una altura, y donde no pudiesen ser ofendidos de los de caballo; y como llegaron los españoles, los del pueblo sin esperar a cosa alguna, comenzaron a pelear con ellos, y desde lo alto echar muchas piedras; . . . que aunque era mucha la ofensa y resistencia que se les hacía, les entraron, aunque hubo mucho heridos. Y como los indios nuestros amigos los siquieron y los enemigos se vieron de vencida, fué tanta la matanza de ellos a manos de los nuestros, y de ellos despeñados, de lo alto, que todos los que allí se hallaron afirman un río pequeño que cercaba casi aquel pueblo, por más de una hora fué teñido en sangre, y les estorbó de beber por entonces, porque como hacía mucha calor tenían necesidad de ello." Both Francisco López de Gómara and Bernal Díaz also described this action in about the same terms although Díaz said there were other sources of water available for the thirsty soldiers and chided Gómara by name for his rendition of the use of the bloody stream (Francisco López de Gómara, *Historia de la conquista de México*, 2 vols. [Mexico, 1943], 2:18; and Díaz del Castillo, chap. 142.)

33. Cortés, *Cartas*, p. 104.

34. Bancroft 1:596 (*See* Appendix 5).

35. Cortés, *Cartas*, p. 104.

36. Ibid.

37. Ibid., p. 105.

38. In his account Bernal Díaz makes no reference to Xiutepec but ascribes this action to Tepoztlan (Díaz del Castillo, chap. 144). H. R. Wagner suggests that some troops may have been dispatchd to Tepoztlan, and Díaz recorded their visit (H. R. Wagner, *The Rise of Fernando Cortés* [Los Angeles, 1944], pp. 341–43). Probably Díaz simply confused the names of the two places, perhaps having forgotten the Xiutepec

name as it was a town of little consequence after the conquest, while Tepoztlan was well known.

39. Díaz del Castillo, chap. 144.

40. López de Gómara, 2:23; and Manuel Orozco y Berra, *Historia antigua y de la conquista de México*, 4 vols. (Mexico, 1880), 4:544, ". . . al acercarse los castellanos quedaban separados de sus contrarios por la profunda barranca, recibiendo de la opuesta orilla una lluvia de flechas pedradas y hondragas, accompañados de grita atronadora."

41. Cortés, *Cartas*, p. 105; and Díaz del Castillo, chap. 149.

42. This battle is admirably outlined by Wagner, pp. 342–43.

43. Díaz del Castillo, chap. 144: ". . . En este pueblo se hubo gran despojo, así de mantas muy grandes como de buenas indias . . ."

44. Cortés, *Cartas;* and Díaz del Castillo, chap. 144.

45. Ixtlilxochitl, 2:545, ". . . El señor se llamaba Yoatzin que se fué retirando á la montaña, y Ixtlilxochitl [leading Cortés' Texcocan allies] le envió á reprender su rebeldía, y que luego se viniese a dar y pedir perdón de lo que hasta allí había hecho; y así luego que amaneció se vinieron á ofrecer al servicio y amparo de los cristianos, promentiendo de ayudarles y ser siempre en su favor como en efecto lo hicieron . . ."

46. Cortés, *Cartas*, p. 125; and Díaz del Castillo, chap. 155.

47. The general outlines of this part of the Introduction were drawn from the well-known modern works of Robert Ricard and P. Mariano Cuevas, S.J., and the contemporary or near-contemporary accounts of Fray Gerónimo de Mendieta, Fray Toribio Motolinía, Fray Juan de Grijalva, Fray Agustín Dávila Padilla, Francisco Cervantes de Salazar, and others. All are listed in the Bibliography.

48. His name appears in the accounts of Cortés, Díaz del Castillo, Gómara, Cervantes de Salazar, and Dávila Padilla.

49. Gerónimo de Mendieta, *Historia eclesiástica indiana*, 4 vols. (Mexico, 1945), 2:94.

50. No available evidence clearly supports such a possibility, however. For want of adequate, exact, and pertinent data, discussion of the earliest phases in the attempted spiritual conquest of any particular area within New Spain is difficult and can only be a summary outline. What follows for the Morelos area is, therefore, necessarily a generalized treatment.

51. Mendieta, 2:94, ". . . fundaron el quinto convento en el pueblo de Cuernavaca. . . . De aquel Convento de Cuernavaca visitaban á Ocuila y a Malinalco y toda la tierra caliente que cae al mediodia hasta la mar del sur."

52. Ibid., 2:112, ". . . del monesterio de Cuernavaca que fué el quinto donde se pusieron frailes, salieron á visitar por la comarca de lo que llaman Marquesado y hallaron la gente en tan buena disposición y aparejo para ser cristianos, como en las pueblos que arriba se ha hecha mención especialmente en las llamadas Yacapichtla [Acapistla] y Guastepec [Oaxtepec] . . ."

53. *Códice Municipal de Cuernavaca. Anónimo del siglo XVI* (Mexico, 1951), pp. 29–31, ff. There is no date given for this *Códice*. The erroneous reference to Philip II as Spain's monarch at the time of Cortés' conquest of the Empire of the Triple Alliance suggests it was written after Philip became king of Spain. More significant is the absence from its list of the town's principales of the names of Don Hernando, principal and governor of the pueblo under Fernando Cortés' agents in the 1530s and 1540s (he died in the late 1540s), and that of his widow, Doña María, who was prominent and active in the 1550s. Eighteenth-century copies of the Códice are included in the Aubin Collection housed in the Bibliothèque Nationale (Paris), Departmente des Manuscrits Mexicaines. No. 291 is the Nahuatl version and no. 292 is the Spanish version; the latter is included herein as Appendix 2.

54. Ibid., p. 29. The friars listed were Fray Luis (possibly Luis de Fuensalida), Fray Francisco de Soto, Fray Andrés de Córdoba, Fray García de Ceros (Cisneros), Fray Martín de Jesús (Coruña), Fray Juan Juárez, and Fray Juan Motolinía (no doubt Fray Toribio Motolinía), all of whom can be identified with the "Twelve Apostles." In the list are four other names, Fray Francisco Martínez, Fray Juan de Serva, Fray Ortiz, and Fray Martín de Silva (see Appendix 2). The last probably was Fray Alonso Ortiz who arrived with the second group of Franciscans who came to New Spain in 1525. Fray Martínez, Fray Serva, and Fray Silva may also have been members of this group.

55. Mendieta, 2:113 and Toribio Motolinía, *History of the Indians of New Spain*, ed. Francis Borgia Steck (Washington, 1951), p. 179.

56. Mendieta, 2:113.

57. AGI, Just. 156, no. 1. Witnesses from the towns of Totolapan, Tlayacapan, Nepopoalco, and Atlatlahuacan indicated that they attended masses many times in Cuernavaca and later in Oaxtepec and Acapistla before the church was built in Totolapan. The *Relación* of Acapistla drawn up in 1580 quotes Indians who said Franciscans converted that area (no. 23, item 8, Joaquín García Icazbalceta Manuscript Collection, University of Texas, Austin, Texas).

58. George Kubler, *Mexican Architecture of the Sixteenth Century*, 2 vols. (New York, 1948) and John McAndrew, *The Open-Air Churches of Sixteenth Century Mexico* (Cambridge, Mass., 1965) treat these temporary churches in detail.

59. Kubler, *Architecture*, 2:480, 522–23; Manuel Mazari, "Códice Mauricio de la Arena," *Anales del Museo Nacional de Arqueología, Historia y Etnografía*, época 4, vol. 4 (1926): 272–79; AGI, Just., leg. 156, no. 1 (Indian witnesses stated that the monastery in Acapistla was originally Franciscan); and Elena Vázquez y Vázquez, *Distribución geográfica y organización de las órdenes religiosas en la Nueva España, siglo XVI* (Mexico, 1965), pp. 63, 92–93.

60. McAndrew, pp. 230–31 and Vázquez y Vázquez, pp. 63, 92–93.

61. Robert Ricard, *La Conquista Espiritual de México* (Mexico, 1947), p. 165.

62. Agustín Dávila Padilla, *Historia de la fundación y discurso de la provincia de Santiago de México de la Orden de Predicadores* (Mexico, 1955), p. 50. It is possible that the Dominican friars were those who went to Oaxtepec in 1528 after the Indians from there came to Tenochtitlan to secure advice on staging a religious procession similar to the one which had been miraculously successful when used in the capital city to stop the crop-ruining rains of that year. This incident was recorded by Motolinía, p. 178.

63. Dávila Padilla, p. 50 ff., and Mendieta, 2:113.

64. Dávila Padilla, p. 617 and Durán, 1:252–53.

65. Kubler, *Architecture*, 2:480, 522–23; McAndrew, p. 122; and Vázquez y Vázquez, pp. 63, 92–93.

66. Ricard, p. 171.

67. Kubler, *Architecture*, 2:521, sets the date at 1536. Indians testified in 1556, however, that the monastery was built in 1533 (AGI, Just., leg. 156, no. 1), and the *Relación* for Totolapan, prepared in 1579, states that it was built forty-five years earlier, or in 1534 (PNE, 6:11).

68. Juan de Grijalva, *Crónica de la Orden de N.P.S. Agustín en las provincias de la Nueva España* (Mexico, 1924), pp. 41–46; Vázquez y Vázquez, pp. 77, 82, 95–96; and McAndrew, pp. 177, 283. Also see n. 18, this chapter.

69. Grijalva, p. 73.

70. Ibid. and Vázquez y Vázquez, pp. 78, 82, 95–96.

71. Vásquez y Vázquez, pp. 78, 95.

72. Cortés' role in the missionary program in the Morelos area is treated in subsequent chapters.

Chapter 2: Encomiendas

1. George Kubler, "Mexican Urbanism in the 16th Century," *Art Bulletin* 24 (1942): 162. Kubler notes therein that for the reconstruction of Tenochtitlan ". . . as far afield as Oaxtepec, fifty miles distant, the entire population labored in the quarries for stone needed in the capital." His cited sources leave no doubt as to the use of labor and material from the Morelos area.

2. Jorge A. Vivó, *Geografía humana de México* (Mexico, 1948), p. 17.

3. Bancroft, 2:38–39 and PNE, 6:283 (*See* Appendix 5).

4. Fernando B. Sandoval, *La industria del azúcar en Nueva España* (Mexico, 1951), p. 21.

5. Cortés, *Cartas*, p. 144. Cortés expressed opposition to the repartimiento-encomienda system as it was known in Cuba in his reports to the crown beginning in 1522, while justifying at the same time the need for his own brand of that system in New Spain.

6. A more detailed discussion of the encomienda system as it developed in New Spain follows in Chapter 3.

7. This system is outlined in Chapter 1 and Appendix 1.

8. Charles Gibson, "The Aztec Aristocracy in Colonial Mexico," *Comparative Studies in Society and History* 2 (1960): 180, and Silvio Zavala, *La encomienda indiana* (Madrid, 1935), pp. 40–61. Discussion of land-holding in New Spain during the first half of the sixteenth century follows in Chapter 5.

9. Charles Gibson, *The Aztecs Under Spanish Rule. A History of the Indians of the Valley of México, 1519–1810* (Stanford, 1964), pp. 257–64. Preconquest land-holding practices are more fully discussed in Chapters 1 and 5.

10. Bancroft, 2:31–32.

11. DII, 26:50–65, 135–48, 163–70 (*See* Appendix 5).

12. Bancroft, 2:132.

13. DII, 13:107; 26:379–80, 429–30, 472–73; 27:23. Numerous modern writers have demonstrated this fact by noting the contemporary correspondence of royal officials and the crown, lawsuit testimony, and the letters of Cortés and others. The preceding citations refer to exemplary items of these data, including the charges and testimony in the "pesquisa secreta" conducted against Cortés in 1529 and Bishop Zumárraga's well-known letter to the crown of August 27, 1529.

14. Información sobre los pueblos que Hernán Cortés tenía al tiempo que fué a la conquista de Honduras, así como lo que rentaron, 1531, AGN, HJ, leg. 265, exp. 5; and France V. Scholes, "The Spanish Conqueror As a Businessman," *New Mexico Quarterly* 27, no. 1 (Spring 1958): 11.

15. AGN, HJ, leg. 265, exp. 5. This proceso initiated by Cortés' attorneys in 1531 was an attempt to secure the revenues from Cortés' encomiendas which Pedro Almindes Cherino, New Spain's first veedor, in alliance with Gonzalo de Salazar, the colony's factor, had seized in 1525 and early 1526 and which were not regained by the Conqueror until his return from Honduras in May 1526. A list of Cortés' holdings was entered in these proceedings by his attorneys, and witnesses testified to its accuracy. This list compares more or less favorably with several others related to the same period. One of these attested by witnesses appears in Antonio Serrano, regidor y vecino de México, con Hernando Cortés, Marqués del Valle, sobre derecho al pueblo de Cuernavaca y sus sujetos, 1530, AGI, Just., leg. 108, no. 1. Another is included in a letter written by Cortés to his father in 1526 after he had regained most of his encomienda towns, recorded in Don Hernando Cortés, Marqués del Valle, con el fiscal de su Majestad sobre el pago de una multa de 62,000 pesos de oro, 1529, AGI, Just., leg. 185, ramo 2.

16. Tetela del Volcán and Hueyapan were granted in encomienda to a member of the

Orozco expedition of 1521 which penetrated that locale (Bancroft, 2:39 and PNE, 1:96; 6:283).

17. *Nuevos documentos relativos a los bienes de Hernán Cortés, 1547–1947* (Mexico, 1946), pp. 143–69; and AGI, Just., leg. 156, no. 1. A letter of 1532 from the Audiencia to the crown indicates the difficulties which resulted from Cortés' organization of tribute-paying towns as encomiendas; the town of Acapistla and its sujetos were an example (ENE, 2:208–21 [see Chapter 1 and Appendix 1]).

18. The alterations made by Cortés in the kinds and amounts of tribute paid are examined in Chapter 3. A detailed discussion of the uses of the Mexican system with modifications in the Valley of México is included in Gibson, *The Aztecs*, pp. 32–97, 194–299.

19. AGI, Just., leg. 108, no. 1 and Just., 156, no. 1; AGN, HJ, leg. 265, exp. 5. For the changes made in 1523 there is considerable evidence, examples of which are included in the following: DII, 12:277–85 and 26:276–80.

20. AGI, Just., leg. 108, no. 1 and Just., 156, no. 1; AGN, HJ, leg. 265, exp. 5.

21. The purposes and events of the Honduras venture are not related here as they are well known and not sufficiently relevant to warrant inclusion.

22. Rodrigo de Paz was the son of Francisca Núñez, a notary of Salamanca, Spain, and Inés de Paz, a sister of Cortés' father. In his youth Cortés lived for a year or more with the Núñez-Paz family in Salamanca. From the later 1520s to the mid-1540s a brother of Rodrigo de Paz named Francisco Núñez, a *relator* of the Royal Council of Castile, served as Cortés' procurador (attorney) in Spain.

23. These data were supplied by Professor France V. Scholes from his study of the trial, torture, and execution of Rodrigo de Paz as recorded in Autos de Inéz de Paz vecina de México, con Gonzalo de Salazar, Pedro Almindes Cherino, y Antonio de Villaroel, tenientes de gobernador en la misma ciudad sobre la sentencia de muerte que pronunciaron contra Rodrigo de Paz, 1531, AGN, Just., leg. 111.

24. ENE, 1:89, ". . . y que el gobernador Hernando Cortés tenía en esta tierra la mayor parte de los indios y los mejores de los otros, los que eran provechosos los daba a sus parientes y criados y allegados por manera que todos los pueblos vivían en estrema necesidad y que agora Gonzalo de Salazar y Pedro Almindez Cherino que quedaron en la gobernación han repartido los indios y remediado los pueblos y acrecentado los vecinos y poblaciones . . ."

25. For example, Cortés had granted the pueblo of Yanhuitlan, one of the most populous towns in the Oaxaca area, as an encomienda to his cousin, Francisco de las Casas, who had come to Mexico after the conquest of the Aztec Confederacy had been attained. It was this Francisco de las Casas whom Cortés sent to Honduras early in 1524 to punish the disloyalty of Cristóbal de Olid (Ronald Spores, *The Mixtec Kings and Their People* [Norman, Okla., 1967], 77–78).

26. AGI, Just., leg. 108, no. 1. Serrano was known earlier as Villaroel but had changed his name by this time. When Inés de Paz, mother of Rodrigo de Paz, instituted criminal proceedings in 1531 before the Second Audiencia of México against Salazar and Cherino on charges relating to the execution of her son, Serrano was named as a codefendant (Professor Scholes' study of AGI, Just., leg. 111).

27. ENE, 1:78–90.

28. AGI, Just., 108, no. 1 and AGN, HJ, leg. 265, exp. 5.

29. Proceso de Tepuztlan y Yautepec contra el Marqués del Valle sobre que no pueden complir [con sus tributos], 1551, AGN, HJ, leg. 289, exp. 100.

30. Aguilar's assumption of authority to make grants of encomienda is attested by documentation in AGI, Just., and AGN, IIJ. During his tenure as governor of New Spain, he issued an interesting series of ordinances relating to the duties and obligations

of encomenderos. This information was supplied by Professor Scholes from his investigation of Martín Vásquez con Hernando Maldonado, vecinos de México, sobre derecho al pueblo de Atoyaque, 1532, AGI, Just., leg. 115, no. 3.

31. Many examples of encomienda grants by Estrada are recorded in the Patronato and Justicia sections of AGI.

32. A listing of these grants is recorded in Pleito de Juan de Burgos, vecino de México, con Hernán Cortés, Marqués del Valle, sobre derecho á un pueblo de indios, 1531, AGI, Just., leg. 113, no. 5.

33. Ibid.; AGN, HJ, leg. 289, exp. 100; and *Nuevos documentos,* pp. 143–69.

34. Record of the residencia proceedings conducted against Velázquez by Altamirano is preserved in Residencia tomada por el lic. Juan Altamirano de Adelantado Diego Velásquez, teniente de gobernador de la isla de Cuba, y a sus alcaldes y regidores, 1524, AGI, Just., leg. 49, no. 1. For more than twenty years thereafter Altamirano served as the principal administrator and legal agent for Cortés' properties and interests in New Spain (see Chapter 6).

35. Ignacio López Rayón, ed., *Sumario de la residencia tomada a D. Fernando Cortés,* 2 vols. (Mexico, 1852–53). These volumes record only a part of the residencia proceedings. Additional portions were printed in DII, 26–29. The entire manuscript record of the residencia preserved in AGI, Just., legs. 220–25 comprises more than 6,800 folios and covers a period extending from 1529 to the 1540s.

36. Tres cuadernos de autos contra bienes de D. Hernando Cortés, 1529, AGN, HJ, leg. 266, exp. 79. These fines included, for example, one of 32,000 pesos which was an attempt to recover funds disbursed in 1523–24 by Cortés from the royal treasury to cover expenditures for the expenses of Cristóbal de Olid's expedition to Honduras.

37. Vasco de Puga, ed., *Provisiones, cédulas, instrucciones para el gobierno de la Nueva España* (Facsimile reprint ed., Madrid, 1945), pp. 82–109.

38. AGN, HJ, leg. 289, exp. 100; and AGI, Just., leg. 108, no. 1.

39. These are the disagreements discussed in the preceding paragraphs.

40. AGI, Just., leg. 113, no. 5.

41. This is suggested by Cortés' contention that the Audiencia took this town from him while he was in Spain (Don Antonio Serrano de Cardona, vezino y regidor de la ciudad de Temistitan [Tenochtitlan] México de la Nueva España contra Don Hernando de [sic] Cortés, Marqués del Valle, sobre las heredades de Cuernavaca, 1532, AGI, Just., leg. 118, no. 2; and DII, 12:5–31) and the testimony in a suit between Cortés and the fiscal in 1533 over Acapistla's sujetos indicating that Cortés took that town from Solís and Holguín after his return from Spain on the basis of his Marquesado grant of 1529 rather than their agreements made in 1528 (*Nuevos documentos,* pp. 143–45).

42. AGN, HJ, leg. 289, exp. 100.

43. Ibid.

44. *Ced. Cort.,* pp. 103–5 (*see* List of Abbreviations).

45. Manuel Orozco y Berra, *Historia de la dominación española en México,* 4 vols. (Mexico, 1938), 2:29–31; and Lucas Alamán, *Disertaciones sobre la historia de la republica mejicana,* 3 vols. (Mexico, 1942), 2:29–30.

46. *Ced. Cort.,* pp. 108–22 and DIU, 9:386–99, 439–47. For a discussion of the crown's position on the encomienda in this period see Zavala, *La encomienda,* pp. 60–61.

47. *Ced. Cort.,* pp. 123–24, 190–92.

48. For the cedulas of July see DII, 4:572–74; 12:404–7. For the later legislation which included the conqueror's appointment as governor of the areas discovered in the Mar del Sur, see DII, 21:379 ff.; 22:289–95.

49. *Ced. Cort.,* pp. 93–95, 122–23.

50. Ibid., 140–41, 168–72, 175–89; DII, 12:406–47; 14:395–440.

51. DII, 12:990-109; 13:191-94 and *Ced. Cort.*, pp. 164-66. For the suit concerned with the costs of the Honduras expedition, see AGI, Just., leg. 185, ramo 2. The order to pay Cortés a certain part of these costs (1531) is included in *Ced. Cort.*, pp. 212-13.

52. *Ced. Cort.*, pp. 125-32, 141-64.

53. Alamán, pp. 296-310 and DII, 13:238 ff. The Pope also legitimized three of his natural children.

54. Puga, p. 75; and DII, 13:237-41.

55. *Ced. Cort.*, pp. 190-92.

56. In AGI, Just., and AGN, HJ the costs of the numerous judicial disputes in which Cortés was plaintiff or defendant in the years 1531 and following are recorded.

57. AGI, Just., leg. 108, no. 1.

58. AGI, Just., leg. 113, no. 5.

59. Bancroft, 2:412; ENE, 2:35-64; and Asiento entre Hernán Cortés y la Audiencia de Nueva España sobre los 23,000 vasallos, 1531, AGI, Patron., leg. 16, no. 2, ramo 30.

60. AGI, Patron. 16, no. 2, ramo 30. Additional data pertinent to the agreement are included in DII, 14:329-47; and DII, 12:514-20.

61. *Nuevos documentos*, pp. 123-69; Proceso del Marqués del Valle contra los licenciados Salmerón y otros sobre lo de Totolapa, 1536, AGN, HJ, leg. 409, exp. 25; ENE, 2:208-21; and PNE, 3:7.

62. Confirmación que S.M. hizo al . . . Marqués del Valle de las 22 villas y lugares que tiene en la Nueva España sin limitación de vasallos . . . , Toledo, 16 Dec., 1560, LC, Hark., vol. 42 (*see* Appendix 5).

63. Proceso del Marqués del Valle con el fiscal sobre la suplicación que interpuso de lo que se cometió al Doctor Quesada en razón de la visita del Marquesado, 1550, AGI, Just., leg. 201B, no. 2, ramo 4.

Chapter 3: Tribute

1. In addition to the materials specifically cited, this discussion of tribute and the encomienda is based upon the encomienda studies of Zavala and Simpson; chapters 4 and 8 of Gibson, *The Aztecs;* and the introduction to Volume 4 of the Scholes-Adams documentary series relating to colonial Mexico (see the Bibliography for complete references).

2. Cortés, *Cartas*, p. 144.

3. Ibid.

4. Ibid., p. 54.

5. See *El libro de las tasaciones de pueblos de la Nueva España. Siglo XVI*, ed. Francisco González de Cossío (Mexico, 1952). This volume records tasaciones for many of New Spain's encomienda and crown towns for the decades between 1530 and 1560. A number of fixed tribute assessments for crown towns were established by the First Audiencia in 1529 (Razón de las ciudades y provincias y lugares que se aplicaron a S.M. para que le vivan y contribugan [sic] por el presidente y oidores de México á 11 Mayo de 1529 y el tante en que se comencieron, 1529, AGI, Contaduría, leg. 657, exp. 4, ramo 4).

6. AGI, Just., leg. 108, no. 1; and AGN, HJ, leg. 265, exp. 5.

7. AGI, Just., leg. 108, no. 1; and AGI, Just., leg. 118, no. 2.

8. Charles Gibson, *The Aztecs Under Spanish Rule. A History of the Indians of the Valley of México, 1519-1810* (Stanford, 1964), pp. 182 and 196. Gibson demonstrates that both calpixques and tequitlatos fell into the general category of tribute collectors and guardian-managers of properties. Tlapixques were also in this category but seem to

have performed different services, supervising labor as opposed to collecting and managing tribute production and payment.

9. AGN, HJ, leg. 265, exp. 5. See Appendix 3.

10. AGI, Just., 108, no. 1.

11. Relación de los tributos de los pueblos del estado del Marqués del Valle, 1550, AGN, HJ, leg. 98, exp. 6; HJ, leg. 289, exp. 100; and HJ, leg. 289, exp. 102. A pierna has been defined as one strip of cloth, varying from twenty-two to thirty inches in width and from one yard to six yards in length, such as was woven on the backstrap looms common to the native peoples of New Spain (Woodrow W. Borah and Sherburne F. Cook, *Price Trends of Some Basic Commodities in Central Mexico, 1531–1570* [Berkeley and Los Angeles, 1958], pp. 26–27). When Serrano formally reclaimed possession of Cuernavaca in May 1529 the Indians brought him a token number of mantas and a *joya de oro* described as "un rosario de cuentas de oro baxo que tenía setenta cuentas del tamaño de avellanas poco mas o menos" (AGI, Just., leg. 118, no. 2). The items of gold jewelry delivered to Cortés with the mantas four times each year were probably of a similar kind.

12. AGN, HJ, leg. 289, exp. 102.

13. A carga was eventually defined as one-half a fanega or fifty Castilian pounds (about 50.7 pounds). Borah and Cook, *Price Trends,* pp. 10–11.

14. AGN, HJ, leg. 289, exp. 100.

15. Ibid. The interrogatory used in questioning witnesses and some of the attorneys' argumentation suggest that these labor services were performed for Burgos. No witnesses, however, attested to either the truth or the falsity of this data.

16. These quarterly payments were defined in the same terms as those of Cuernavaca.

17. Much of the cotton utilized in weaving the mantas must have been secured through trade (primarily with Cuernavaca, Oaxtepec, and their sujetos) as little was produced in the Yautepec-Tepoztlan area (none by Tepoztlan and its sujetos). AGN, HJ, leg. 289, exp. 100 and HJ, leg. 289, exp. 102.

18. AGN, HJ, leg. 289, exp. 100 and HJ, leg. 289, exp. 102.

19. The exact location of these mines is unknown although the Yopes were peoples of the preconquest señorío de Yopitzinco which was located in the central part of the present state of Guerrero.

20. AGN, HJ, leg. 289, exp. 100 and HJ, leg. 289, exp. 102.

21. Ibid.

22. AGN, HJ, leg. 265, exp. 5. See Appendix 3.

23. See Appendix 3. The total figure was computed by using the 6,000 pesos de oro de minas as the annual revenues for three years (1522–25); 5,040 pesos de oro de minas for two years (1526–28); and 3,120 pesos de oro de minas for one year (1529). The figure for 1526–28 allows for the loss of Tepoztlan and Yautepec which in the early 1530s contributed about 16 percent of the total tribute collected; the figure for 1529 allows for the loss of all the encomiendas but Cuernavaca with its 52 percent of the total figure (based on the early 1530s, AGN, HJ, leg. 265, exp. 5; HJ, leg. 289, exp. 100; and HJ, leg. 289, exp. 102).

24. See Chapter 2 for a discussion of the circumstances which produced cessation of these revenues.

25. AGI, Just., leg. 108, no. 1 and Just. 113, no. 5.

26. AGN, HJ, leg. 289, exp. 100.

27. AGN, HJ, leg. 289, exp. 100 and HJ, leg. 289, exp. 102; and ENE, 3:120–23.

28. AGN, HJ, leg. 289, exp. 100 and HJ, leg. 289, exp. 102.

29. Ibid. Apparently when Cortés resided in Cuernavaca in the years 1526–28 he lived in the house formerly occupied by the señor of the town. That house evidently

made way, at least in part, for the new palace constructed by Cortés (Proceso de Doña María, viuda muger que fué de Don Hernando de Cuernavaca, contra el Marqués sobre las cañas y tributo de Amanalco y otras cosas, 1551, AGN, HJ, leg. 398, exp. 1 and HJ, leg. 293, exp. 144).

30. Razón de ciertos pueblos del Marqués del Valle, 1536, AGN, HJ, leg. 377, exp. 1.

31. AGN, HJ, leg. 289, exp. 100. These specialists evidently were carry-overs from the preconquest period. According to Indian witnesses they paid no tribute and in fact were supported by the community in return for their painting.

32. AGN, HJ, leg. 377, exp. 1; DII, 14:142–47; and ENE, 3:120–23. The medalla de oro was described by the principales of Oaxtepec as "que las cuesta 4 cargas de mantas y 2 mantas que dan al platero que le haze" (AGN, HJ, leg. 377, exp. 1).

33. AGN, HJ, leg. 289, exp. 100; HJ, leg. 289, exp. 102; and *Nuevos documentos relativos a los bienes de Hernán Cortés, 1547-1947* (Mexico, 1946), pp. 198–202. The prices suggested in these sources by Cortés' agents and witnesses were 4½ to 5 pesos a carga for mantas, 10 pesos a carga for colchas, and 25 pesos a carga for camisas and naguas. The peso de oro común was worth about 300 maravedís in this period as compared with 450 maravedís for the peso de oro de minas. In 1535–36 Viceroy Mendoza set the peso de oro común at 272 maravedís.

34. Ibid.

35. DII, 14:142–47," . . . dan al dicho Marqués comida para su dispensa y casa que es menester en cada un día de la semana que les cabe a servir, que es de dos semanas, la una, y la otra semana dan los otros pueblos del valle [Oaxtepec, Acapistla, Tepoztlan, and Yautepec] de la manera que la comida de todo el año esta partida por medio e una semana la da sola Cuernavaca, y la otra todos los pueblos del valle . . ."

36. AGN, HJ, leg. 289, exp. 100; HJ, leg. 289, exp. 102; and HJ, leg. 377, exp. 1.

37. Ibid.

38. DII, 14:142–47; AGN, HJ, leg. 289, exp. 100; HJ, leg. 289, exp. 102; and HJ, leg. 377, exp. 1.

39. AGN, HJ, leg. 289, exp. 100; HJ, leg. 289, exp. 102; and HJ, leg. 377, exp. 1.

40. DII, 14:142–47; ENE, 3:1–4; AGN, HJ, leg. 289, exp. 100; HJ, leg. 289, exp. 102; and HJ, leg. 377, exp. 1.

41. Ibid.

42. Gibson, *The Aztecs*, Appendix 4, p. 448 and Appendix 5, p. 452.

43. DII, 14:142–47. The principales declared that in addition to the tribute they paid and the labor services they performed they also gave Cortés' criados, when they needed them, wet nurses for their children. They said they took some to Juan Altamirano's wife and five to the wife of Juan de Salamanca. In addition they had supplied to Martín Sánchez (calpixques in Yautepec) "dos indias para su servicio."

44. ENE, 3:1–4.

45. ENE, 3:120–23. Mayorga was stationed at the Dominican missionary-church near Oaxtepec. From time to time, for almost twenty years after this date, he appeared in lawsuits as a witness friendly to the Indians and their various causes.

46. *Ced. Cort.*, pp. 251–52.

47. Providencias del gobernador del estado [del Marqués del Valle], 1539-1630, AGN, HJ, leg. 201; HJ, leg. 289, exp. 100; HJ, leg. 289, exp. 102; and Proceso de Oaxtepec y Amilpas contra el Marqués del Valle sobre que no puedan cumplir [con sus tributos], 1551, AGN, HJ, leg. 418, exp. 1.

48. AGN, HJ, leg. 377, exp. 1.

49. Ibid.

50. Relación de los pueblos que estan en la cabecera del Marqués del Valle y de lo

tributan, 1535–37(?), AGI, Patron., leg. 17, ramo 21; AGN, HJ, leg. 201; HJ, leg. 289, exp. 100; HJ, leg. 289, exp. 102; HJ, leg. 377, exp. 1; and HJ, leg. 418, exp. 1.

51. Gibson, *The Aztecs*, Appendix 4, p. 445 and Appendix 5, p. 452.

52. The data employed in preparing Table 2 were drawn from the manuscript items cited in n. 50 and from material in *Nuevos documentos,* pp. 198–212.

53. See Table 2.

54. AGI, Patron., leg. 17, ramo 21; AGN, HJ, leg. 201; HJ, leg. 289, exp. 100; HJ, leg. 289, exp. 102; HJ, leg. 377, exp. 1; and HJ, leg. 418, exp. 1.

55. Item prices utilized in establishing this estimated monthly figure were taken from several manuscript sources cited in n. 38, and from Borah and Cook, *Price Trends.*

56. AGN, HJ, leg. 289, exp. 100 and HJ, leg. 289, exp. 102.

57. *Nuevos documentos,* pp. 31–32; AGN, HJ, leg. 289, exp. 100; and HJ, leg. 289, exp. 102.

58. See Chapter 4, in which the labor services performed and the compensation received for them are discussed.

59. AGN, HJ, leg. 289, exp. 100 and HJ, leg. 289, exp. 102.

60. AGN, HJ, leg. 289, exp. 100; HJ, leg. 289, exp. 102; HJ, leg. 418, exp. 1; and AGI, Just., leg. 201B, no. 2, ramo 4.

61. See Tables 2 and 13.

62. AGN, HJ, leg. 418, exp. 1.

63. See Table 13.

64. AGN, HJ, leg. 289, exp. 100; HJ, leg. 289, exp. 102; HJ, leg. 418, exp. 1; and AGI, Just., leg. 201B, no. 2, ramo 4.

Chapter 4: Labor

1. See Chapter 2.

2. AGN, HJ, leg. 289, exp. 100; HJ, leg. 289, exp. 102; HJ, leg. 293, exp. 144; and HJ, leg. 377, exp. 1. The buildings and lands acquired were expropriated, purchased, and rented from local and Aztecan nobles, officials, communities, and institutions. For further discussion see Chapter 5.

3. See Table 3. AGN, HJ, leg. 289, exp. 100; HJ, leg. 289, exp. 102; HJ, leg. 293, exp. 144; and HJ, leg. 377, exp. 1.

4. Ibid.

5. AGN, HJ, leg. 289, exp. 100 and HJ, leg. 289, exp. 102.

6. AGN, HJ, leg. 289, exp. 100; HJ, leg. 289, exp. 102; HJ, leg. 377, exp. 1; ENE, 3:1–4; and DII, 14:142–47.

7. AGN, HJ, leg. 289, exp. 100; HJ, leg. 289, exp. 102; and HJ, leg. 377, exp. 1.

8. *Ced. Cort.,* pp. 103–5.

9. AGN, HJ, leg. 289, exp. 100; HJ, leg. 289, exp. 102; and HJ, leg. 377, exp. 1.

10. Ibid.

11. AGN, HJ, leg. 201. This delivery may have been part of an exchange of sugar for Negro slaves between Cortés and the Seville-based firm of Marín and Lomelín (see Ruth Pike, *Enterprise and Adventure: The Genoese in Sevilla and The Opening of the New World* (New York, 1966), pp. 65–67.

12. AGN, HJ, leg. 201.

13. Ibid.

14. See Woodrow W. Borah and Sherburne F. Cook, *Price Trends of Some Basic Commodities in Central Mexico, 1531–1570* (Berkeley and Los Angeles, 1958), and Sherburne

F. Cook and Lesley Byrd Simpson, *The Population of Central Mexico in the Sixteenth Century* (Berkeley and Los Angeles, 1948).

15. See Silvio Zavala, *Los esclavos indios en Nueva España* (Mexico, 1967), pp. 2–25 and Hojas sueltas [del estado del Marqués del Valle], n.d., AGN, HJ, leg. 107, exp. 31. In the last of these, purchases (by the manager of the Tlaltenango mill) of two convict laborers at later dates (1548 and 1558) are recorded. See Chapter 3 for additional discussion of the slaves secured by Cortés.

16. Zavala, *Los esclavos,* pp. 26, 27, 54 and Proceso de Serrano de Cardona contra el Marqués del Valle sobre ciertas pesos . . . e sobre la madera, 1531, AGN, HJ, leg. 9, exp. 31.

17. Ibid.

18. *Doc. inéd.,* pp. 225–99 (*see* Appendix 5).

19. AGN, HJ, leg. 9, exp. 31.

20. *Doc. inéd.,* pp. 225-99.

21. Ibid.

22. A brief discussion of the establishment and early history of Atlacomulco mill follows in Chapter 5.

23. Gonzalo Aguirre Beltrán, "El trabajo del indio comparado con el del negro en Nueva España," *México Agrario,* 4 (1942): 203–7 and Zavala, *Los esclavos,* pp. 66–75.

24. Fernando B. Sandoval, *La industria del azúcar en Nueva España* (Mexico, 1951), pp. 51–53 and Relación de las haciendas y granjerías que el Marqués tiene en Nueva España y en tierras de su estado, 1556, AGN, HJ, leg. 267, exp. 26. The relación lists 150 Negro slaves, including children, 50 Indian wage earners and no Indian slaves as employed at Tlaltenango in 1556.

25. Gonzalo Aguirre Beltrán, "Comercio de esclavos de México por 1542," *Afroamerica* 1 (1945): 25–40; Gonzalo Aguirre Beltrán, "The Slave Trade in Mexico," *Hispanic American Historical Review* 24 (1944): 421–31; Wilbur Zelinsky, "The Historical Geography of the Negro Population of Latin America," *Journal of Negro History* 34 (1942): 153–221; and Peter Boyd-Bowman, "Negro Slaves in Early Colonial Mexico," *The Americas* 26 (1969): 134–51.

26. Pike, p. 65.

27. Pike, pp. 65–67 and Rubén García, *Aspectos desconocidos del aventurero Hernán Cortés* (Mexico, 1956), pp. 28–31.

28. Testimonio y probanza sobre cien esclavos entregados al Marquesado por L. Lomelín, 1542, AGN, HJ, leg. 247, exp. 8.

29. Cuentas de los azucares y algodon que ha recibido García Morón para la contratación. Ingenio de Cuernavaca, 1540–43, AGN, HJ, leg. 235, exp. 10, 11.

30. García, *Aspectos,* pp. 70–72 and AGN, HJ, leg. 201.

31. AGN, HJ, leg. 9, exp. 31.

32. *Doc. inéd.,* pp. 225-99.

33. Ibid.

34. Ibid. This Morisco slave may have been of North African origins (Arabic-Berber) as he claimed Cafi as his original home.

35. See Chapter 2.

36. AGN, HJ, leg. 9, exp. 31 and AGI, Just., leg. 118, no. 2. Among these employees were Pedro Gómez, Juan Gonzalez, Nuño de Burgos, Diego de Rivera, Francisco Rodríguez, Hernán Rodríguez, and Francisco Baeza. At times the last two of these were also members of Cortés' management staff (See Chapters 2 and 6).

37. AGN, HJ, leg. 9, exp. 31; HJ, leg. 289, exp. 100; HJ, leg. 289, exp. 102; AGI, Just., leg. 118, no. 2; and *Doc. inéd.,* pp. 225–99.

38. AGI, Just., leg. 201B, no. 2, ramo 4 and *Doc. inéd.,* pp. 225–99.

128 NOTES

39. AGN, HJ, leg. 201. For example, in August 1556 the Marquesado's governor-administrator arranged a one-year contract with one Pedro Hernández Rey, a labrador or cultivator from Castilblanco in Castile. The contract specified that Hernández Rey would provide for his food and lodging as he sowed "trigo y otras semillas" or wheat and other seeds in such areas as he was directed. At the end of the contract period (August 10, 1557) he was to receive a wage-payment of 100 pesos de oro de minas.

40. These figures are based upon the sale prices of Negro slaves noted in preceding paragraphs.

41. Zavala, *Los esclavos*, pp. 66–75.

Chapter 5: Land

1. For this consideration of pre- and postconquest land utilization in New Spain exclusive of the Morelos area (for which specific citations are included) reference was made to the following: Alfonso Caso, "La tenencia de la tierra entre los antiguos mexicanos," *Memoria de el Colegio nacional* 4 (1958–60): 29–54; François Chevalier, *La formación de las grandes latifundias en México* (Mexico, 1956); Charles Gibson, "The Aztec Aristocracy in Colonial Mexico," *Comparative Studies in Society and History* 2 (1960): 169–96 and *The Aztecs Under Spanish Rule: A History of the Indians of the Valley of Mexico, 1519–1810* (Stanford, 1964); and Paul Kirchoff, "Land Tenure in Ancient Mexico: A Preliminary Sketch," *Revista mexicana de estudios antropológicos* 14 (1954–55): 351–61.

2. Gibson, *The Aztecs*, pp. 257–64.

3. Chevalier, pp. 18–26.

4. *Ced. Cort.*, pp. 103–5.

5. AGN, HJ, leg. 289, exp. 100; HJ, leg. 289, exp. 102; and HJ, leg. 377, exp. 1.

6. AGN, HJ, leg. 377, exp. 1.

7. *Códice Municipal de Cuernavaca. Anonimo del siglo XVI* (Mexico, 1951). See Appendix 2.

8. AGN, HJ, leg. 289, exp. 100 and HJ, leg. 289, exp. 102.

9. See Chapter 1.

10. AGN, HJ, leg. 289, exp. 100 and HJ, leg. 289, exp. 102.

11. See Chapter 2.

12. AGI, Just., leg. 118, no. 2.

13. Ibid.

14. See Chapter 2.

15. AGI, Just., leg. 118, no. 2 and AGN, HJ, leg. 9, exp. 31.

16. El Marqués del Valle con Antonio de la Cardena y Isabel de Hojeda sobre ciertos aprovechamientos de leña y agua de un ingenio [Atlacomulco], 1547, AGI, Just., leg. 146, no. 4.

17. AGI, Just., leg. 146, no. 4 and AGN, HJ, leg. 9, exp. 31.

18. For instance, Don Martín Cortés, Marqués del Valle con Isabel de Ojeda, viuda vecina de la ciudad de México, sobre el ingenio de azúcar de Atlacomulco, 1568, AGI, Just., leg. 174, no. 3.

19. AGN, HJ, leg. 398, exp. 1 and HJ, leg. 293, exp. 144.

20. AGN, HJ, leg. 293, exp. 144.

21. Ibid.

22. ENE, 3:120–23; DII, 17:142–47; and AGN, HJ, leg. 289, exp. 100.

23. AGN, HJ, leg. 398, exp. 1.

24. Fernando B. Sandoval, *La industria del azúcar en Nueva España* (Mexico, 1951),

pp. 90–91 and Cortés Papers, Conway Collection of Hispanic Documents, no. 95-2a, Gilcrease Institute, Tulsa, Oklahoma.

25. *Doc. inéd.*, pp. 225-99.

26. Woodrow W. Borah, *Silk Raising in Colonial Mexico* (Berkeley and Los Angeles, 1943), pp. 18–19, 72.

27. See n. 24.

28. AGI, Just., leg. 118, no. 2.

29. See preceding paragraphs in this chapter and, for a discussion of the agrarian goods Cortés received as tribute from his Morelos encomiendas, see Chapter 3.

30. Borah, *Silk*, pp. 5–6 and Sandoval, pp. 23–27.

31. ENE, 1:136–52 and AGN, HJ, leg. 289, exp. 100; HJ, leg. 289, exp. 102.

32. Ibid.

33. See preceding paragraphs in this chapter.

34. *Doc. inéd.*, pp. 284–86.

35. AGN, HJ, leg. 289, exp. 100 and *Doc. inéd.*, p. 281.

36. AGN, HJ, leg. 289, exp. 100; HJ, leg. 289, exp. 102; HJ, leg. 377, exp. 1; and Borah, *Silk*, p. 18.

37. Borah, *Silk*, p. 19 and *Doc. inéd.*, pp. 291–97.

38. AGN, HJ, leg. 289, exp. 100 and Borah, *Silk*, p. 19.

39. *Doc. inéd.*, pp. 291–97.

40. Borah, *Silk*, p. 19 and Sandoval, p. 27.

41. Sandoval, pp. 27–29.

42. See preceding paragraphs in this chapter.

43. See Chapter 2.

44. AGN, HJ, leg. 377, exp. 1 and AGI, Just., leg. 108, no. 1.

45. See preceding paragraphs in this chapter.

46. *Doc. inéd.*, p. 242 and Sandoval, pp. 27–29.

47. AGN, HJ, leg. 235, exp. 10:11.

48. Ibid. These account sheets kept by Morón show that the sugar was delivered in arrobas and Castilian pounds by types of sugar: *blanco* (refined white), *mascabado* (raw and unrefined), and *espumas y panelas* (slightly refined and brown). The price of azucar blanco is listed as three pesos de oro de minas per arroba with three arrobas of azucar mascabado equal to two of azucar blanco, and two of espumas y panelas equal to one of azucar blanco.

49. See Chapter 2.

50. Relación de los testimonios de azucares que parece haber venido de la Nueva España hechas desde 1 Sep. 1544 hasta 12 Sep. 1548 y ha recibido los factores de Leonardo Lomelín en el dicho tiempo, 1548, AGN, HJ, leg. 228, exp. 3 and Ruth Pike, *Enterprise and Adventure: The Genoese in Sevilla and the Opening of The New World* (New York, 1966), pp. 65–67.

51. Autos seguidos por la parte de Marqués del Valle contra Leonardo Lomelín sobre azucares, 1548, AGN, HJ, leg. 335, exp. 1 and Pike, pp. 65–67.

52. AGN, HJ, leg. 228, exp. 3.

53. Comparison of the cultivated acreage supporting the Atlacomulco mill with that supporting the Tlaltenango operation provided a basis for the computation of this figure (see Table 11).

54. AGN, HJ, leg. 377, exp. 1.

55. AGN, HJ, leg. 289, exp. 100.

56. See Table 11.

57. *Doc. inéd.*, pp. 246, 248, 268, 285, 288–91.

Chapter 6: Management and Revenues

1. ENE, 14:148–55; *Códice Municipal de Cuernavaca. Anonimo del siglo XVI* (Mexico, 1951), see Appendix 2; and AGI, Just., leg. 108, no. 1. The Francisco de la Peña mentioned here may have been one Diego de la Peña who was acting in 1536 as attorney for the señor of Cuernavaca, Don Hernando, in a suit with Cortés (AGN, HJ, 293, exp. 144).

2. See Chapter 1.

3. *Códice municipal* (see Appendix 2).

4. AGN, HJ, leg. 293, exp. 144. See Chapter 5.

5. *Códice municipal* (see Appendix 2).

6. El Marqués del Valle sobre residuos de los pueblos que el tenía al tiempo que salia para Castilla, 1531, AGN, HJ, leg. 264, exp. 6 and AGI, Just., leg. 108, no. 1. Also see Chapters 2 and 5.

7. *Nuevos documentos relativos a los bienes de Hernán Cortés, 1547–1947* (Mexico, 1946), pp. 97–98 and AGN, HJ, leg. 108, no. 1.

8. ENE, 1:136–52; AGI, Just., leg. 108, no. 1, Just., leg. 146, no. 4, and Just., leg. 185, ramo 2; and AGN, HJ, leg. 264, exp. 6 and HJ, leg. 265, exp. 5.

9. AGI, Just., leg. 118, no. 2 and Just., leg. 185, ramo 2.

10. See Chapters 2 and 5.

11. Ibid.

12. See Chapters 3, 4, and 5.

13. AGN, HJ, leg. 289, exp. 100 and AGI, Just., leg. 118, no. 2.

14. AGN, HJ, leg. 9, exp. 31 and HJ, leg. 289, exp. 102; DII, 14:142–47; and *Doc. inéd.*, p. 275.

15. DII, 14:142–47; AGI, Just., leg. 118, no. 2; and AGN, HJ, leg. 289, exp. 102.

16. AGN, HJ, leg. 9, exp. 31; HJ, leg. 289, exp. 100; and HJ, leg. 289, exp. 102.

17. AGN, HJ, leg. 9, exp. 31 and AGI, Just., leg. 118, no. 2. See Chapters 2 and 5 for a discussion of the Serrano affair and Chapters 3, 4, and 5 for details pertinent to the construction of Cortés' house in Cuernavaca.

18. See Chapter 2.

19. Información recibide en México a pedimiento de Hernán Cortés, sobre no ser cierta la calumnia que se le imponia de haber despuesto que se ausentasen de sus tierras los Indios que debian contar para el completo de los 23,000 vasallos, 1532, AGI, Patron., leg. 16, no. 2, ramo 31; AGI, Just., leg. 118, no. 2; and AGN, HJ, leg. 9, exp. 31.

20. *Nuevos documentos*, pp. 124–25; DII, 14:142–47; AGI, Just., leg. 118, no. 2; and AGN, HJ, leg. 264, exp. 6 and HJ, leg. 398, exp. 1.

21. DII, 14:142–47; AGI, Just., leg. 118, no. 2; and AGN, HJ, leg. 264, exp. 6.

22. See Chapters 3, 4, and 5.

23. AGN, HJ, leg. 289, exp. 100 and HJ, leg. 289, exp. 102.

24. *Doc. inéd.*, pp. 196–224.

25. Ibid. Subsequent paragraphs provide discussion of the new contract.

26. Bancroft, 2:419–27. Those aspects of Cortés' Mar del Sur expeditions which are pertinent to the development of the Marquesado in Morelos are discussed in Chapter 2.

27. Bancroft, 2:419–27.

28. *Doc. inéd.*, pp. 212–13, ". . . la posesión e señorío real e corporal de las mis villas e pueblos jurisdición, que yo he y tengo e me pertenecen, según que en el privilegio que de Su Majestad tengo se guarde con la jurisdición civil e criminal, alta e baxa, mero mixto imperio, e con los oficios, pechos e derechos e tributos de los dichos pueblos; e para que sobre ello e lo dello dependiente o anexo e conexo, pueda hacer e haga las diligencias que convengan e le parecieren necesarias; . . ."

29. Ibid., pp. 213–19.

30. AGN, HJ, leg. 377, exp. 1.

31. Sec Chapter 5.

32. Proceso de los indios de Cuernavaca contra Juan de Carasa sobre que les apremia la parte de la Marquesa que hagan servicios personales, 1547, AGN, HJ, leg. 276, exp. 84. Also see Chapters 3 and 4.

33. AGN, HJ, leg. 289, exp. 100 and HJ, leg. 289, exp. 102.

34. *Doc. inéd.*, pp. 196–224.

35. Ibid.

36. Ibid.

37. AGN, HJ, leg. 289, exp. 100.

38. Poder de Don Hernando Cortés, a favor de su primo Licenciado Juan Altamirano, 1539, AGN, HJ, leg. 201, exp. 1.

39. AGN, HJ, leg. 289, exp. 100 and HJ, leg. 289, exp. 102; AGI, Just., leg. 146, no. 4, and Just., leg. 201B, no. 2, ramo 4.

40. AGN, HJ, leg. 289, exp. 100; HJ, leg. 289, exp. 102 and AGI, Just., leg. 146, no. 4.

41. See Chapter 5.

42. See Chapters 3, 4, and 5.

43. AGN, HJ, leg. 235, exp. 10, 11.

44. The suit prompted sequestration of Lomelín's properties in Mexico City and Veracruz as well as some goods (mostly sugar) which he had already transferred to others for shipment and sale elsewhere (see Chapter 5 for additional details). Among Lomelín's agents and sometimes partners were Simón Pasqua, Antonio Fesco (or Fiesco), Pablo Bernan, Nicolás Caçona (or Ascona), Juan Bautista de Marín, Leonardo de Vergara, and Martin de Pisuela. All of these men except the last two, Vergara and Pisuela, were clearly identified as Genoese, and all but Marín, as *estantes* (temporary residents) of Veracruz or Mexico City (AGN, HJ, leg. 335, exp. 1).

45. AGN, HJ, leg. 418, exp. 1. Also see Chapters 3 and 4.

46. Sec Chapters 3 and 4.

47. AGN, HJ, leg. 276, exp. 84.

48. El fiscal de Su Majestad contra el Marqués del Valle y sus mayordomos y criados sobre los tributos demasiados y malos tratamientos del Marquesado, 1544, LC, Hark., 6 and AGN, HJ, leg. 276, exp. 84. Also see Chapters 3, 4, and 7.

49. See Chapter 7.

50. See Chapter 2.

51. AGN, HJ, leg. 9, exp. 31. In 1531, for instance, Cortés argued that his alcalde mayor (in Cuernavaca) was not subordinate to the audiencia. The crown and council responded negatively to the argument and ruled accordingly.

52. See Altamirano's assigned responsibilities as governor of the Marquesado (discussed in preceding paragraphs). Sr. Bernardo García Martínez treats of the señorial rights enjoyed by Cortés and his heirs as well as the status of the Marquesado as a señorío in his *El Marquesado del Valle: Tres siglos de régimen señorial en Nueva España* (Mexico, 1969). His contentions as to both matters for the years 1522–47 are not those reflected in this, or the preceding and subsequent paragraphs of this chapter; that is, the señorial rights enjoyed by Cortés were more limited than he suggests, and the Marquesado was only in the broadest sense a señorío. Cortés enjoyed no rights of land assignment, tribute assessment, or judicial privilege and power which were not circumscribed—subjected to appellate review not by the crown and council in Spain but by the governing agencies in New Spain—or denied.

53. See Chapter 2.

54. Ibid.

55. According to Licenciado Altamirano, who reported in 1551 as to the holdings of

the Conqueror's heir, Don Martín, the Marquesado included some "villas y lugares por merced de su majestad con la jurisdición civil y criminal como es Cuernavaca y Guastepeque [Oaxtepec] y Yautepec [including Acapistla] y Tepuztlan [Tepoztlan], y Teguantepeque [Tehuantepec and probably including nearby Jalapa] y otros pueblos" and others also "por merced de su majestad" but "sin jurisdición . . . como Estotuca [Toluca], Guaxaca [Oaxaca], Etla [in the Oaxaca area], Cuylapa [also in the Oaxaca area], Cuyoacan [Coyoacan] y otros" (AGN, HJ, leg. 289, exp. 100). Also see the territorial and señorial definition of the entire Marquesado in García Martínez, *El Marquesado*.

56. See Chapter 3.

57. See Chapter 3 for discussion of the tribute revenue figure cited. The figure indicated as that of the revenues obtained by Cortés from the sale of agricultural goods produced by his Morelos landholdings is an estimate. It is based upon occasional citations as to amounts of goods produced and the prices for which those goods sold in the various documentary sources cited in Chapter 5.

58. See n. 57. In computing the figure shown for the profits derived from the sale of agricultural goods, the increase in the amount of land owned and used by Cortés in the Morelos area after 1531 was given consideration (see Chapter 5).

59. See Table 2 and nn. 57 and 58 above.

60. See Table 2 and nn. 57 and 58 above.

61. See Chapters 3 and 5.

62. See Chapters 3 and 4.

63. The gross revenue figures employed here and in preceding paragraphs are, again, estimates. Of the several items utilized in developing that estimate, the tribute revenue figures were the most numerous and reliable.

64. In several instances Cortés, his agents and, later, Don Martín and those associated with him in the administration of the Marquesado noted profit fluctuations of the sort suggested.

65. AGN, HJ, leg. 98, exp. 6.

66. These figures and percentages are, again, estimates.

67. The estimated share of the Marquesado's total gross revenues produced by its Morelos portion was taken from the income-expense accounts in AGN, HJ, leg. 98, exp. 6. Those data indicate that the Morelos properties produced about 54 percent of the Marquesado's revenues in 1550–51 and about 59 percent in 1551–52 (see concluding paragraphs of Chapter 7).

68. Arthur S. Aiton, *Antonio de Mendoza, First Viceroy of New Spain* (Durham, North Carolina, 1927), pp. 35–36.

69. Hayward Keniston, *Francisco de Los Cobos, Secretary of the Emperor Charles V* (Pittsburgh, 1958), pp. 317, 419–22.

Chapter 7: The Morelos Marquesado in 1547

1. These population figures are drawn from a census of the Morelos encomiendas made in 1551. They are not completely accurate for the population of these encomiendas four years earlier or even for the time of the census. They do seem adequate for use as a probable minimum estimate, however, as no plagues or other disasters appear to have diminished that population in the years 1547–51. Doubtless not included (as attorneys for the Marquesado argued, although with apparent exaggeration) were many of the

mayeques of the señores and principales of the several cabecera and important sujeto communities as well as some of the tributary and labor service-providing macehuales excluded ("hidden") from the count by their Indian overlords. The census reveals the following town-by-town population data:

(1) Cuernavaca—tributary vassals, 9,018; total population, 33,130, of which 18,370 were adults and 14,760 were children.

(2) Yautepec—tributary vassals, 4,211; total population, 13,828; adults, 7,676; children, 6,152.

(3) Tepoztlan—tributary vassals, 2,438; total population, 7,870; adults, 4,135; children, 3,735.

(4) Acapistla—tributary vassals, 4,861; total population, 16,461; adults, 8,756; children, 7,705.

(5) Oaxtepec—tributary vassals, 2,508; total population, 5,763; adults, 3,341; children, 2,422.

(6) Las Amilpas (made up of settlements which in 1547 were sujetos of Oaxtepec)—tributary vassals, 2,430; total population, 4,800; adults, 2,800; children, 2,000.

These figures, if compared with those assigned to the Cuernavaca towns in 1519 (see Chapter 1), even allowing for the towns subsequently split off from the old Aztec provinces of Oaxtepec and Cuernavaca (see Chapter 2), suggest either a shocking death rate or a gross error in the Borah-Cook computation of the 1519 figures. The census of 1551 is recorded in AGN, HJ, leg. 289, exp. 100; HJ, leg. 289, exp. 102 and AGI, Just., leg. 201B, no. 2, ramo 4.

2. The details of the buildings owned by Cortés in the Morelos area, their use, and pertinent contents were taken from the inventory made of Cortés' Cuernavaca properties in 1549 (*Doc. inéd.*, pp. 225–99).

3. Although no data presently available describe the palace furniture other than a few items such as chairs and trunks, no doubt it included numerous chairs, benches, cushions, and tables.

4. G. R. G. Conway, *Postrera voluntad y testamento de Hernán Cortés, Marqués del Valle* (Mexico, 1940), p. 11.

5. Ibid., pp. 44–47.

6. Ibid., pp. 37–38.

7. AGN, HJ, leg. 276, exp. 84. See Chapters 3, 4, and 6 for discussion of this lawsuit.

8. AGI, Just., leg. 146, no. 4. Cadena purchased one-half of Isabel's interest in the mill in an agreement concluded November 7, 1546, securing thereby a three-sevenths share in its ownership. See Chapter 5 for some discussion of the Ojeda-Cortés dispute over the mill.

9. See n. 8 above. One part of that litigation is included in AGI, Just., leg. 174, no. 3.

10. See Chapters 3, 4, and 6 for discussion of the legal proceedings of 1544.

11. AGI, Just., leg. 201B, no. 2, ramo 4.

12. Ibid.

13. Los indios de Cuernavaca contra el Marqués del Valle sobre tierras, 1551, AGN, HJ, leg. 276, exp. 79; HJ, leg. 289, exp. 100; HJ, leg. 289, exp. 102; and HJ, leg. 398, exp. 1.

14. Don Martín Cortés Marqués del Valle con el fiscal de Su Majestad y el Lic. Juan Altamirano, vecino de México, sobre cumplimientos de unas cláusulas de testamiento otorgado por Don Fernando Cortés, el padre . . . 1569, AGI, Escribanía de Camara, leg. 160A, no. 4:5 and AGI, Just., leg. 146, no. 4.

15. AGN, HJ, leg. 98, exp. 6.

16. Ibid.

Chapter 8: Coda

1. Charles Gibson, *The Aztecs Under Spanish Rule. A History of the Indians of the Valley of Mexico, 1519–1810* (Stanford, 1964), pp. 263–67.

2. Jorge L. Tamayo, *Geografía general de México,* 4 vols. (Mexico, 1962), 4:64–65 (Table); and Nathan L. Whetten, *Rural Mexico* (Chicago, 1948), p. 575 (Table 1).

Appendix 1: The Cuernavaca Area in 1519

1. Except where otherwise noted, province and town names were taken from the *Códice Mendocino* and their modern equivalents supplied in parentheses. The modern locations of the towns and provinces were taken, in most instances, from R. H. Barlow, *The Extent of the Empire of the Culhua Mexica* (Berkeley and Los Angeles, 1949).

2. Barlow leaves this town as well as Molotla and Yztepec unlocated. All three were among the sujetos to Cuernavaca in postconquest times.

3. Barlow lists these four towns, nos. 17–20, (not listed in either the *Códice Mendocino* or *Matrícula de tributos*) as a part of the province of Cuernavaca. They all appear in the earliest postconquest listing of Cuernavaca's sujetos (see Appendix 4) and seem to have been a part of the province in preconquest times.

4. Determination of the number of payments made each year and the amounts of the goods included in each was made by the author in a reading of the sources cited for these data (see Chapter 3).

5. A troje is defined as a granary, and colonial sources show it as having comprised from 4,000 to 5,000 *fanegas* [see *Códice* and France V. Scholes and Eleanor B. Adams, eds., *Información sobre los tributos que los Indios pagaban a Moctezuma. Año de 1554* (Mexico, 1957)]. A fanega was a unit of dry measure of approximately 1.6 bushels.

6. Chia is defined as a species of sage in the *Diccionario de la Lengua Española* published by the Real Academia Española.

7. Huautli is defined by Robert L. Dressler, "The Pre-Columbian Cultivated Plants of Mexico," Harvard University *Botanical Museum Leaflets* 16, no. 6 (December 4, 1953): 120.

8. Xochimilçacinco and Ahuehuepan apparently no longer exist. Barlow cites evidence of their previous location. Both towns were sujetos to Oaxtepec during the 1530s and 1540s.

9. Çompanco, Tepoztla, Tehuizco, and Atlhuelic are left unlocated by Barlow. Tepoztla was probably Tepoztlan (see Chapter 1). In postconquest times Tepoztlan was a cabecera town; Çompanco, a sujeto to Oaxtepec; Tehuizco, a sujeto to Tepoztlan; and Atlhuelic, a sujeto to Yautepec.

10. Barlow lists these three towns (nos. 27–29) as a part of the province of Oaxtepec although they are not included in either the *Matrícula* or the *Códice*. A Tetela appears on the Cortés list cited previously, but it could not have been Tetela del Volcán (see Chapter 2). Barlow's evidence is convincing. In postconquest times Tetela del Volcán and Hueyapan were cabecera towns, not a part of the Morelos Marquesado (see Chapter 2). Ocopetlayuca can be identified with a postconquest sujeto to Yautepec.

11. For these data I used the Scholes-Adams document as well as the sources cited in Chapter 3.

Appendix 2: Códice Municipal de Cuernavaca

1. This item was transcribed from an eighteenth-century copy (apparently only a part of the original) made rather carelessly by Pere José Antonio Pichardo and presently a part of the Aubin Collection of the Bibliothèque Nationale (Paris), Departmente des Manuscrits, Mexicain no. 292 (see Chapter 1, n. 53).

2. In 1951 Vargas Rea published an ineffectively rendered edition (in 100 numbered copies) of the item cited in n. 1 under the title *Códice Municipal de Cuernavaca. Anónimo del Siglo XVI.* For his edition—a part of his Biblioteca de Historiadores Mexicanos, Colección Historica Estado de Morelos—Vargas employed an earlier published version from the *Boletín y Revista Eclesiástica de Cuernavaca* 12 (see Chapter 1, n. 53).

Appendix 3: Encomiendas Held by Cortés

1. This list was taken from a proceso of 1532 in which Cortés was attempting to regain the revenues he lost when the encomiendas enumerated were taken from him by Gonzalo de Salazar and Pedro Almindes Cherino (AGN, HJ, leg. 265, exp. 5).

Appendix 4: Morelos Encomienda Towns and Their Sujetos as Reported in 1531–32

1. This list is based upon memorials drawn up in 1531 and 1532 both by Cortés' attorneys and by an *escribano* of the Audiencia of México (Información hecha ante los señores presidente y oidores de la audiencia y chancelleria real desta Nueva España a pedimiento del Marqués del Valle, 1532, AGI, Patron., leg. 16, no. 2b, ramo 32 and DII, 12:554–63).

2. The names in parentheses are those of the preconquest provinces and towns as shown in Appendix 1.

Bibliography

Manuscript Materials

The manuscript materials used in the preparation of this study are preserved in the Archivo General de Indias, Seville (AGI); the Archivo General de la Nación, Mexico (AGN); the Library of Congress (LC); the Library of the University of Texas; the Gilcrease Institute; and the Bibliothèque Nationale (Paris). The author investigated some of these materials in their respective depositories during visits to Spain, Mexico, Oklahoma, and Texas and used transcripts or photocopies of others supplied him by the depositories or by his generous mentor, Professor France V. Scholes.

The most important block of documentation relative to the properties of Fernando Cortés in New Spain, including those in Morelos, is the Ramo de Hospital de Jesús (HJ) of the Archivo General de la Nación, Mexico. This ramo contains records of the Marquesado dating from the 1520s to the mid-1800s. Utilized in this study were property inventories, revenue and expenditure accounts, lawsuits, letters, reports, management instructions and orders, and other items. These papers yielded considerable data on encomienda towns, size, location, organization, and tribute assessments, as well as on acquisition and use of land, the employment of labor, and the development and management of agricultural and manufacturing enterprises. Most of this material was unfortunately deficient in references to the pre-1530 period but contained a considerable amount of information for the years after 1531. Of particular value were the following lawsuits: (1) Proceso de Tepuztlan y Yautepeque contra el Marqués del Valle sobre que no pueden complir [con sus tributos], 1551, AGN, HJ, leg. 289, exp. 100; (2) Proceso de la villa de Cuernavaca contra el Marqués del Valle sobre que no pueden complir [con sus tributos], 1551, AGN, HJ, leg. 289, exp. 102; (3) Razón de ciertas pueblos del Marqués del Valle, 1536, AGN, HJ, leg. 377, exp. 1; and (4) Proceso de Doña María, viuda muger que fue de Don Hernando de Cuernavaca, contra el Marqués sobre las cañas y tributo de Amanalco y otras cosas, 1551, AGN, HJ, leg. 398, exp. 1; and the inventory made of Cortés' Morelos Estate in 1549, which the author used in its published form (*Documentos inéditos relativos a Hernán Cortés y su familia*, pp. 220–95).

Most of the manuscript materials utilized from the Archivo General de Indias of Seville (AGI) were examined in Spain during the fall and winter of 1962–63. Some data were secured from the Indiferente General, Patronato, and Contaduría sections of that archive, but most, and certainly the richest, were gleaned from the Justicia section (Papeles de Justicia) which contains lawsuits heard by the Council of the Indies, usually on appeal from the audiencias of Spain's New

World colonies. Among these are a number involving Cortés and his properties in Morelos, the most valuable of which were: (1) Antonio Serrano, regidor y vecino de México, con Hernando Cortés, Marqués del Valle, sobre derecho al pueblo de Cuernavaca y sus sujetos, 1530, AGI, Just., leg. 108, no. 1; and (2) Proceso del Marqués del Valle con el fiscal sobre la suplicación que interpuso de lo que se cometió al Doctor Quesada en razón de la visita del Marquesado, 1550, AGI, Just., leg. 201B, no. 2, ramo 4.

Supplementing these manuscripts were a few items utilized in photocopy form from the Harkness Collection of the Library of Congress (LC, Hark.) and the Bibliothèque Nationale (Paris), and some investigated in the Joaquín García Icazbalceta Collection of the University of Texas Library (1963) and the Hispanic Documents (Cortés Papers) Collection of the Gilcrease Institute, Tulsa, Oklahoma (1968). One item, Los indios de la villa de Cuernavaca contra el Marqués del Valle sobre tierras, 1544, LC, Hark., 6 was especially useful in the writing of Chapter 4, which deals with Cortés' landholdings in the Morelos area.

The reader will find pertinent citations to specific documents or documentary series within these manuscript collections in the notes to the several chapters of this study.

Printed Materials

This listing was limited to useful items which appeared in print prior to July 1970.

Acosta, Joseph de. *Historia natural y moral de las Indias.* Edited by Edmundo O'Gorman. Mexico, 1940.

Aguirre Beltrán, Gonzalo. "Comercio de esclavos en México por 1542." *Afroamerica* 1 (1945): 25–40.

———. "El trabajo del indio comparado con el del negro en Nueva España." *México agrario* 4 (1942): 203–7.

———. "The Slave Trade in Mexico." *Hispanic American Historical Review* 24 (1944): 412–31.

Aiton, Arthur S. *Antonio de Mendoza, First Viceroy of New Spain.* Durham, North Carolina, 1927.

Alamán, Lucas. *Disertaciones sobre la historia de la república mejicana, desde la época de la conquista que los españoles hicieron, á fines del siglo XV y principios del XVI, de las islas y continente americano hasta la independencia.* 3 vols. Mexico, 1942.

Alcedo, Antonio de. *Diccionario Geográfico-Histórico de las Indias Occidentales o América: es a saber: de los Reynos del Peru, Nueva España, Tierra Firma, etc.* Madrid, 1967.

Alvarado Tezozómoc, D. Hernando. *Crónica mexicana.* Mexico, 1878.

Arteaga Garza, Beatriz, y Guadalupe Pérez San Vicente, eds. *Cedulario Cortesiano.* Mexico, 1949.

Bancroft, Hubert Howe. *History of Mexico*. 6 vols. San Francisco, 1883–88.

Barlow, Robert H. *The Extent of the Empire of the Culhua Mexica*. Berkeley and Los Angeles, 1949.

Borah, Woodrow W. *Silk Raising in Colonial Mexico*. Berkeley and Los Angeles, 1943.

———, and Sherburne F. Cook. *Price Trends of Some Basic Commodities in Central Mexico, 1531–1570*. Berkeley and Los Angeles, 1958.

———. *The Aboriginal Population of Central Mexico on the Eve of the Spanish Conquest*. Berkeley and Los Angeles, 1963.

Boyd-Bowman, Peter. "Negro Slaves in Early Colonial Mexico." *The Americas* 26 (1969): 134–51.

Carrasco, Pedro. "Tres libros de tributos del Museo Nacional de México y su importancia para los estudios demográficos," in Congreso Internaciónal de Americanistas 35, Mexico, 1962, *Actas y Memorias*, 3 (1964): 373–78.

———. "The civil-religious hierarchy in Meso-American Communities: pre-Spanish background and colonial development." *American Anthropologist* 63 (1961): 483–97.

Carrera Stampa, Manuel. "The Evolution of Weights and Measures in New Spain," *Hispanic American Historical Review* 29 (1959): 2–24.

Cartas de Indias. Madrid, 1877.

Caso, Alfonso. "La tenencia de la tierra entre los antiguos mexicanos." *Memoria de el Colegio nacional* (Mexico) 4 (1958–60): 29–54.

Catalogue des manuscrits mexicaines de la Bibliothèque Nationale. Paris, 1899.

Cervantes de Salazar, Francisco. *Crónica de Nueva España*. Madrid, 1914.

Chevalier, François. *La formación de las grandes latifundias en México. Tierra y sociedad en los siglos XVI y XVII. Problemas agricolas e industriales de México*, Vol. VIII, No. 1 (Mexico, 1956).

Codex Mendoza. Edited and translated by James Cooper Clark. 3 vols. London, 1938.

Códice Chimalpopoca. Anales de Cuauhtitlan y Leyenda de los soles. Edited and translated by Primo Francisco Velásquez. Mexico, 1945.

Códice Mendocino. Edited by Francisco del Paso y Troncoso. Mexico, 1925.

Códice Municipal de Cuernavaca. Anónimo del siglo XVI. Mexico, 1951.

Colección de documentos inéditos relativos al descubrimiento, conquista, y organización de las antiguas posesiones españolas de América y Oceania. 42 vols. Madrid, 1864–84.

Colección de documentos inéditos relativos al descubrimiento, conquista, y organización de las antiguas posesiones españolas de Ultramar. Second Series. 25 vols. Madrid, 1885–1932.

Conway, G. R. G., ed. *Postrera voluntad y testamento de Hernán Cortés, Marqués del Valle*. Mexico, 1940.

Cook, Sherburne F., and Woodrow Borah. *The Indian Population of Central Mexico, 1531–1610*. Berkeley and Los Angeles, 1960.

———, and Lesley Byrd Simpson. *The Population of Central Mexico in the Sixteenth Century*. Berkeley and Los Angeles, 1948.

Cortés, Hernán. *Cartas de Relación*. Mexico, 1960.

Cuevas, Mariano, ed. *Cartas y otros documentos de Hernán Cortés novísimamente descubiertos en el Archivo General de Indias de la ciudad de Sevilla.* Seville, 1915.

———. *Documentos inéditos del siglo XVI para la historia de México.* Mexico, 1914.

———. *Historia de la iglesia en México.* 5 vols. El Paso, Texas, 1921–28.

Dávila Padilla, Agustín. *Historia de la fundación y discurso de la provincia de Santiago de México de la Orden de predicadores.* Mexico, 1955.

Denhardt, Robert M. "The Truth About Cortés' Horses." *Hispanic American Historical Review* 17 (1937): 525–32.

Díaz del Castillo, Bernal. *Historia verdadera de la conquista de la Nueva España.* 2 vols. Mexico, 1939.

Diccionario de la Lengua Española. Madrid: Real Academia Española, 1956.

Diccionario Porrua de Historia, Biografía y Geografía de México. Mexico, 1964.

Diccionario Universal de Historia y Geografía. 10 vols. Mexico, 1853–56.

Díez, Domingo. *Bibliografía del estado de Morelos.* Mexico, 1933.

———. *El Cultivo e Industria de la caña de azúcar, el problema agrario y los monumentos históricos y artísticos del Estado de Morelos.* Mexico, 1919.

———. *Observaciones críticas sobre el Regadio de Estado de Morelos.* Mexico, 1919.

Documentos inéditos relativos a Hernán Cortés y su familia. Mexico, 1935.

Dorantes de Carranza, Baltasar. *Sumaria relación de las cosas de la Nueva España con noticia individual de los descendientes legítimos de los conquistadores y primeros pobladores españoles.* Mexico, 1902.

Dressler, Robert L. "The Pre-Columbian Cultivated Plants of Mexico," Harvard University *Botanical Museum Leaflets* 16 (1953): 115–72.

Durán, Diego. *Historia de las indias de la Nueva España y islas de tierra firma.* 2 vols. and atlas. Mexico, 1867–80.

Dusenberry, William H. *The Mexican Mesta: The Administration of Ranching in Colonial Mexico.* Urbana, Illinois, 1963.

El libro de las tasaciones de pueblos de la Nueva España. Siglo XVI. Edited by Francisco González de Cossío. Mexico, 1952.

Estrada, Pedro. *Nociones estadísticas de estado de Morelos.* Cuernavaca, 1887.

Foronda y Aguilera, Manuel de. *Estancias y viajes del Emperador Carlos V.* Madrid, 1914.

Galindo y Villa, Jesús. *Geografía de México.* Mexico, 1950.

García, Rubén. *Aspectos desconocidos del aventurero Hernán Cortés.* Mexico, 1956.

García Cubas, Antonio, ed. and comp. *Cuadro geográfico, estadístico e histórico de los Estados Unidos Mexicanos.* Mexico, 1885.

García Icazbalceta, Joaquín, ed. *Códice franciscano.* Mexico, 1940.

———. *Colección de documentos para la historia de México.* 2 vols. Mexico, 1856–66.

———. *Nueva colección de documentos inéditos para la historia de México.* 5 vols. Mexico, 1888–92.

García Martínez, Bernardo. *El Marquesado del Valle: Tres siglos de régimen señorial en Nueva España*. Mexico, 1969.

García Pimentel, Luis, ed. *Relación de los obispados de Tlaxcala, Michoacan, Oaxaca y otros lugares en el siglo XVI*. Mexico, Paris, Madrid, 1904.

Gayangos, Pascual de, ed. *Cartas y relaciones de Hernán Cortés al Emperador Carlos V*. Paris, 1866.

Gibson, Charles. "Llamamiento general, repartimiento, and the Empire of Acolhuacan." *Hispanic American Historical Review* 36 (1956): 1–27.

———. "The Aztec Aristocracy in Colonial Mexico," *Comparative Studies in Society and History* 2 (1960): 169–96.

———. *The Aztecs Under Spanish Rule. A History of the Indians of the Valley of México, 1519–1810*. Stanford, California, 1964.

Gómez de Orozco, Federico. *El convento franciscano de Cuernavaca*. Mexico, 1943.

Grijalva, Juan de. *Crónica de la Orden de N. P. S. Agustin en las provincias de la Nueva España en quatro edades desde el año de 1533 hasta el de 1592*. Mexico, 1924.

Haring, Clarence H. *The Spanish Empire in America*. New York, 1947.

Herrera y Tordesillas, Antonio de. *Descripción de las Indias Occidentales. Historia general de los hechos de los castellanos*. 17 vols. Madrid, 1936–56.

Ixtlilxóchitl, Fernando de Alva. *Obras históricas*. 2 vols. Mexico, 1952.

Jiménez Moreno, Wigberto. "Síntesis de la historia precolonial del Valle de México." *Revista mexicana de estudios anthropológicos* 14 (1954–55): 219–36.

Keniston, Hayward. *Francisco de Los Cobos, Secretary of the Emperor Charles V*. Pittsburgh, 1958.

Kirchoff, Paul. "Land Tenure in Ancient México, a Preliminary Sketch," *Revista mexicana de estudios antropológicos* 14 (1954–55), 351–61.

Kirkpatrick, F. A. "Repartimiento-encomienda." *Hispanic American Historical Review* 19 (1939): 372–79.

———. "The landless encomienda." *Hispanic American Historical Review* 22 (1942): 765–74.

Kubler, George. *Mexican Architecture in the Sixteenth Century*. 2 vols. New Haven, 1946.

———. "Mexican Urbanism in the 16th Century." *Art Bulletin* 24 (1942): 160–71.

———. "Population Movements in Mexico." *Hispanic American Historical Review* 22 (1942): 606–43.

Las Casas, Fray Bartolomé de. *Historia de las Indias*. 3 vols. Mexico, 1951.

Lens, Hans and Federico Gómez de Orozco. *La industria papelera de México*. Mexico, 1940.

Lewis, Oscar. *Life in a Mexican Village: Tepoztlan Revisited*. Urbana, Illinois, 1963.

López de Gómara, Francisco. *Historia de la conquista de México*. Edited by Joaquín Ramírez Cabañas. 2 vols. Mexico, 1943.

López de Velasco, Juan. *Geografía y descripción universal de las Indias*. Madrid, 1894.

López Rayón, Ignacio, ed. *Sumario de la residencia tomada a D. Fernando*

Cortés, Gobernador y Capitán General de Nueva España (1508, 1529) 2 vols. Mexico, 1852–53.

MacGregor, Luis. *Tepoztlan*. Mexico, 1958.

Marquina, Ignacio. *Arquitectura prehispánica*. Mexico, 1954.

Mazari, Manuel. "Códice Mauricio de la Arena." *Anales del Museo Nacional de Arqueología, Historia, y Etnografía*, época 4, tomo 4 (1926): 273–78.

McAndrew, John. *The Open-Air Churches of Sixteenth Century Mexico*. Cambridge, Massachusetts, 1965.

McBride, George McCutchen. *The Land Systems of Mexico*. New York, 1923.

Mendieta, Gerónimo. *Historia eclesiástica indiana*. 4 vols. Mexico, 1945.

Miranda, José. *El tributo indijena en la Nueva España durante el siglo XVI*. Mexico, 1952.

Motolinía, Toribio. *Motolinía's History of the Indians of New Spain*. Edited and translated by Francis Borgia Steck. Washington, 1951.

Müller, Florencia. *Historia antigua del Valle de Morelos*. Mexico, 1949.

Muró Orejón, Antonio. "Hernando Cortés, exequias, almoneda e inventario de sus bienes, con otros noticias de su familia." *Anuario de Estudios Hispano-Americanos* 23 (1966): 1–72.

Noguera, Eduardo. *Zonas arqueológicas de Estado de Morelos*. Mexico, 1946.

Nuevos documentos relativos a los bienes de Hernán Cortés, 1547–1947. Mexico, 1946.

Orozco y Berra, Manuel. *Apéndice al Diccionario Universal de Historia y Geografía*. 3 vols. Mexico, 1853–56.

———. *Apuntes para la historia de geografía en México*. Mexico, 1881.

———. *Historia antigua y de la conquista de México*. 4 vols. and atlas. Mexico, 1880.

———. *Historia de la dominación española en México*. 4 vols. Mexico, 1938.

Oviedo y Valdés, Gonzalo Fernández de. *Historia general y natural de las Indias*. 5 vols. Madrid, 1959.

Paso y Troncoso, Francisco del, ed. *Epistolario de Nueva España*. 16 vols. Mexico, 1939–42.

———. *Papeles de Nueva España*. 9 vols. Madrid, 1905–48.

Peñafiel, Antonio, ed. *Colección de documentos para la historia mexicana*. 6 vols. Mexico, 1897–1903.

———. *Ciudades coloniales y capitales de la República Mexicana*. 5 vols. Mexico, 1909.

———. *Monumentos del arte mexicana antigua*. 3 vols. Berlin, 1890.

———. *Nombres geográficos de México. Catalogo alfabetico de los nombres de lugar pertenecientes al idioma "nahuatl."* 2 vols. Mexico, 1885.

Pike, Ruth. *Enterprise and Adventure: The Genoese in Sevilla and The Opening of the New World*. New York, 1966.

Piña Chán, Román. *Ciudades arqueológicas de México*. Mexico, 1963.

Plancarte y Navarrete, Francisco. *Apuntes para la geografía del estado de Morelos*. 2nd ed. Cuernavaca, 1913.

———. *Tamoachan: El estado de Morelos y el principio de la civilización en México*. Mexico, 1911.

Prescott, William H. *History of the Conquest of Mexico.* New York, 1949.

Puga, Vasco de, ed. *Provisiones, cédulas, instrucciones para el gobierno de la Nueva España.* Facsimile reprint. Madrid, 1945.

Reyes, Vicente. *Onamatología geográfica de Morelos.* Mexico, 1888.

Ricard, Robert. *La Conquista Espiritual de México. Ensayo sobre el apostolado y los metodos misioneros de las ordenes mendicantes en la Nueva España de 1523–24 a 1572.* Mexico, 1947.

Robelo, Cecilio A. *Cuernavaca.* Cuernavaca(?), 1894.

———. *Nombres geográficos indigenas de estado de Morelos. Estudio critico de varias obras de topomatologia nahoa.* 2nd ed. Cuernavaca, 1897.

Sahagún, Bernardino de. *Historia general de las cosas de Nueva España.* 5 vols. Mexico, 1938.

Sandoval, Fernando B. *La industria del azúcar en Nueva España.* Mexico, 1951.

Schäfer, Ernesto. *Indice de la Colección de Documentos Inéditos de Indias, editadad por Pacheco, Cárdenas, Torres de Mendoza y otros (1. ser., tomos 1–42) y la Real Academia de la Historia (2. ser., tomos 1–25).* 2 vols. Madrid, 1946.

Scholes, France V. "The Spanish Conqueror as a Businessman." *New Mexico Quarterly* 27 (1958): 1–29.

———, and Eleanor B. Adams, eds. *Información sobre los tributos que los Indios pagaban a Moctezuma. Año de 1554.* Mexico, 1957.

Simpson, Lesley Byrd. *Exploitation of Land in Central Mexico in the Sixteenth Century.* Berkeley and Los Angeles, 1952.

———. *The Encomienda in New Spain: the Beginning of Spanish Mexico.* Berkeley and Los Angeles, 1950.

Solís, Antonio de. *Historia de la conquista de México, población y progresos de la América septentrional, conocida por el nombre de Nueva España.* 2 vols. Madrid, 1783–84.

Spores, Ronald. *The Mixtec Kings and Their People.* Norman, Oklahoma, 1967.

Suárez de Peralta, Juan. *Noticias históricas de la Nueva España.* Madrid, 1878.

Tamayo, Jorge L. *Geografía general de México.* 4 vols. Mexico, 1962.

Torquemada, Juan de. *Monarquía indiana.* 3 vols. Mexico, 1943–44.

Vaillant, George C. *The Aztecs of Mexico. Origin, Rise and Fall of the Aztec Nation.* Baltimore, 1966.

Vázquez y Vázquez, Elena. *Distribución geográfica y organización de las ordenes religiosas en la Nueva España, Siglo XVI.* Mexico, 1965.

Velasco, Alfonso Luis. *Geografía estadística de la república mexicana.* 13 vols. Mexico, 1889–93.

Veytia, Mariano D. *Historia antigua de México.* 2 vols. Mexico, 1944.

Vivó, Jorge A. *Geografía humana de México.* Mexico, 1948.

Wagner, Henry R. *The Rise of Fernando Cortés.* Los Angeles, 1944.

Whetten, Nathan L. *Rural Mexico.* Chicago, 1948.

Zavala, Silvio. *La encomienda indiana.* Madrid, 1935.

———. *Los esclavos indios en Nueva España.* Mexico, 1967.

Zelinsky, Wilbur. "The Historical Geography of the Negro Population of Latin America." *Journal of Negro History* 34 (1949): 153–221.

Zorita, Alonso de. *Historia de la Nueva España.* Madrid, 1909.

TABLE 1

Tribute: Morelos Encomiendas, 1522–1530

Year		Cotton Textiles					Foodstuffs					Firewood and Fodder					Slaves					Building Materials					Gold, Jewelry, Feathers					Encomenderos
		Cue	Oax	Tep	Yau	Aca	Cue	Oax	Tep	Yau	Aca	Cue	Oax	Tep	Yau	Aca	Cue	Oax	Tep	Yau	Aca	Cue	Oax	Tep	Yau	Aca	Cue	Oax	Tep	Yau	Aca	
1522-1523		X	X	X	X	X	X	X	X	X	X	X	X	X	X	X	X	X	X	X	X			X	X	X	X	X				Cortés
1523-1524		X	X	X	X	X	X	X	X	X	X	X	X	X	X	X	X	X	X	X	X			X	X	X	X	X				Cortés
1524-1525		X	X	X	X	X	X	X	X	X	X	X	X	X	X	X	X	X	X	X	X			X	X	X	X	X				Cortés
																																Cortés
1525-1526		X		X	X		X		X	X		X		X	X		X		X	X		X					X					Serrano
				X	X				X	X				X	X				X	X												Ordaz
																																Cherino-Salazar
1526-1527		X	X	X	X		X	X	X	X		X	X	X	X		X		X	X		X					X	X				Cortés
				X	X				X	X				X	X				X	X												Ordaz
1527-1528		X	X	X	X		X	X	X	X		X	X	X	X		X		X	X		X					X	X				Cortés
				X	X				X	X				X	X				X	X												Ordaz
1528-1529		X		X			X		X			X		X			X	X	X			X					X	X				Cortés
				X	X				X	X				X	X				X	X												Burgos
				X	X				X	X				X	X				X	X												Ordaz
						X					X					X					X											Holguín-Solís
1529-1530		X		X			X		X			X		X			X		X			X					X					Serrano
				X	X				X	X				X	X				X	X												Burgos
				X	X				X	X				X	X				X	X												Verdugo
		X				X	X				X	X				X	X				X											Holguín-Solís

(Town abbreviations: Cue = Cuernavaca, Oax = Oaxtepec, Tep = Tepoztlan, Yau = Yautepec, Aca = Acapistla. The six category groups — Cotton Textiles, Foodstuffs, Firewood and Fodder, Slaves, Building Materials, Gold, Jewelry, Feathers — fall under the heading "Tribute"; the town columns fall under the heading "Encomiendas.")

TABLE 2

Prices Per Carga and Annual Revenue Value of
Tribute in Cotton Textiles
Supplied to Fernando Cortés by the Morelos
Encomiendas, 1536–1544

Year	Mantas		Colchas		Camisas and Naguas		All Cotton Textiles
	Price Per Carga	Annual Value	Price Per Carga	Annual Value	Price Per Carga	Annual Value	Annual Value
1536-37	7	12,488	10	240	25	700	13,428 (8116+)
1537-38	8	14,272	10	240	25	700	15,212 (9217+)
1538-39	10	17,840	11	264	27	756	18,860 (11,399+)
1539-40	12	21,408	12	288	28	784	22,480 (13,587+)
1540-41	12	21,408	12	288	28	784	22,480 (13,587+)
1541-42	25	44,600	12	288	30	840	45,728 (27,640+)
1542-43	25	44,600	12	288	30	840	45,728 (27,640+)
1543-44	25	44,600	12	288	30	840	45,728 (27,640+)
Total		221,216		2,184		6,244	229,644 (138,826+)

All figures represent pesos de oro común except those in parentheses in the last column; those therein represent pesos de oro de minas.

TABLE 3
Labor Services: Morelos Encomiendas, 1522–1530

Year	Encomenderos	IS Cuernavaca	IS Oaxtepec	IS Tepoztlan	IS Yautepec	IS Acapistla	TM Cuernavaca	TM Oaxtepec	TM Tepoztlan	TM Yautepec	TM Acapistla	AG Cuernavaca	AG Oaxtepec	AG Tepoztlan	AG Yautepec	AG Acapistla	CN Cuernavaca	CN Oaxtepec	CN Tepoztlan	CN Yautepec	CN Acapistla	MN Cuernavaca	MN Oaxtepec	MN Tepoztlan	MN Yautepec	MN Acapistla	HH Cuernavaca	HH Oaxtepec	HH Tepoztlan	HH Yautepec	HH Acapistla
1522-1523	Cortés	X	X	X	X	X	X	X	X	X	X																X				
1523-1524	Cortés	X	X	X	X	X	X	X	X	X	X																X				
1524-1525	Cortés	X	X	X	X	X	X	X	X	X	X																X				
	Cortés	X	X	X	X	X	X	X	X	X	X																X				
1525-1526	Serrano	X					X					X															X				
	Ordaz			X	X				X	X														X	X						
	Cherino-Salazar					X					X																				
1526-1527	Cortés	X	X				X	X																			X				
	Ordaz			X	X	X			X	X	X													X	X						
1527-1528	Cortés	X	X				X	X																			X				
	Ordaz			X	X				X	X														X	X						
	Cortés					X					X																	X			
1528-1529	Burgos		X															X					X					X			
	Ordaz			X	X				X	X														X	X						
	Holguin-Solís					X					X																				
1529-1530	Serrano	X					X					X															X				
	Burgos		X															X					X					X			
	Verdugo			X	X				X	X																					
	Holguin-Solís					X					X																				

Labor Services: Indios de Servicio (IS), Tamemes (TM), Agrarian Labor (AG), Construction Labor (CN), Mine Labor (MN), Household and Other (HH)

TABLE 4

Origins of the Indian Slaves Utilized by
Fernando Cortés in Morelos, 1549

PLACE*	SEX		TOTAL
	Male	Female	
Acamalote		1	1
Acatlan		1	1
Aculhuacan	1		1
Aguitlan	1		1
Capanala		1	1
Chalco	1	1	2
Chiapa		1	1
Cholula		1	1
Cicuaque	4	3	7
Cocotlan	1		1
Colima	1		1
Coxotepeque		1	1
Cuexco		1	1
Cuicatlan		1	1
Cuyacan		1	1
Cuzcatlan	2	1	3
Extapalapa		1	1
Guatemala	2		2
Guaxaca	2	3	5
Guaximalpa	1		1
Guaxuapa		1	1
Guazacualco	2		2
Inala		1	1
Ixtintepec	1		1
Izucar	3	1	4
Macuyl		1	1
Macyltepec		1	1
México	4	4	8
Mextitlan	2	1	3
Mila		1	1
Oxitipan	1	1	2
Pango	1	2	3
Pantla	1	2	3
Papalotla	1		1
Soconusco	1		1
Suchipila	1		1
Tamanalco	1		1
Taxcolula		1	1
Taxiquiaco	1		1
Tecomastlavaca	2		2
Teguantepec		2	2
Tejalputepeque	1		1
Tepeaca	5	3	8
Tepespa		1	1
Tepozcolula	2		2
Tezapotitlan	1		1
Texcoco	8	5	13
Tlamaca	1		1
Tlamintla	1		1
Tlaxcala	9	12	21
Tocotla	1		1
Toquitla	1		1
Toluca		1	1
Tonala	2		2
Totlan	1		1
Toxquitapilco	1		1

TABLE 4 (con't.)

| PLACE* | SEX | | TOTAL |
	Male	Female	
Tutci		1	1
Tututepecque	1		1
Tuzapan		2	2
Tuxpa	1	1	2
Xalco		1	1
Xapopotla		1	1
Yanquitlan	2	7	9
Yavaluca		1	1
Zacatlan	2		2
Zapotepeque		1	1
Zapotitlan	1		1
Zapotlan		3	3
Undisclosed	1		1
Subtotal	80	77	157
Morelos Area			
Atlachuluaya	1		1
Chiautla	3	2	5
Ecatepeque	1		1
Guacintla		1	1
Guastepeque		1	1
Guautlan	2		2
Guaxacango	1		1
Mazatepec		1	1
Nanacatepeque		1	1
Poxotla		1	1
Quauhnahuac	3	3	6
Teocatzingo	1		1
Tenestequipaqui		1	1
Teltelpa	1		1
Xocotla		1	1
Xiutepec	3	1	4
Subtotal	16	13	29
TOTAL	96	90	186

* Place names rendered as given in source (*Doc. inéd.*, pp. 225–99).

TABLE 5

Sex and Age of the Slaves Employed by Fernando Cortés in Morelos, 1549

AGES IN YEARS	INDIAN Male	Female	NEGRO Male	Female	Ladino*	OTHER**
9 and under			9	15		3
10-19			2	1	(2)	
20-29			6	4	(8)	
30-39	4	4	12	12	(20)	
40-49	50	45	19	10	(22)	2
50-59	35	40	11		(8)	
60 and over	7	1	1	1	(2)	
Total	96	90	60	43	(62)	5

* Ladinos were Negro slaves who spoke Spanish.

** Of the five slaves owned by Cortés who were not technically classified Negro or Indian, three were mulatto children, one was a mulatto adult male, and the other was an adult Morisco (probably of Spanish and mulatto parentage).

TABLE 6

Distribution by Location of the Cortesian Slaves Employed in Morelos, 1549

LOCATION	INDIAN ADULTS Male	Female	NEGRO ADULTS Male	Female	CHILDREN	OTHER*
Cuernavaca Headquarters and Household	11	5		8	7	3
Cuernavaca Tlaltenango Sugar Mill	82	83	42	21	17	1
Atelinca Ranch	1	1	1			1
Tlaltizapan Ranch	1	1	1			
Atlicaca Ranch	1					

* The "other" slaves located in Cuernavaca were mulatto children. The one at Tlaltenango was a mulatto male, and the one at Atelinca was a Morisco.

TABLE 7

Distribution of Specialized Skills Among the Slaves Employed by Fernando Cortés in Morelos, 1549

SPECIALIZED SKILL	LOCATION	NUMBER OF SLAVES*		
		Negro	Indian	Other
Miller	Cuernavaca	1		
Tailor	"		1	
Gardener	"		1	
Lace-maker	"		1	
Butcher	"		1	
Cook	Cuernavaca and Tlaltenango	1	1	
Blacksmith	Tlaltenango	1	1	
Tiller	"		1	
Oxen Drivers	"	5	11	
Boiler Workers	"		11	
Sugar-makers	"		5	
Fullers and Weavers	"		17	
Master Sugar-maker	"			1
Cartwrights	"	3		
Master Boiler Worker	"	1		
Ranch hand (cowboy)	Atelinca			1
Total		12	51	2

* All of the skilled workers among the slaves were male. The master sugar-maker listed as "other" was a male mulatto; the *vaquero,* or ranch hand, was a Morisco.

TABLE 8

Origins and Sex of the Slaves Employed
in Serrano's Atlacomulco Sugar Mill, 1549

PLACE	SEX Male	Female	LADINO	TOTAL
*NEGROES**				
Africa				
Bañol	1		(1)	1
Berbesi	2			2
Biafara	3		(1)	3
Bran	1	1	(2)	2
Gelofe	3		(1)	3
Mandinga	4		(2)	4
Manicongo	1			1
Mozambique	1			1
Zape	2			2
Undisclosed	1		(1)	1
Subtotals	19	1	(8)	20
*INDIANS**				
New Spain				
Chietla	1			1
Coyuca	1			1
Guachinango	1			1
Guatemala	1			1
Tepexi		1		1
Tlaxcala	2			2
Subtotals	6	1		7
Totals	25	2		27

* Adults only.

TABLE 9

Sex and Ages of the Slaves Employed in the
Atlacomulco Sugar Mill, 1549

AGES IN YEARS	INDIAN		NEGRO		Ladino
	Male	Female	Male	Female	
9 and under			3*		
10-19					
20-29			2	1	(1)
30-39	1	1	5		
40-49	2	1	4		(4)
50-59	2		6		(3)
60 and over			1	1	
Totals	5	2	21	2	(8)

* These three children were males, *negrillos,* and were, at the time of the inventory in 1549, in Tenochtitlan-México.

TABLE 10

Origins of the Negro Slaves Utilized
by Cortés in Morelos, 1549

PLACE	SEX Male	Female	LADINO	TOTAL*
AFRICA				
Bañol	2	2	(4)	4
Berbesi		4		4
Biafara	7	5	(11)	12
Bran	15	6	(18)	21
Cazanga	1		(1)	1
Cibalo		1		1
Gelofe	6	5	(9)	11
La Gomera	1		(1)	1
Mandinga	3	2	(4)	5
Manicongo	1		(1)	1
Mozambique	1			1
Samuco	1		(1)	1
Tierra Nueva		1	(1)	1
Tucuxuy	1		(1)	1
Zape	3		(3)	3
EUROPE				
Portugal	1		(1)	1
UNDISCLOSED	7	3	(6)	10
Totals	50	29	(62)	79

* Includes only Negro adults. Home origins were not cited (in the inventory of 1549) for children and mulattoes. The Morisco (not included here) claimed home origins in Cafi (Africa).

TABLE 11

Cortesian and Other Spanish Land-Holdings in Morelos, 1549:
Location, Use, and Acreage

Owner	Location	General Use							
		Houses, Barns, Mills, etc.	Corrals, Stables, etc.	Orchards and Gardens	Sugar Cane Fields	Vineyards	Wheat Fields	Mulberry Groves	Total Acres
	CUERNAVACA*	5**	1	9					15
	Tlaltenango	5			769.3	11.7			786
	Xiutepec							40	40
	Acatliquipa							17	17
	Atelinca	8							8
	Atlicaca	8							8
	Zinaguatin							18	18
	Atlacomulco	0.3		0.5			9		9.8
Cortés	Tetela-Iztayaca				103				103
	YAUTEPEC*			17			40	44	101
	Tlacomulco	2							2
	Tlaltizapan	8							8
	OAXTEPEC*			1			260		261
	Texcalpa		8						8
	ACAPISTLA	2		8.3				7	17.3
	Total Acres	38.3*	9	35.8	872.3	11.7	309	126	1402.1
Serrano-Ojeda	CUERNAVACA*			3.0					3.0
	Atlacomulco	1.8							1.8
	Tetela-Iztayaca				618		54		672
	Total Acres	1.8		3.0	618		54		676.8
Castillo	CUERNAVACA*								
	Amanalco	1.5**		2*	3**				6.5
	Total Acres	1.5		2	3				6.5
TOTALS		41.6	9	40.8	1493.3	11.7	363	126	2085.4

The sources utilized in preparing this listing recorded the size of the land-holdings in brazas which were defined as of ten palmas each. The palma was equal to approximately 8¼ inches; the braza, therefore, was of about 82¼ inches, and a square braza contained approximately 5.251 square yards. The square brazas in each piece of land listed were determined and, using the above equation, converted into square acres (approximately 921.9 square brazas per acre).

* Cabecera towns are capitalized; sujetos follow in lower case.
** Estimated acreage.
*** One seventh share of Serrano-Ojeda holdings (Atlacomulco mill and lands).

TABLE 12
A. Governing and Administrative Organization
of The Marquesado, 1531–1547

Colonial Bureaucracy	Viceroy (governor), New Spain		
	Audiencia, México		
First Level Marquesado Officials	Governor		
	Justicia Mayor		
			Spaniards
Second Level	Mayordomos (Cuernavaca, Tlaltenango)	Alcalde Mayor (Cuernavaca)	Area Tribute Collector
Marquesado Officials		Alguacil (Cuernavaca)	
	Governors and Señores (Cabecera Towns)		
	Principales (Alguaciles) (Cabecera and Sujeto Towns)		Indians
	Tlapixque and Calpixque (Sujeto Settlements)		

B. Governors and Principal Administrators
of The Marquesado, 1522–1551

1522-1524	Fernando Cortés	
1524-1525	Rodrigo de Paz	(Mayordomo)
1525-1526	Francisco de Las Casas	(Mayordomo)
1526-1528	Fernando Cortés	
1528-1530	Lic. Juan Altamirano, Diego de Ocampo and Pedro Gallego	(Mayordomos)
1531-1534	Fernando Cortés	(Governor)
1534-1536	Lic. Juan Altamirano	(Governor)
1536-1539	Fernando Cortés	(Governor)
1539-1549	Lic. Juan Altamirano	(Governor)
1549-1551	Pedro de Ahumada Sámano	(Governor)
1551	Tristán de Arellano	(Governor)

C. Alcaldes Mayores, Cuernavaca, 1531–1548

1531-1534	Lic. Juan Altamirano
1534-1536	Juan Zimbrón
1536-1539	Lic. Juan Altamirano
1540-1547	Juan de Carasa
1548	Jorge Cerón de Saavedra

TABLE 13

Estimated Gross Annual Revenues Produced by the Morelos Marquesado, 1522–1547

Year	Agricultural Goods		Tribute		Gross Revenues
	Sugar	Other	Cotton Textiles	Other	
1522-23		350	6,000	1,000	7,350
1523-24		350	6,000	1,000	7,350
1524-25		350	6,000	1,000	7,350
1525-26					
1526-27		350	5,040	1,000	6,390
1527-28		350	5,040	1,000	6,390
1528-29		350	3,120	1,000	4,470
1529-30					
1530-31					
1531-32		931	6,642	3,106	10,679
1532-33		931	6,642	3,106	10,679
1533-34		931	6,642	3,106	10,679
1534-35		931	6,642	3,106	10,679
1535-36		1,296½	6,642	3,106	11,044½
1536-37		1,296½	8,116	1,080	10,492½
1537-38	3,165	1,296½	9,217	1,080	14,758½
1538-39	3,165	1,296½	11,399	1,080	16,940½
1539-40	3,165	1,296½	13,587	1,080	19,128½
1540-41	3,165	1,296½	13,587	1,080	19,128½
1541-42	3,165	1,296½	27,640	1,080	33,181½
1542-43	3,165	1,296½	27,640	1,080	33,181½
1543-44	3,165	1,296½	27,640	1,080	33,181½
1544-45	5,396	2,823	21,933	1,080	31,232
1545-46	5,396	2,823	21,933	1,080	31,232
1546-47	5,396	2,823	7,311	1,080	16,610
Total	38,343	25,961½	254,413	33,410	352,127½

All figures represent pesos de oro de minas.

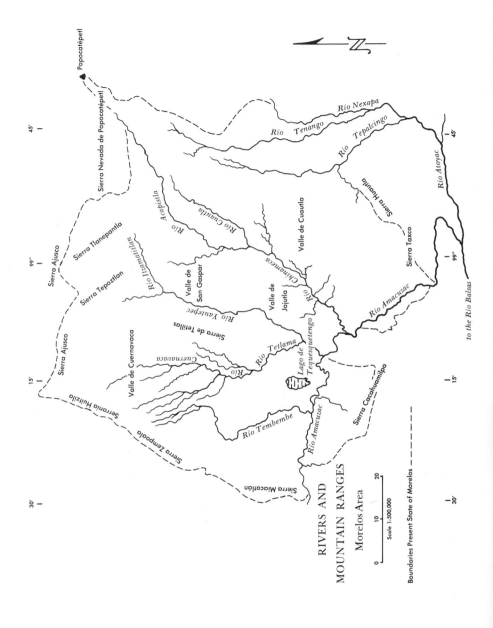

RIVERS AND
MOUNTAIN RANGES
Morelos Area

Scale 1:500,000

0   10   20

Boundaries Present State of Morelos — — — —

Popocatépetl

Sierra Nevada de Popocatépetl

Sierra Ajusco

Sierra Tlanepantla

Sierra Tepoztlan

Sierra Ajusco

Serranía Huitzilac

Sierra Zempoala

Sierra Miacatlán

Río Itzamatitlán

Acapistla

Río Yautepec

Río Cuautla

Valle de
San Gaspar

Valle de
Jojutla

Río Chinameca

Valle de Cuautla

Sierra Huautla

Sierra Taxco

Río Tenango

Río Nexapa

Río Tepalcingo

Río Atoyac

Río Amacuzac

to the Rio Balsas

Sierra de Tetillas

Valle de Cuernavaca

Río
Cuernavaca

Río Tetlama

Lago de
Tequesquetengo

Sierra Cacahuamilpa

Río Amacuzac

Río Tembembe

45'

99°

15'

30'

45'

99°

15'

30'

N

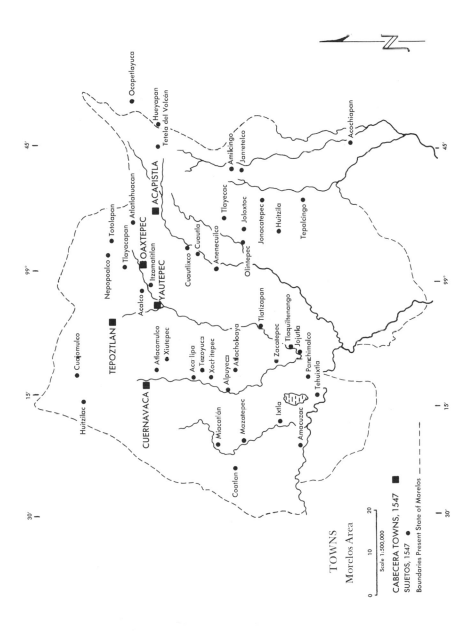

The Conquest of Morelos: Detail from a Mural by Diego Rivera

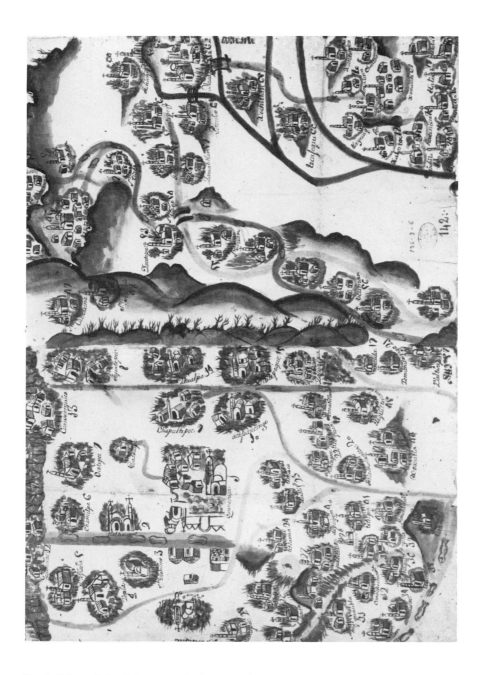

Early Map of the Marquesado in Morelos

Sugar Cane Cultivation on the Marquesado in Morelos:
Detail from a Mural by Diego Rivera

Yautepec

Tepoztlan

Oaxtepec

Cuernavaca

Acapistla

Mazatepec

Olintepec

Tlatizapan

Acatlicpac
(Acatlipa)

Acatzinco
(Acaçingo)

Xiutepec

Nahuatl Symbols for Cabecera Towns in Morelos

Index

RENEWALS 458-4574
DATE DUE

MAR – 9			
GAYLORD			PRINTED IN U.S.A.